CARMELITE

St. Teresa of Avila:
A Woman for Her Times,
Her Culture, Her Church
and of the Living Spirit

Edited by
John Sullivan, OCD
Chairman, ICS

Christus
Publishing, LLC

WELLESLEY, MA
www.ChristusPublishing.com

Christus Publishing, LLC
Wellesley, Massachusetts
www.ChristusPublishing.com

Peter J. Mongeau is the Founder and Publisher of Christus Publishing, LLC.

Library of Congress Cataloging in Publication Data
Catholic University Symposium (1982)
Centenary of St. Teresa.
(Carmelite studies ; 3)
Includes bibliographical references.
1. Teresa, of Avila, Saint, 1515-1582—Congresses. I. Sullivan, John, 1942- II. Catholic University of America. III. Title. IV. Series.

BX4700.T4C2851982   282'.092'4   2012937522

ISBN 978-1-936855-10-0 (pbk.) — ISBN 978-1-936855-11-7 (e-book)

Printed and bound in the United State of America

10   9   8   7   6   5   4   3   2   1

Text design and layout by Peri Swan
This book was typeset in Garamond Premier Pro and ITC Legacy Sans.

Contents

◆ ◆ ◆

Teresa and Her Church

Teresa of the Living Spirit

Abbreviations

◆ ◆ ◆

For references to the major works of either St Teresa of Jesus or St John of the Cross we will continue to use the following abbreviations adopted in previous volumes of *Carmelite Studies:*

ST TERESA OF JESUS
L = The Book of Her Life
W = The Way of Perfection
C = The Interior Castle
F = Book of the Foundations

In C the first number indicates the Dwelling

ST JOHN OF THE CROSS
A = The Ascent of Mount Carmel
N = The Dark Night
C = The Spiritual Canticle
F = The Living Flame of Love

In A and N the first number indicates the book

Introduction

This volume of *Carmelite Studies* offers a set of articles which were originally given as talks in the symposium that honored St Teresa of Jesus at Catholic University of America on the occasion of the Fourth Centenary of her passing from this life to the eternal dwelling places. The whole range of centenary festivities was broader than just a symposium—including, as it did, an exhibit, concert, festive Eucharist and several receptions at various other sites in Washington, D.C. More than 500 persons attended the events planned (over several years) for the weekend of October 15-17, 1982, and now we are glad to present the reflections of the ten speakers in printed form to the public at large.

Their names and their affiliations will assure the reader that this collection of studies is marked by a high level of competence. Those who spoke Teresa's praises in Catholic University's Hartke Theater would easily have been granted Teresa's own seal of approval and awarded the title of *letrados* by her for their work. Far more importantly, however, they formulated their contributions to our knowledge about the Church's first woman doctor in terms of devotion, devotion for her and also a devotion flowing from their own obviously deep spiritual lives. They would thereby gain a further accolade of *la Madre* that is housed in the following remarks of her L, 10, 9:

> As much as I desire to speak clearly about these matters of prayer, they will be really obscure for anyone who has not had experience . . . These things I'll say from what the Lord has taught me through

1

experience and through discussions with very learned men *(letrados)* *and* persons who have lived the spiritual life *(personas espirituales)* for many years.

Put in a different way, and up against the background of what could be called in contemporary jargon a remedy for "misinformation," Teresa says a little later on in L that "the devils have a tremendous fear of that learning which is *accompanied by* humility and virtue; and they know they will be discovered and go away with a loss." How gratifying it is to be in a position to introduce studies that are so worthy of Teresa herself.

While it is obvious that several symposia could have been organized, with each of them devoted to any one of the sub-themes covered by these authors, the ten articles provide more than adequate treatment of the overall theme of the Fourth Centenary Celebration: "Teresa of Avila / A Woman / for Her Times / Her Culture / Her Church / and of the Living Spirit." In several articles some facets of Teresa's life experience and thought show up over and over again. To point out where these appear and reappear through frequent editor's notes would have seemed an intrusion, so we leave to the reader the happy task of discovering these *ritornellos* and enjoying how several treatments of one and the same thing (such as Teresa's assimilation of Osuna's teaching on contemplative prayer) provide broad, interdisciplinary perspectives on the same phenomenon. Furthermore, the final article of Monika Hellwig indicates how some of the other articles cluster around similar topics.

To close out these words of introduction it would be good to mention that the contributions of the ten authors, as originally delivered, are available on tape (along with introductions to each sub-theme and question-and-answer periods) from Ministr-O-Media/ P.O. Box 155 / Pomfret, MD 20675. Then, there is another feature of the Centenary Celebration which appears in this third volume of *Carmelite Studies*.

May this book pay fitting tribute in its own way to Teresa who so loved to enjoy traces of God's beauty wherever they could be found, and who started her great treatise on the dwelling places with these wonderfully consoling words: "I don't find anything comparable to the magnificent *beauty* of a soul and its marvelous capacity . . . (because) he created us in his own image and likeness."

JOHN SULLIVAN, OCD
EDITOR

A WORD OF APPRECIATION

These talks will most likely be referred to as the "CU Papers," and it is only fitting that some expression of thanks be made to The Catholic University of America in this volume. From the highest-placed members of its administration, through the deans of its schools, and on to both faculty with their assistants and the students, all provided expert collaboration with the Carmelites and gracious hospitality to participants from over 25 states at the Centenary Symposium, Exhibit, and Concert in the Fall of 1982. Without their able assistance much of what occurred then would not have been as successful or as pleasant for either the planners or the public. May the Lord prosper their work and their careers on behalf of quality education.

J.S.

Teresa the Woman

St Teresa of Avila: A Directress of Formation for All Times

◆ ◆ ◆

Susan Muto, Ph.D.

Susan Muto is Director of Duquesne University's Institute of Formative Spirituality. She has enriched America's supply of spiritual reading by a steady flow of books and articles, and has even written a book about "doing" spiritual reading entitled A Practical Guide to Spiritual Reading.

INTRODUCTION

Numerous studies focus on St Teresa's life and times, her methods of prayer, her Carmelite spirituality.[1] My interest is not to duplicate these commentaries but to draw out further insights into the saint's gifts as a directress of souls. The major source for these reflections will be chapters 1 to 18 of W.[2]

Were we asked to describe the ideal spiritual directress, we might say that above all she should understand the trials and errors of formation on the basis of her own experience. Did she struggle to remain faithful in the face of doubt? Did she follow God's will despite the pull of pride? Did she persevere in her calling however badly she might have been misunderstood? Through the uniqueness of her personality, we would like her to radiate the attitudes of Christ. While hoping that she would respond seriously to serious questions, we would not want her to lose her sense of humor. She should demonstrate the right balance of gentleness and firmness, nearness and distance, subjectivity and objectivity. If she spoke of prayer, we would like to feel behind each word the weight of first hand experience. Were her responses to life questions rooted in reality? Did an honest inquiry merit an equally honest reply? Was she a balanced, down-to-earth person, who could see meaning in human suffering? In her presence, did we really feel understood? Could she anticipate the longing we felt for the Lord and facilitate our quest?

Adrian van Kaam suggests some signs by which to determine if a directress is genuinely summoned by God to care for persons in this way. One sign is the invitation from fellow Christians to assist them in their journey to the Lord. Another sign of the divine appeal includes a peaceful awareness that one does have a certain ability for direction. This appears together with the assurance that the Church does not object to one's serving as a spiritual guide among a segment of the faithful.

If these two primary criteria are fulfilled, then secondary indications of this calling can be found in one's spiritual knowledge and experience, in one's wisdom and maturity, and in the fact that people who know one in daily life acknowledge such qualities. Other signs include: a temperament suited for presence to others' problems in patience and respect, availability of time and energy, and a profound capacity for transcendent presence in prayer. These factors indicate if God is calling one to participate in the spiritual journey of another person or persons at this time.[3]

An ideal model of such a directress would be none other than St Teresa of Avila, reformer, mystic, doctor of the Church, directress of formation for all times. When St Teresa founded the monastery of St Joseph's in 1562, her intention was to establish a new way of life for "thirteen poor little women" consecrated to prayer. The problem she encountered was that most of the books on prayer available at the time were forbidden due to their being listed on the *Index*. The solution was simple and typically Teresian. The sisters needed this kind of instruction from their trusted directress. Therefore, she would write such a book herself, submit it to the harshest censors to be sure it contained no errors, and then encourage her sisters to make as many copies of it as they wished. Teresa's other writings, notably her L (1565), the C (1577), the F (1573-82), were in the main autobiographical reflections on her personal formation journey in both the interior and exterior realms. She wrote these texts in the hope that her confessors would be better able to understand her. She would not allow her sisters to read these books during her lifetime.[4]

By contrast, according to Rodriguez, she composed W as a didactic book. Its intention was to explain both why sisters are drawn to that particular form of life and how they can concretely set about living it. She saw W as a teaching tool to fill in a gap until the *Constitutions,* written between 1563 and 1567, were ready. She probably wrote her first redaction of W in 1566. The text was the only book Teresa allowed to be read publicly in the refectory while she was alive. She did all in her power to have it printed, though it was only in 1583, a year after her death, that the first edition appeared. She made none of these efforts in regard to her other writings. Thus we can assume how important it was for her to pass on to her sisters the wisdom and practice contained in this book. It was to be her legacy to them, containing the essence of her life as a way of formation in the Lord.

The book presents advice and counsel to her religious sisters, living according to the primitive *Rule* of our Lady of Mount Carmel. She writes it specifically in response to persistent requests from the sisters that she teach them more about prayer. She accepts this challenge, confident that she can "say something about the mode and manner of life proper to this house."[5] Experience tells her that before she can explain the art and discipline of mental prayer, it is necessary to depict the formative atmosphere essential for such a life. Thus, prior to her presentation of the practicalities of meditation, beginning with chapter 19, Teresa senses the wisdom of outlining in detail the prerequisites. She will speak in terms of ordinary things they all know to be true. Moreover, she will say nothing about what she has not experienced herself, or seen in others, or received understanding of from the Lord in prayer.[6]

FIELD OF FORMATION

Teresa begins by reflecting in general on the liberating effects of following the three evangelical counsels, poverty, chastity and obedience. She never wavers in her intention to show her sisters the immense importance of a life freed from worldly concerns, graced by a good conscience, and devoted to praying for the Church. Such a life, modeled on the primitive *Rule* of Carmel, takes as its cornerstone ceaseless prayer, complemented by fasts, disciplines and silence. Hard work must flow from lofty thoughts. Before saying anything about these interior matters, she pauses to state what dispositions are necessary if one wants to advance in the service of the Lord. In the vast ocean of prayer, she will launch them on three safe ships—three trustworthy carriers of the foundations of human and Christian formation:

> Do not think, my friends and daughters, that I shall burden you with many things; please God, we shall do what our holy fathers established and observed, for by walking this path they themselves established they merited this title we give them. It would be wrong to seek another way or try to learn about this path from anyone else. I shall enlarge on only three things, which are from our own constitutions, for it is very important that we understand how much the practice of these three things helps us to possess inwardly and outwardly the peace our Lord recommended so highly to us. The first of these is love for one another; the second is detachment from all created things; the third is true humility, which, even though I speak of it last, is the main practice and embraces all the others.[7]

In this oft-quoted paragraph, certain key words stand out, words like "path," "practice," "peace." This threefold path of formation, when sincerely practiced, will lead to peace. If one puts into practice these basic, Christ-like dispositions, one will live in the light of his peace and by implication enjoy the rest and refreshment of the Holy Spirit in contemplative prayer. How formative and foundational are these three directives? Do they address not only Carmelite nuns but all true seekers? We shall show in this paper that Teresa's insight is not confined to a specific locale in sixteenth-century Spain. The W spans the ages and is rightly designated a classic.[8] The examples Teresa uses to embellish each of these dispositions necessarily contain some time-bound accretions, but her underlying intuition about the centrality of these three directives is timeless.

Ongoing consonant formation depends on the love we receive from parents, friends and peers.[9] Love received increases our capacity to give love in return. The formation of humanity in compassion depends on this uniquely human capacity to love one another beyond the self-preserving instinct.

Consonant formation becomes dissonant when we lose our freedom by clinging excessively to other people or by grasping possessions in an inordinate way. We lose our peace when people disappoint us or we fail them. Wealth, fame and worldly accomplishments pale in importance as the years pass. Even if we do not focus consciously on detachment, it happens to us. We are detached from our parents and our careers by the liberating agents of aging, illness and death. Teresa felt obliged to teach that detachment from passing people, events and things is essential so that we can be liberated for the Eternal.

To love unselfishly, to let go of obstacles to freedom, to follow God's call, we must learn day by day the painful truth of who we are. The basic fact of being human means being made by God. We are not sufficient unto ourselves. We depend for our life itself on the formation mystery, on the God who calls us forth from *humus*, from the dust of the earth. We have been made in his image and likeness. This constitutes our original dignity, our substantial union with God that can never be destroyed. The fall into pride and sin separated us from

God. We were exiles in a land of unlikeness. Human pride marred our likeness to God, but through the mediation of Jesus, Lord and Savior, we gained the help we needed to reenter the land of likeness.[10] Humility embraces the two foundations of charity and detachment, for it reminds us at once that God loved us first and that we are called to sever the bonds that keep us from returning to him in the union of love. Humility signifies the misery that evoked God's mercy, the nothingness that he raises to the heights of nobility. Life in many ways is a journey from pride and ignorance of the Transcendent to humility and openness to the Transcendent.[11]

These three directives apply not only to human formation; they also impart in a lively way the wisdom of the Christian revelation. To love one another is ultimately only possible because God has first loved us (1 Jn 4:10). To live realistically in detachment leads us from the bondage of the pride form to the freedom of the children of God, who lay aside their former way of life and acquire a fresh, spiritual way of thinking (Eph 4:22-23). To be humble is to imitate Christ, who humbled himself for our sakes, becoming one of us in all things but sin (Phil 2:6-7).

These dispositions, to quote van Kaam, facilitate the release on all levels of our being of the Christ form of the soul.[12] We experience intimacy with others by uniting ourselves with the Lord, who alone can teach us the art of selfless loving. We detach ourselves from narcissistic needs so we can cultivate true community with Christ at the center. We gain our deepest spiritual identity in transcendent presence to the Sacred when we give up our egocentric striving for perfection. Thus Christian spirituality as such is built on the three pillars of charity, renunciation and truth, or of love for one another (chastity), detachment (poverty of spirit), and humility (obedience). Chaste, respectful loving, letting go of excess, listening to God's will as disclosed in each situation—these three foundations reflect the trinitarian bond between Father, Son and Holy Spirit.

Teresa's treatment of this threefold path reveals the realistic, humorous, gentle quality of her gifts as a directress of formation.[13] Eloquent and shrewd, observant and penetrating, she discloses the essential framework of a life in Christ that simultaneously respects uniqueness and fosters community. The way she proposes is simply a portrait of her own person. She was not only writing about love, detachment and humility. She was herself a living witness to their validity as foundational directives of formation.

LOVE

In regard to the first directive—love for one another—Teresa is well aware that we err either because our love is excessive or defective. We love too much or too little, too possessively or too indifferently. The problem of possessive love is especially treacherous in the close confinement of a contemplative community where it may flourish under the guise of virtue and piety. However, such love, directed toward anyone but God, becomes a detriment to the soul that ought to be totally occupied in loving him. In keeping with her own experience, Teresa cautions that this excessive love is likely to be found among women more than men. Its symptoms are well known to her, as it gives rise to the following:

> . . . failing to love equally all the others; feeling sorry about any affront to the friend; desiring possessions so as to give her gifts; looking for time to speak with her, and often so as to tell her that you hold her dear and other trifling things rather than about your love for God. For these great friendships are seldom directed toward helping one love God more. On the contrary, I think the devil gets them started so as to promote factions in religious orders. For when love is in the service of His Majesty, the will does not proceed with passion but proceeds by seeking help to conquer other passions.[14]

Instead of cultivating in a domineering way one friend over another, Teresa says that in a house where no more than thirteen women live, all must be friends, all must be loved, held dear, helped. The Lord does not play favorites and neither must they.

To clarify further this foundation of community life, Teresa distinguishes between two kinds of love: purely spiritual or unselfish and spiritual mixed with sensuality or selfishness. The first love takes into account our affective, somewhat controlling nature, but does not stop there. Compared to the greater love of God that grips every fiber of one's being, lesser loves for pleasure and power seem like shadows. Other loves weary one compared to the endless refreshment of the love of God. One does what one can and must for others, but one avoids becoming preoccupied with their lives to the point of becoming forgetful of God. Perfect lovers trample underfoot the comforts the world has to offer since they cannot tolerate being apart from God. No affliction is too great for such a love, no sacrifice too much to ask. Such lovers are more inclined to give than to receive, for theirs is a "precious love that imitates the Commander-in-chief of love, Jesus, our good!"[15] This love is happiest when it sees others progressing likewise in non-manipulative, non-seductive, self-donating service.

These latter traits—manipulation, seduction, self-serving versus self-giving —characterize the lesser love Teresa cautions the sisters to avoid at all costs. If they keep Christ as their model, they will feel compassion and respond accordingly to each one's needs. They will cultivate truly spiritual friendships, take time for recreation, and keep the rule of chastity with great perfection. Phrases like "my life," "my soul," "my only good" will be words of endearment kept only for one's Spouse.

Teresa is adamant about the elevation of love from sensual to spiritual. Firmness must guide gentleness in this regard. She says that if anyone is found to be the cause of such disruption, it is best to send the person to another monastery. Her advice here allows for little compromise:

> Get rid of this pestilence; cut off the branches as best you can, and
> if this is not enough pull up the roots. And if that doesn't work, do
> not let the one who is taken up with these things leave the prison
> cell. That's much better than letting so incurable a pestilence infect
> all the nuns. Oh, how great an evil it is! God deliver us from the

monastery where it enters; I would rather that the monastery catch fire and all be burned.[16]

The impassioned language Teresa uses shows just how strongly she feels about making anyone but Christ the center of our love life. Later she enlarges on this matter in reference to the actual operation of her religious house, but suffice it to say that the vital impulse to love has to be tamed by the transcendent inspiration to love one another as Christ has loved us.

DETACHMENT

In regard to the second directive—detachment from all created things—Teresa immediately casts this rather negative sounding disposition in a positive light. She says that detachment "if . . . practiced with perfection, includes everything . . . because if we embrace the Creator and care not at all for the whole of creation, His Majesty will infuse the virtues."[17] Teresa is in no way advocating a posture of hatred or disparagement of creation. She was obviously a lover of life and nature. What she does advise is an inner attitude of care freeness from the vicissitudes of creation. All things come and go, rise and fall, stay for a while and pass away. If we become absorbed in these things, we lose our freedom. We can no longer soar without worry to God.

In this regard, Teresa tackles a concrete problem she may have had trouble with herself: attachment to relatives other than one's parents, for they "seldom fail to help their children, and it is right for us to console them in their need."[18] As contemplatives must discipline their relations to friends, loving all equally, so they must moderate their memories, anticipations and fantasies where relatives are concerned. The mortification implied here is mainly an interior reformation of memory, anticipation and imagination.[19] If one vows to leave the world, this movement cannot be only geographical; it must be deeply interior, in response to the Lord's directive to leave mother, father, brothers and sisters to follow him (Mk 10:28-30). Teresa does not like people to fool themselves. It is only when they have left the world and gone into the desert of Carmel that the real work of detachment begins: disentangling oneself from bodily comforts that lead to disobedience of the *Rule;* avoiding heroic penances that lack discretion and increase vanity; practicing silence; ceasing to complain about slight sicknesses, since "When the sickness is serious, it does the complaining itself"; in short, practicing the "long martyrdom" of interior mortification.[20] Only if we go against our own will, gradually without knowing how, relying on grace, we shall find ourselves at the summit. St Teresa would agree with St John of the Cross that the way is rigorous, but the reward is great, for in giving up all, we gain the All.

HUMILITY

Teresa insists that humility goes hand in hand with charity or love of others and detachment or diminished seeking of self-satisfaction. It is the ground of these dispositions and the source of our strength, especially when it comes to resisting demonic plays on human pride. Great progress in holiness occurs when we resist vain reasoning and defensive postures; take on lowly tasks; avoid the privileges of rank and power; disengage ourselves from excesses of praise or blame; and bear with dishonor, ridicule and misunderstanding, for "it calls for great humility to be silent at seeing oneself condemned without fault."[21] Only in this way do we imitate the humility of Jesus and Mary with real determination, not wavering for reasons of worldly honor.

In one of her most memorable comparisons, Teresa places humility within a game of chess. She says:

> The queen is the piece that can carry on the best battle in this game, and all the other pieces help. There's no queen like humility for making the King surrender. Humility drew the King from heaven to the womb of the Virgin, and with it, by one hair we will draw

him to our souls. And realize that the one who has more humility will be the one who possesses him more; and the one who has less will possess him less. For I cannot understand how there could be humility without love or love without humility; nor are these two virtues possible without detachment from all creatures.[22]

In this beautiful text, Teresa sums up her program of foundational formation in the virtues of charity, detachment and humility. This foundation is both a preparation for and a consequence of the practice of mental prayer. She does say emphatically that "meditation is the basis for acquiring all the virtues, and to undertake it is a matter of life and death for all Christians."[23] By the same token, to progress to the higher stage of contemplation, one must put these three virtues into constant practice, for they must be possessed in as high a degree as possible as a prerequisite for contemplative prayer. "I say that the King of glory will not come to our soul—I mean to be united with it—if we do not make the effort to gain the great virtues."[24]

Contemplatives must diligently practice humility lest their state of life breed a proud, holier-than-thou attitude. They ought to seek the lowly path so God himself can lead them higher. For, ultimately, contemplation is his gift, not our doing. Teresa herself admits to spending fourteen years unable to practice meditation without reading. Lack of delights in contemplation enabled her to walk with humility, in great security, waiting upon the Lord's will. She affirms in this regard that "true humility consists very much in great readiness to be content with whatever the Lord may want to do . . . and in always finding oneself unworthy to be called his servant."[25]

Enduring trials is always good for the soul. Contemplatives can wager they are on the right path if "they . . . keep the flag of humility raised and suffer all blows they receive without returning any."[26] Bearing the Cross without complaint signifies one's growth in Christ-like love. Such love is another sign that one is on the way to union. For real advancement is manifested in deeds done for one's own spiritual growth and for the good of others, "not in having more delights and raptures in prayer, or visions, or favors of this kind that the Lord grants . . ."[27] There is more wisdom in detaching oneself from these extraordinary phenomena than in pursuing them under the guise of spiritual awakening. Here humility joins mortification and careful obedience to the rules governing the common life.

CONCLUSION

In conclusion, Teresa says:

> . . . these are the virtues I desire you to have, my daughters, the ones you must strive for and about which you should have only holy envy. As for those other devotions, there's no need to be sorry about not having them; having them is an uncertain matter. It could be that in other persons they may be from God, whereas in your case His Majesty may permit them to be an illusion of the devil and that you be deceived by him, as were other persons . . . Why desire to serve the Lord in a doubtful way when you have so much that is safe?[28]

From this point onward in the text, Teresa begins to discuss mental prayer as such and in the light of the Our Father. This article has concentrated on her threefold plan for human and Christian formation. Anyone, in any walk of life, seeking liberation from egoism and union with the Lord, can benefit from her advice and counsel. She offers sensible, clear directives to all. Humility assures us that we shall find our most unique, congenial self in Christ. Detachment enables us to live in each situation with a high degree of compatibility. We can be simultaneously near to others in genuine care while maintaining a certain respectful distance. Charity flows over into compassion for our own weaknesses and for the vulnerability of those who people our world.

Teresa was not only a fine directress of formation. She was also an obedient directee. She placed herself under the guidance of spiritual directors, confessors and superiors. She knew how important it was to find combined in a confessor both learning and goodness. Lacking one or the other, a confessor might do great harm to a penitent. This happened in Teresa's case. She tells about the time she spoke of a matter of conscience with a confessor who had gone through the whole course of theology. He did her a great deal of harm by telling her that some matters did not amount to anything. She trusts that he did not intend to misinform her, but that he simply did not know any more. The ideal is to speak to learned persons, who are also spiritual. She says emphatically: "If the appointed confessor is not spiritual and learned, they [the nuns] should at times seek out others."[29] Even if a confessor has these qualities, it is still good to consult with others because it is possible for him to be mistaken.

Learning, spirituality, and experience—these are Teresa's own gifts.[30] They emerge from her life as well as from solid reading of Scripture and the classics. She combines in her writings a womanly sensitivity with a sharp intellect and an innate capacity for playful, perceptive reflection. She is not baffled by the paradoxes of Christian living but handles these with gracious wisdom. She shows that it is possible to experience deep relationships while preserving recollection. She herself functions in a "man's world" while experiencing the heights of mystical union. If one lives with Christ as the Center of one's life, one can serve the Church tirelessly while maintaining inner tranquility.

Teresa is a living witness to the marriage of ministry and mysticism. This marriage is grounded in humility, detachment and love. These dispositions constitute a trinity of virtues modeled on the Triune Mystery and embodied fully in Jesus Christ. He is the humble, detached, charitable Person we are called to be like, whether we go forth in service or seek solitude and prayer. These memorable words certify for all ages Teresa's place as God's directress of souls:

Let nothing disturb you,
Nothing affright you.
All things are passing;

God never changes.

Patient endurance

Attains to all things.

Whoever possesses God

Is wanting in nothing.

God alone suffices.

NOTES

1. See, e.g., Marcelle Auclair, *St Teresa of Avila* (New York: Pantheon Books, 1953);
E. Allison Peers, *Mother of Carmel: A Portrait of St Teresa of Jesus* (Wilton, CT: More-
house-Barlow Company, 1944); Peter-Thomas Rohrbach, *Conversation with Christ: An
Introduction to Mental Prayer* (Chicago: Fides Publishers, 1956); and Teresa M. Boer-
sig, "Teresian Spirituality," *Contemplative Review,* 15 (Fall, 1982), 37-42.

2. *The Collected Works of St Teresa of Avila* vol 2, trans. Kieran Kavanaugh and Otilio
Rodriquez (Washington: ICS Publications, 1980), pp. 37-106. EDITOR'S NOTE: All
references to the works of St Teresa hereinafter will cite (dwelling place) chapter and
paragraph after the conventional letter identifying the work itself. Pagination will be
given only where this adds clarity.

3. See Adrian van Kaam, *The Dynamics of Spiritual Self Direction* (Denville, NJ:
Dimension Books, 1976), p. 425.

4. I am indebted for these observations to Fr Otilio Rodriguez, *The Teresian Gospel*
(Darlington Carmel: unpublished *pro manuscripto* edition, 1974), pp. 13-17.

5. W, Prologue, 1.

6. Ibid., Prologue, 3.

7. Ibid, 4, 4.

8. According to van Kaam:

Human subjects have much in common. Spiritual masters over the centuries have
experienced and expressed how the universal subjectivity of man is affected by grace
and follows certain stages of spiritual unfolding. Successive generations of spiritual men
and women recognized that these masters had really described the universally possible
experiences of persons who obeyed the call of grace. Their writings were given the status of "classics" of the spiritual life.

See *The Dynamics,* p. 288. See also Susan Annette Muto, *A Practical Guide to Spiritual Reading* (Denville, NJ: Dimension Books, 1976).

9. For insights into the meaning of formation consonance and the implied difference between consonance and dissonance, see Adrian van Kaam, "Provisional Glossary
of the Terminology of the Science of Foundational Formation," *Studies in Formative
Spirituality,* 2 (1981), 509-10. Van Kaam also speaks of the seminal event in initial formation when the parents bestow upon the child the "foundational formative triad" of
faith, hope, and consonance or love. He discusses at length the results of giving or with-

holding this triad on life's formation in *The Science of Formative Spirituality: An Introduction* I (New York: Crossroad Publishing Co., 1983), chap. 15 [in press].

10. See Aelred of Rievaulx, *Spiritual Friendship*, trans. M. E. Laker (Kalamazoo: Cistercian Publications, 1977). Coll. "Cistercian Fathers Series," 5. For Aelred the experience of faithful friendship constitutes one of the main means by which we leave the land of unlikeness, whose soil is selfish sensuality, and journey to the land of likeness, whose soil is Christian charity.

11. According to Adrian van Kaam "Formation ignorance is an ignorance of the true transcendent nature of formation, an ignorance common to people since the Fall." Its remote cause is the fallen state of human formation; its first main proximate cause is the autarchic pride form. See his glossary of terminology pertinent to the science of formation in *Studies in Formative Spirituality*, 1 (1980), 458-59.

See also *The Steps of Humility and Pride* in *The Works of Bernard of Clairvaux* V, trans. M. A. Conway (Washington: Cistercian Publications, 1974). Coll. "Cistercian Fadiers Series," 13.

12. See Adrian van Kaam, *The Mystery of Transforming Love* (Denville, NJ: Dimension Books, 1982).

13. The phrase "threefold path" is taken from Adrian van Kaam, *The Vowed Life* (Denville, NJ: Dimension Books, 1968).

14. W, 4, 6.

15. Ibid., 6, 9.

16. Ibid., 7, 11.

17. Ibid., 8, 1.

18. Ibid., 9, 3.

19. See Adrian van Kaam, "Formative Dispositions and Traditions," in *The Science of Formative Spirituality* II (New York: Crossroad Publishing Co., 1983—in progress).

20. W, 11, 1 and 12, 2.

21. Ibid., 15, 1. Teresa adds: "The truly humble person must in fact desire to be held in little esteem, persecuted and condemned without fault even in serious matters. If she desires to imitate the Lord, in what better way can she do so?"

22. Ibid., 16, 2.

23. Ibid., 16, 3.

24. Ibid., 16, 6.

25. Ibid., 17, 6.

26. Ibid., 18, 5.

27. Ibid., 18, 7.

28. Ibid., 18, 9.

29. Ibid., 5, 4.

30. Teresa seems to manifest this list of qualities characteristic of a Christian leader, according to St Bonaventure. They are: zeal for righteousness, mutual love, patience, an exemplary life, discretion and devotion to God. See Philip O'Mara, *St Bonaventure, The Character of a Christian Leader: A Modern Version* (Ann Arbor, MI: Servant Books, 1978), p. viii.

Elements of a Feminist
Spirituality in St Teresa

◆ ◆ ◆

Sonya A. Quitslund, Ph.D.

*Dr Sonya Quitslund is an Associate Professor of Religion
at George Washington University in Washington, D. C.
Her academic interests are constantly guided by a concern
for Christian unity and she founded "Christian Feminists"
in 1974, an organization dedicated to raising consciousness
regarding the Christian dimension of the feminist movement*

INTRODUCTION

There is no value to a hypothetical spirituality—only a lived spirituality
brings with it the elements of realism and authenticity that can engen-
der not only genuine admiration but even more importantly, emulation.
To dwell on the special spiritual gifts and experiences—transverbera-
tions, raptures, locutions—as a means to determine if in fact moments
of a feminist spirituality are to be found in Teresa's spirituality, will
bring us to about as much understanding of the real Teresa as drawing conclusions about the character and values of a stranger on the
basis of an inventory of the gifts friends bring to a birthday party, or a
house-warming, or a shower—and that is assuming we have experience
of such occasions. Very few of us have extensive acquaintance with the
mystical experience of others. Gifts say as much about the giver as about

the recipient, and in the final analysis, they remain ambiguous to the outside observer, because the motive of the giver may range the gamut from deep love, to pity, to indifference or even a desire to shame the individual. At best, the real nature of the gift remains a secret between the giver and the recipient.

Our approach to Teresa will perhaps seem a trifle unorthodox to some. We shall try to demonstrate from the details of her life, the contents of her works and letters, that Teresa was both an exceptional woman well worthy of ecclesiastical recognition and yet an extraordinarily ordinary woman. In fact, this sixteenth-century woman's message of hope and encouragement could well have been addressed directly to the twentieth-century middle-aged woman coming to grips with her own personhood, with both her religious and personal identity; to the woman who for the first time in the silence created by the death of a spouse, an empty nest, divorce or job insecurity, hears a voice within— the real self—trying to break forth, urging her to become who she really is meant to be. It is the time when our "inner selves begin to speak more truthfully as we cast off the various masks we've worn . . . a loving Father invites us to become more aware of the spirit within us."[1]

It is a frightening thing to wake up at age forty or fifty and suddenly to realize life is surely half over, and where has the first half gone? Who am I? Can I really stand me? What games have I been playing with myself all these years when I should have been *being* and *becoming* myself? It is a moment when the God-question becomes very real. Some of us suppress the piercing cry of this small voice and drown it out by simply turning up the volume of our life. Teresa mastered this trick as a young nun. Never really impressed with her father's brand of spirituality, she took it upon herself to teach him to pray. However, already blessed with the prayer of union by the age of twenty-three, Teresa soon tired of it all—like spoiled children tire of fancy toys; and when her father continued to come, seeking spiritual conversation, she would prolong her frivolous chatter with her worldly friends, rather than risk revealing her own spiritual emptiness and immaturity to him.

He humbly accepted the slight, but soon stopped coming. Listening to idle prattle had become a waste of time for him. Only his death in 1543 would bring her to her senses; never again would she abandon prayer—no matter how long and painful the aridity.[2] But what pain and shame must have haunted her for the rude way she had treated her father, and for the precious lost moments of spiritual sharing and encouraging with her father. "If only I had . . . "—the mark of missed opportunities was as much a part of Teresa's experience as ours. But we are getting ahead of ourselves.

Teresa of Avila comes out of a specific context—sixteenth-century Spain. Feminists today have been known to refer disparagingly to the "male macho mystique" and even to identify it with the Hispanic world. Moreover, the sixteenth century is hardly remembered as being a particularly liberating century as far as women are concerned. In fact, the Reformation took away the one option for quasi "independent living"—I refer to vowed or consecrated celibate life—and in so doing called into question for the entire Western world, the very wisdom of the institution. After all, does not I Timothy read: "But women shall be preserved through the bearing of children, if they continue in faith and love and sanctity with self-restraint" (1 Tm 2:15)? In Teresa's case, fears of the consequences of child bearing were very real. Her own mother died at the age of thirty-three after bearing nine children in eleven years, when Teresa was only thirteen. But Teresa also had a seeming horror at the very thought of being subject to a man, and these were among the motivating factors that drove her to the convent, not an overwhelming desire to serve God.[3]

As such, she is extraordinarily ordinary: like most teenage girls, she weighed her options and then plunged in blindly, not knowing what she was bargaining for and then when boredom or disappointment set in, as it most generally does—regardless of the choice—she found ways to accommodate the demands of the state of what suited her whim of the moment. Rare are the individuals who catch themselves at this game: the housewife who decides to make excessive homemaking her excuse for not growing in mind or spirit, for not bearing witness in the community; the woman who turns to soap operas, alcohol, drugs, as her escape from tedium, boredom, an unresponsive husband or unappreciative children; or the professional woman who simply marks time waiting for retirement. The scenario is not foreign to Teresa: she has walked the same path, only to be rudely awakened at about age forty-five, and told by God it was high time she do something constructive—like reform the Carmelite Order—but it took a great deal of convincing. She is so human she is lovable—the big issue for her was not lack of experience in reforming religious orders but the inconvenience it would cause her. She was very comfortable in her little cell at the Incarnation. She had it arranged just to perfection, and now, to have to leave that! This was asking a lot: after all, it had taken her almost twenty years to create her little oasis.[4] In comparison to the crying needs of the Church in the 1550s, it may seem incredible that such a trivial thing could have mattered. But that is why she is so extraordinarily ordinary. It is the trivial, petty little things that do us in, that create the greatest obstacles to becoming our true selves, and Teresa knew it from personal experience.

We shall develop this ordinary side of Teresa in more detail shortly, but first, to bring her a little closer to our time and as a fundamental argument for the contemporaneity of her age to ours, let us recall briefly some facts to substantiate this claim, because I am sure many objections to any proposed parallels between sixteenth-century Spain and twentieth-century America immediately come to mind.

Moreover, even though women have been around since the creation of humankind, the adjective "feminist" does not conjure up the same definition in all minds; nor for that matter, does the term "spirituality." If we expect to say anything intelligible and of lasting value on feminist spirituality, we need to begin our analysis of its presence or absence in Teresa's life from a commonly agreed-upon starting point. You may not agree with my definition, but at least you will know from where I am coming and be better equipped to assess the logic or lack thereof in the arguments to follow.

SOME HISTORICAL PARALLELS

On the four-hundredth anniversary of Teresa's death, the Catholic Church is in a ferment not unlike that experienced by the Church of Teresa's day. The Council of Trent ended just as she began her reform. She died barely twenty years after its end; today we stand in a similar distance from Vatican II. Both ages had to face reforms —some useful, some not, some even seemingly detrimental to basic spirituality. Religious life was in a state of chaos as much from the spirit of the age as from the upheaval caused by the Reformation or the spiraling inflation and depressed economy of the period. The cost of living increased an incredible 400% between 1571 and 1581.[5] The very challenge posed to the validity of religious life itself as a Christian way of life raised in the sixteenth century has not been without parallel in the twentieth.

But the major religious issue of the sixteenth century was: in which camp is true Christian orthodoxy to be found? In terms of this broader debate, Teresa was somewhat isolated since the Protestant Reformation as such failed to penetrate the Iberian peninsula in her day. She knew however that the unity of the Church was clearly at stake. In a sense the situation is much more complex today. As Christians struggle to reestablish the broken unity, the broader issue has become religious commitment in general.

While we more readily recognize religious value in non-Christian religions, we in the Western world are increasingly faced with a new phenomenon, the de-Christianization of a formerly "Christian" world, creating an even more ambiguous religious situation in which to raise our young. Nevertheless, the religious upheaval or chaos that marked the sixteenth century is not necessarily any more dramatic than that which the twentieth century faces; both situations were equally unexpected by most believers. However, there is a new dimension we must add to the picture of the twentieth century, the ferment represented by the feminist movement in both the secular and ecclesiastical arenas. Do feminists perhaps represent the prophetic voice within the twentieth-century Church, raising a justified protest in both the Protestant and Catholic churches about issues of human dignity and justice, just as some Protestant reformers did in the sixteenth century about other issues of human dignity and justice?

TOWARD A DEFINITION OF FEMINIST SPIRITUALITY

Having tried to make a case for at least some fundamental similarity between our age and Teresa's, isn't it stretching things just a bit too far to then propose that we can find elements of a feminist spirituality in Teresa's life and thought? Would not Teresa recoil at the very idea that her spiritual legacy could produce a Teresa Kane or foster a Women's Ordination Conference, or motivate women to pursue theological educations or pastoral ministries?

On the other hand, do feminists even want a woman proposed as their spiritual model and guide, and identified with their movement who frequently referred to herself as a "vile, rotten worm," "filthy slime," a "befouled body" and who candidly admitted that the very thought she was a woman made her "wings droop?"[6] What possibly can she have in common with feminists? She must have been a loyal, docile daughter of the Church to have been canonized, let alone proclaimed a doctor of the Church—for these processes are exclusively in the hands of men, and would they propose anything as unsettling as a genuine feminist as a model for women in the Church?

Obviously before proceeding any further we need to define "feminist spirituality," if we are to discuss how Teresa may have anticipated or contributed to it. More is finally being written on the subject, as women recognize no movement can long endure without some philosophy or spirituality to nourish it.[7] A feminist is generally described as one who affirms the full personhood of woman, with all that we associate with personhood in terms of freedom to explore one's potential without being automatically stereotyped because of one's sex. The definitive feminist spirituality has yet to be produced and ideally it should never be more than a temporary stage on the way to a fuller human spirituality.[8] It will include a "vision of the world in which genuine mutuality, reciprocity and equality" prevail, and include such elements as "sisterhood, and non-competitive, non-hierarchical and non-dominating modes of relationships among humans."[9]

EXTRAORDINARILY ORDINARY

Too often we think of Teresa simply as the great mystic and reformer, we miss the human dimension, the simplicity and love that marked her as a woman. Her motto was: to act, to suffer, to love—an equally appropriate spiritual program for the post-Vatican II woman.

Because she loved deeply, she was not immune to human pain. From her earliest years she had been haunted by the concept of "loving for ever" and wondered if anyone really understood what it meant. Throughout her life she remained extremely sensitive to displays of love or their lack. In 1576 she wrote to Mother Mary: "My chief complaint against you now is that you cared so little to be with me at Seville." She continues with how keenly hurt she was "at not meeting the same simplicity and love" from her.[10] To another nun she said: "if you love me . . . I love you in return and like to hear you tell me so." Teresa also had a sweet tooth. From time to time she mentions her desire or expresses appreciation for sweets of pink sugar or orange flower water and oil. She even wonders whether Gratian will forget to send her her Easter cake.[11]

Gratian meant a great deal to her but in 1581 he did not accompany her as far as she expected. It took her a while to get over the hurt but she finally wrote him: "I must remind you . . . that, after all, the flesh is weak, and what has happened has made me sadder than I could have wished to be; it has been a great blow to me. I have been very lonely here."[12] How deep this love for Gratian must have been is reflected in one of her last letters to him: "How overwhelmed I have felt lately; however, my pain melted away when I heard that you were well."[13] Of even greater interest is the love between John of the Cross and Teresa. Initially John did not even want to meet Teresa because he tried to avoid conversing with women.[14] Teresa once said: "There is no way of talking of God with John of the Cross because he immediately falls into ecstasy and you with him." His demands frightened her. She would have liked to love him still more. He in turn loved her more than he allowed himself to love any other human being. He would have liked to admire her less for he did not wholly approve of her. He nevertheless admitted to suffering from being separated from her and ultimately burned all her letters because of his attachment to them.[15]

But this love was not limited to Carmelites. She maintained strong family attachments and loyalties, although toward the end of her life she no longer derived pleasure from personal contacts or relationships unless they were of a spiritual nature. Writing to her brother Lawrence about his intended return from South America, she reflects on her joy at his presence: "I have so little earthly comfort that perhaps God means to grant me this . . . "[16] But to Alonso Ramirez she directs a loving reprimand: "Had I so much leisure as you, I should not be so tardy in writing as you are—although I do not lack time to pray for you."[17] On more than one occasion she complains of those who do not answer her letters.[18]

In general there was something truly maternal and protective about Teresa in her personal relations. It is clear from her life and writings that being a saint does not mean one stops being human or ceases to love family and friends. She clearly realized "the stronger we are the greater our obligation to stoop in tenderness toward those to whom a mere nothing often causes great suffering."[19]

In rereading Teresa's works for this article I kept in mind that for the first twenty years of her adult life she basically let herself be swept with the tide, her heart divided between God and the world. At fifteen she used cream, rouge and perfume. She even plucked her eyebrows.[20] She was a typical teenager. But at the convent boarding school of Our Lady of Grace she was made to realize she was not perfect—that she had an incapacity to understand and to feel.[21] Nevertheless she made decisions that presaged the determination and zeal that would later be so characteristic of her: for example, she rejected as suitable for her temperament the Augustinians who taught her. Generous and impulsive, she wanted something more demanding. But once she was safely in the "more demanding" convent, and favored with special spiritual gifts, including the prayer of union,[22] she found ways to manipulate the system to her advantage—to gain the maximum of freedom for herself, so that she drifted into a state of spiritual mediocrity which lasted almost two decades. Looking back she would later comment that it is better to marry beneath one's station than to be in an uncloistered convent —unless one is very devout. She readily admitted that especially in contrast to married women, nuns were free from the great trials of the world.[23]

In these early years we find the typical woman committing the typical womanly sins: extremely anxious to please, to be loved, even if it meant doing things she disliked,[24] yet manipulating others and rules to her own advantage. For eighteen years she ran from her own emptiness, her lack of self-acceptance and self-love. She reached out to others not because of real love but because of a need to be loved by others, to be approved and reassured.[25] Part of this anxiety for social acceptance and fear of rejection may well have been due to her Jewish ancestry—a liability she apparently tried to keep concealed.[26] In short, she was guilty of not being honest with others or herself, of blinding herself to the possibility that something might be wrong with herself as well as the society in which she lived, and so of failing to do something about it.

The main difference between Teresa and the Christian feminist today is that we not only recognize the devastating consequences of these games, we insist they are the dark side of sexist structures—the survival tactics devised by victims of sexist oppression, and so conclude both the tactics and the structures are sinful and must go. Teresa clearly recognized the tactics were sinful, and ultimately demeaning to the human person, but she nevertheless continued to use some of the "tricks of the trade" to the end, as the only way to function usefully within the system. "If the General sees we are obedient and if, from time to time, we show him some little civility in token of our submissiveness, no harm will come to us," wrote Teresa in July of 1581.[27]

Teresa did not propose to change the system, but that does not mean she approved of it. Her call, however, was not to reform the structures of society at large, just the Carmelites, primarily by founding convents of Reformed Carmelites as models for the rest. Nevertheless, like any person she wanted to be taken seriously and demanded the right to be heard because her womanly contribution merited it.[28] "She expected a fruitful interaction between her typically womanly religious experience and the theology of men. She appreciated the fact that theology and mysticism need each other for their own authenticity."[29]

Various authors have attempted to psychoanalyze Teresa. Bernadette Lorenzo in an as yet unpublished paper given at the Mariological Congress in Zaragoza, Spain, in 1979, suggests paternal images were actually stronger than maternal ones in Teresa, perhaps because of the emotional trauma of the loss of her mother at the age of thirteen. Accordingly, she transferred her love to Mary and asked her to be her mother; she even called St Anne her grandmother. In short, Lorenzo argues, Teresa did not have a positive model in her feminine identification because her own mother was but a child when she married and died so young. Still, Teresa seldom speaks of Mary; paternal images are stronger than the maternal ones. It is Jesus who initiates her into the joys and sorrows of Mary to help teach her how to be more human,[30] perhaps to provide her with a feminine role model.

It is interesting to note that at the age of sixty Teresa had a vision of Mary alone which lasted several days, and several years earlier when she had become prioress of the Incarnation (against her will and that of the community too), she placed the statue of Mary in the prioress' stall.

Another contemporary writer, J. Ruth Aldrich, sees Teresa as the model "self-actualized woman." She notes that "Teresa had advised . . . (women) they must 'live in their own century' and the saint practiced what she preached . . . Women are expected to be humble in the presence of authoritarian figures, contrite when confronted by reprimand; and Teresa like all self-actualizers, knew how to live within the confines of the Establishment and to make it work for her."[31]

That this is an accurate assessment is supported by a comment in Teresa's L about a serious reprimand:

> I did not want to excuse myself; I had been determined about what I did . . . I begged to be pardoned and punished . . . I saw clearly that in some matters they condemned me without any fault on my part . . . But in other matters I knew plainly they were speaking the truth . . . None of what they said caused me any disturbance or grief although I let on that it did so as not to give the impression I did not take to heart what they said to me . . . I gave the explanation in such a way that neither the Provincial nor those who were present found anything to reprimand me for.[32]

On the other hand, Teresa refused to be inhibited by traditional or conventional behavior when confronted with something she "decided was necessary or important."[33] Although in these circumstances she never lied, she had the art of disclosing nothing she wished to hide.[34]

Rare is the person, let alone the woman who never feels just a little oppressed or repressed. In one of her earlier works, W, Teresa observed:

> Jesus found more faith and no less love in women than in men;

and then in a dialogue with Jesus, she says:

> I do believe, Lord, that this could be true of your goodness and justice, for you are a just judge and not like those of the world. Since the world's judges are sons of Adam and all of them men, there is no virtue in woman that they do not hold suspect. I see that these are times in which it would be wrong to undervalue virtuous and strong souls, even though they are women.[35]

On the other hand, she herself could be reprimanded in 1571 by the Lord: "You always desire trials, and on the other hand you refuse them."[36] Indeed Teresa wryly admits to her own confessor what she considers one of the weaknesses of women: "We women are not so easy to know through and through. You hear our confessions for years and then one day you are surprised at having understood us so little. Women don't know themselves. You judge them on what they tell you."[37] If she felt her prayer life inconsistent with her faults,[38] the Lord could be much more explicit. He told her just how wicked she had been, how vain her will was and then rebuked her for seeking comfort in prayer after being scolded by her confessor. But then God often granted her a favor after first humbling her.[39] Teresa is a woman through and through—with our weaknesses and strengths in a fine balance, an extraordinarily ordinary woman.

While Teresa certainly recognized a difference between men and women in terms of academic accomplishment and psychological maturity,[40] she did not accept this as a permanent ontological reality. The *Constitutions* state that a duty of a prioress is to help teach illiterates who applied for admission to Carmelite monasteries to read.[41] Moreover, she expected everyone received to be fit to be prioress or to fill any other office,[42] and believed they should have the qualities any ordinary man has a right to expect in his wife—and fervor too![43] In fact, it would seem both Jesus and Teresa were more than a little annoyed with the way Paul, and especially the pastoral letter attributed to him, Timothy, was used to keep women in their place. On one occasion Jesus said: "Tell them they should not follow just one part of Scripture but that they should look at other parts, and ask them if they can by chance tie my hands."[44]

If Teresa identified more with her father, it probably had less to do with the loss of her mother and more to do with her temperament and the fact that males were the achievers and the doers in sixteenth-century Spain. Teresa's occasional disparaging remarks about being a woman are to be understood in the light of the limitations society placed on women, which were especially onerous for women with the boundless energy and vision she enjoyed. Moreover, if she deals at times with the psychologically immature, it is because the whole psychological conditioning by culture and the Church kept women psychologically immature. She never rejected her womanhood, nor did she seek to evade sisterhood. In fact, her energies are expended tirelessly on behalf of women—religious and lay—even to the point of hastening her own death. Moreover, her defense of women was so clear and forceful in the first version of W that the censor intervened and she was obliged to revise it considerably.[45] In addition, she was adamant that even women's prayer is a work of the Church,[46] and her insistence on freedom for cloistered nuns in the choice of their confessors was later accepted by Church law.[47]

Teresa loved children and thought each convent ought to have one, but not more than one.[48] She allowed Gratian's sister Isabel to enter when only eight years old,[49] as well as her own niece Teresita who had been born in Quito, and a Casilda. Until 1583 girls not old enough to be novices continued to be admitted.[50]

Far from being a person who denied her femininity, Teresa has a heart ever ready to mother—even to the extent that she raised her own younger sister and the grandchild of her Uncle Francis in her own cell in the Incarnation.[51] Her rejection of marriage was certainly not a rejection of family life and maternal values. She delighted in children and was as concerned about the education and proper marriages of her own nieces and nephews as if they had been her own children. If in F she reminds the nuns of the gratitude they owe God for choosing them for his service and thus rescuing "them from being subject to some man, who very often brings a woman's life to an end—and God grant he may not also ruin her soul,"[52] she willingly prays for children for the childless.[53] This gift of self to and for women is nowhere more dramatically demonstrated than in her last trip, done in sheer agony but under obedience, to bless an approaching birth with her presence, a trip that proved unnecessary—the child arrived prematurely but unfortunately lived only four days. This trip contributed nothing tangible to the reform and surely hastened her death, for she collapsed upon her arrival at Alba de Tormes and was dead in less than two weeks.

Her letters yield a particularly insightful glimpse into Teresa the woman, although undoubtedly some of the best have been forever lost because John of the Cross destroyed all he had.[54] And only eighty addressed to Gratian are extant, even though she wrote him almost daily during the years of persecution, sometimes sending copies of the same letter by different routes in the hopes that at least one would reach him—so miserable was the postal system of her day. Probably only one third of her letters have been found. The fact that each letter no matter how long consists of one sentence may be said to be indicative of the passionate outpouring they generally represented.

In one letter Teresa notes that the "learned men here are shocked at the things (the nuns at Seville) have been obliged to do for fear of excommunication . . . Here we made a point of looking at what we were told to sign before doing so, with the result we gave then nothing they could use against us."[55] Undoubtedly ecclesiastical politics as well as a desire to be able to read the spiritual classics contributed to her insistence that Carmelite nuns be literate.

She also admits to difficult mortifications and her emotional states'—for example, the two hardest mortifications were imposed by Gratian who commanded her to write her general confession which forced her to analyze her feelings, to define the indefinable and so to deepen her self-knowledge, (and, then he never even heard or read it!) and to have her portrait done.[56] In 1576 she writes to Fr Marian that she desires insistence on virtues not austerities; furthermore she admits she is not given to penances herself and tells her zealous brother that it is a greater penance to moderate mortification.[57] Less than a year before she died she wrote: " . . . His Majesty is pleased to punish me by only granting me fresh favors, though for one who knows herself even that is no light punishment."[58] But the last written account of her soul is the most enlightening for the humanity it reveals in this woman who has suffered and loved so much, and who had been so favored with mystical gifts. The state described corresponds to the seventh dwelling place:

I seem more careful as regards my health and body and less mortified respecting my food and penances; this is not the case with my desire for mortification which appears to have increased. (She enjoys) "continual intellectual visions of the three Persons and the Sacred Humanity." (But her soul cares nothing for self-interest) "this makes me fear sometimes lest my soul should have become dulled and that I am doing nothing because I perform no penances, but the doubt does not disturb and grieve me as it used to do . . . I seem to live to eat and sleep and to avoid pain, and even this does not grieve me, except . . . occasionally . . . I am afraid I am being deluded. But . . . as far as I know, I am not dominated by attachment to any creature nor to all the bliss of heaven, but only by love for this God of mine. This love does not diminish: indeed, I believe it increases with the longing that all may serve him . . . (I have) lost the excessive and interior grief that used to torment me when I witnessed the loss of souls or doubted whether I had not offended God . . . I no longer need to consult theologians . . . I only want to satisfy myself as to whether I am on the right road and can do some work."[59]

If we were to present no further evidence, it would seem this letter alone would justify Teresa's relevance, especially to the older woman, as a fitting model of a sound, balanced, truly feminist spirituality: a spirituality that recognizes not only the spiritual reality of the older person but also her psychological and physical reality. It is no wonder that people were astonished she was considered a saint, because she behaved so naturally, she was so extraordinarily ordinary.

By 1580 she had overcome her need to be loved: "For I tell you honestly I do not care whether the nuns take any notice of what I say or no, so long as I hear they are making a point of fulfilling their obligations."[60] But there are other facets to her personality that we must at least mention in passing—the serious side, which called forth lengthy letters regarding two sisters who had lied about Gratian. Teresa is concerned that Christian mercy be shown them and yet insists on the need for discipline and punishment because their lies had potentially disastrous consequences in the days of the Inquisition.[61] On the other hand, there are touches of humor: "Tell Sr Jeronima who signs herself "dungheep" that I hope her humility is not merely a matter of words."[62]

"We are not angels," Teresa once said, "we have a body . . ."[63] But our real problem is we have either too much or too little love. We must not let ourselves be conquered by our affections. She recognizes two kinds of love: purely spiritual and a spiritual love mingled with sensuality and weakness. But even this is still a worthy love. We must realize how insubstantial affection is, even though we soon tire of life without love.[64] Teresa believed "perfect love warns others of their mistakes, avoids flattery and secret blame, submits to criticism without bearing a grudge." Throughout her life she begged the nuns to reprove her when she deserved it and she accepted criticism humbly.[65]

But regarding love of God, she explained why we do not learn to love God perfectly in a short time. We think "we are giving all to God, whereas the truth of the matter is that we are paying God the rent or giving him the fruits and keeping for ourselves the ownership and the root."[66] In the final analysis, "The measure for being able to bear a large or small cross is love."[67] Teresa learned the hard way. She wanted instant mysticism but it took from ages 23-41 to realize that true growth is slow. Sanctity is learning to accept reality, being open to God's word.[68]

FEMININE IMAGERY

If sanctity is learning to accept reality, being open to God's word, spirituality is the path that leads to sanctity. As such, Teresa's spirituality reflects an ongoing process of learning to accept reality and of God helping her to bear up under the reality of being a woman in sixteenth-century Spain.[69] Teresa truly hungered and thirsted for God and when Valdés prohibited the publication and reading of Scripture in the vernacular, Teresa was beside herself.[70] How was she to nurture herself on the Word of God, let alone be open to it, if the Bible were to become effectively off limits for her—for as a woman, excluded from higher education, she had never learned Latin. Even God apparently agreed this was a gross injustice to the devout; for he opened the pages of Scripture to her and especially helped her understand the meaning of the Song of Songs without even knowing the Latin.[71]

Even though Teresa could urge her nuns to be strong and courageous as men, it was to distance her nuns from what was considered characteristic of women—petty rivalries and factions, and to astonish men so they would appreciate the true worth of women.[72] Teresa did not impose a masculine spirituality on them. Indeed, for years she herself was tormented with the thought that her style of prayer was not authentic prayer because it did not follow the mode then in vogue.[73]

Unceasing prayer constituted the essence of Carmelite life for which peace is necessary. Through her own experience and perhaps also womanly intuition, Teresa therefore chose not to burden her nuns but stressed three practices: love of neighbor, detachment and humility.[74] Moreover, she recognized individual differences and urged her prioresses to get to know each nun thoroughly so she could better guide her spiritually.[75] In the first dwelling place she insisted any undue constraint or limits in prayer is bad. Above all she realized God was the real spiritual director and God was sovereignly free to do as he pleased—to call some to the heights of prayer with little or no spiritual consolations, to shower others with all sorts of gifts. Teresa was normal enough to wonder about this and God just as quick to let her know it was none of her business.[76]

Nevertheless, in a day when Ignatian spirituality was rapidly spreading throughout the Catholic world and given the fact that many of her spiritual directors were Jesuits, it is interesting to note the truly feminine dimension that emerges in her spirituality in the area of imagery, specifically what we might describe as womb imagery. Welch considers her a pioneer, in producing images and categories to image what was going on in her.[77] Teresa's comment on this subject is to the point, "since we women have no learning, all of this imagining is necessary that we may truly understand that within us lies something incomparably more precious than what we see outside ourselves. Let's not imagine that we are hollow inside."[78]

Such imagery certainly was not new to the Christian tradition. We see its earliest appearance in Paul's citation of the Greek Epimanander: "In God in whom we live, move and have our being"[79]—God, as pregnant mother. Nor did the Early Church and Church Fathers hesitate to refer to the baptismal fount and/or the Church as womb,[80] and what is the Church but the Body of Christ, extended in time and space? So natural and fitting was this image to express a profound awareness, not only of the reality of God but also of our relationship to God, that saints and mystics alike did not hesitate to address God and Jesus as Mother—for example, Anselm, Bernard, Julian of Norwich.[81]

Whether Teresa was aware of this legacy is not known, but her portrayal of the soul's relation to God as a journey inward through many dwelling places to the interior castle wherein dwells the Trinity is but another version of this womb symbol. Contrary to Epimanander's sense of being within the womb of God, Teresa suggests by this image that God dwells within the "womb" of the soul. Had she limited her presentation of the symbol to this one exposition, her theology might well have been faulted—even though she claims this insight came not from herself but a vision granted her by the Lord. Given Teresa's Jewish ancestry, it is also interesting to speculate on whether any Jewish mystical influence is to be perceived here, an influence transformed of course from a feminine perspective, for the earliest form of Jewish mysticism, Merkabah mysticism, consisted in a perilous journey outward through the seven Hakhaloth halls, into the presence of the throne of God. A later development, considered heretical, would reverse the direction to a descent inward, the soul would become the throne.[82]

While the image of the interior castle is counterbalanced by other images like the cocoon or specific sayings of Jesus, it is important to note what may be inferred from the contrasting uses of the womb symbol. The more traditional use, in which God is the womb in which we dwell clearly suggests the importance of the individual in the life of God—to the point that one is almost overwhelmed in pursuing the analogy. One recalls how the pregnant mother is affected by the growing child within, how her lifestyle is changed and limits are increasingly placed on her as she approaches term. This analogy is equally applicable to the growth of the soul maturity where the limitation the pregnant God experiences is reflected in the gift of freedom given to the individual, and all that implies in terms of the evolving spiritual relationship.

But to focus exclusively on the soul as in the womb of God can undercut the importance of human responsibility because we rarely discuss the responsibilities of the unborn child to its mother. In fact, our society seems willing to accept with few reservations that the unborn has no rights and only one responsibility: not to be a burden to its mother or to society.

The first three dwelling places of C outline what is achievable through human effort and the ordinary help of grace suggesting yet another dimension to human spirituality—the responsibility to assume the quest for the innermost core of our being, God. In fact, in 1577 Teresa said the C is about God; the journey in prayer is ultimately the work of God's love.[83] By placing God in the hidden recesses of our "womb", we sense the fragile nature of this human-divine relationship. The divine-human encounter is as chancy and unpredictable as human conception. Some who very much want a child never conceive; some who could care less do conceive and then either abort or bring an unwanted child into the world which they may then abuse and batter. God is this mysterious potential within us that in some cases forever seems to remain hidden, an untapped potential. In others there may well be some initial mystical encounter, a Presence yearning for a conscious relationship but whose very presence, whose very existence at the conscious level is threatened by any of a multitude of reasons, some of them already noted in the early life of Teresa.

Teresa learned that although union was a gift, it was not necessarily achieved overnight or a permanent possession.[84] Just as the child once conceived still takes up to nine months to become a viable person, so does the divine-human relationship require a sometimes lengthy period of careful nurturing. The point of C is that the nurturing process is a shared responsibility. Union remains a gift, not a reward for good behavior, but a fragile gift that unless properly appreciated and handled with care can be damaged or even destroyed. That is why Teresa could wonder, even after years of intimacy with the Godhead, whether she was in fact, "doing enough."

The simile of the child nursing at its mother's breast is particularly good at expressing the nurturing, mothering side of God. This is a comparison the Lord put in her mind which she uses to explain the prayer of quiet:

> The Lord desires that the will, without thinking about the matter, understand that it is with him and that it does no more than swallow the milk His Majesty places in its mouth and enjoy that sweetness ... If the will goes out to fight with the intellect so as to give a share of the experience, by drawing the intellect after itself, it cannot do so at all; it will be forced to let the milk fall from its mouth and lose the divine nourishment.[85]

Achieving the proper balance between "doing" and simply "being" so that one might "become" was a task that even Teresa had difficulty mastering—another reassuring message for the contemporary woman torn between so many needs and concerns.

Other images of interest in exploring Teresa's feminist dimension include water, cocoon, bee, butterfly, dove, silkworm. Water frequently has functioned as a womb symbol or in more general terms as source of life. It first enters written literature in the epic *Enuma Elish,* with the mother goddess Tiamat as saltwater. In Christian mystical literature it appears as a well developed image in Origen's presentation of the spiritual life as a journey from water hole to water hole based on the Exodus of the ancient Israelites.[86] Water is certainly a central theme in Teresa but less attention has been given to the other images, so we shall say just a word or two about them.

In the fifth dwelling place, Jesus becomes the cocoon in which we die and then are transformed as a butterfly. Like butterflies we cannot return to the cocoon, we are powerless to bring about the favor of union until God grants it.[87] We should also note that the silkworm must die. Seeing oneself in the new life helps one die. It is in union through conformity of wills that we must put the silkworm to death and this requires much effort.[88]

The social dimension of the Christian life is especially apparent in this image. Once transformed by the womb experience, one is sent forth like the butterfly to witness to the glory of God. As uncertain as existence is for the butterfly, so is it for the transformed Christian, but it can no more enter into its cocoon than the Christian can experience union, without the direct aid of God. It is sent forth with a mission to accomplish and insofar as it performs this task, it achieves the purpose for which it was created. The dove image functions in a way similar to the butterfly; it is always bearing fruit for itself and others, it never stops to rest because it never finds its true repose.[89]

Another aspect of this social dimension is the fact we can profit from the spiritual tradition of the past and so actively cooperate in the process of putting to death the old person so a new one may be born.

Teresa also likens the soul to a bee, in the first dwelling place. Flying from flower to flower is like emerging from self-knowledge to flights of meditation. Interestingly enough in the Old Testament the bee is also a symbol for God, especially in the holy war context, and the name of the first prophet in Israel, Deborah, means bee.[90]

A CHALLENGE

One final dimension of Teresa's teaching on prayer we might explore from a feminist perspective is that prayer leads to a natural overflow in activity in the world, an intensified gift of self to and in the world.

Activity reflects the real fruit of union —that is, union consists not in closeness but in oneness with the will of God. To enter heavenly prayer we must first enter our soul to know self and what we owe God.

In the sixth dwelling place Teresa utters a deep sigh that has been reechoed down through the centuries by many Christian feminists: she refers to the pain caused by the obstacle of sex which prevents apostolic activity in the world.[91] Unlike other mystics of note, for example, Bridget of Sweden, Catherine of Siena, Teresa never received revelations for the Church. Her mystical life was one of the inner experience of the content of revelation which brought faith into sharper focus.[92] Nevertheless, from start to finish her spirituality has a decidedly ecclesial dimension that translates readily into the ecumenical age in which we live. The documents of Vatican II, especially *The Dogmatic Constitution on the Church* and *The Pastoral Constitution on the Church in the Modern World* help us understand her commitment to the Church.

She did not hesitate to argue for her sacramental rights. On one occasion when a new foundation was denied daily Mass because the local ordinary was having second thoughts about approving it, Teresa requested daily confession. To her confessor's objections she retorted, "Don't be stingy with other people's riches." In view of the limitations of clerical ministry, for we know that she both profited and suffered from the official ministry of the Church, it is not surprising she also considered spiritual direction her responsibility; for with her personal call to sanctity came a mission to lead others to perfection. Indeed, Peers claims her mission was less to found convents than to help millions live the life of prayer.[93] As more and more women sense a call to the spiritual ministry of the Church, it is a challenge to the rest of us not only to listen to see if we are called, but also to listen to see if the healing love of Christ is being mediated through their ministry. We must remember that the holy relative that played such a great role in Teresa's own life was a lay person.

Teresa was quite sensitive to the pitfalls of women. Our sisters can be equally sensitive to those weaknesses in us too, for example, trying too much, thinking ordinary experiences are transcendental, becoming depressed at our lack of devotion.

Teresa as spiritual director is eminently practical. She does not try to fog us in with abstractions but comes right to the point—as she did with Sr "Dungheep."

THE REAL CHALLENGE

Up to this point we have focused essentially on the positive elements and images of Teresa's spirituality that merit feminist recognition. But the woman facing mid-life crises and career changes may well balk at taking the crucial step of total surrender to God that Teresa deems imperative if she is to escape ultimate mediocrity. No all-convincing argument can be presented to persuade each and every person that she or he is called to be a mystic. Instant mysticism is not promised by Teresa, even though Teresa suggests women do "have a mystical vocation because they are more open to and vulnerable to God's grace"—a case of strength in weakness.[94] Teresa does not mince words. No progress in the spiritual life is made so long as we are not loving neighbor more than self. But the more we love our neighbor, the more we'll love God.[95] However, it is not just a case of loving. Suffering is involved too. Commenting on the words of the Our Father, "thy will be done," Teresa asks what those mean who beg God to fulfill his will in them and yet are afraid to pray for trials lest they be given? "If you love him, strive that what you say to the Lord may not amount to mere polite words; strive to suffer what His Majesty desires you to suffer."[96] In W she also said it is foolish to accept only those crosses we feel we have a right to expect and to reject the others. Such a person should "return to the world."[97]

Teresa knew the Lord was prepared to wait days, even years for us to respond.[98] After all, hadn't he waited almost twenty years for her? This is perhaps why she is so open about her own spiritual failures—to reassure us today. She tells us that when she was about forty she decided to amend her life but nothing came of her good intentions. The priest she consulted wanted instant perfection which brought her to the brink of despair. Then a holy relative came into the picture who could put up with her failures. We too should be prepared to accept help from unexpected sources. She attributes her own salvation to the fact this relative knew how to treat her—which is no small tribute.[99]

The next clue she gives us is that the confessor she finally found who truly helped her, led her by the way of love, not oppression. This does not mean one seeks a gentle hand that will tolerate self-indulgence instead of self-discipline. The same confessor suggested to Teresa that her ill health was perhaps sent because she avoided penances.[100] To her surprise, Teresa ultimately found prayer contributed to her good health and seemingly endless energy. In fact, after suffering from cancer and other ailments probably for over a year prior to her collapse at the convent of Alba de Tormes (several weeks before her death), she confessed when she had to be put to bed immediately: "This is the first time I have gone to bed before midnight in nearly twenty years."[101]

Probably one of the most reassuring words from the Lord at least for those struggling with prayer, came several years after her mystical marriage, and after she had received infused knowledge of the Trinity along with other extraordinary favors. Even though this increased her strength tenfold, it was not for her delight, but to serve.[102] Teresa was still far from perfection and this troubled her considerably, yet her concern only brought the following reassurance from Jesus: "Be patient, for as long as you live a wandering mind cannot be avoided." Indeed, she once referred to her mind as being like wild horses so hard was it to control, and apparently in 1575 it was still giving her trouble. She admits not every imagination is by nature able to meditate, but every soul is able to love God.[103] This should be adequate encouragement for the individual willing to take up Teresa's challenge.

The spirituality she proposes is not complicated. It consists of two essentials: love and humility, supported by courage and fortitude, for without the courage to face up to self-knowledge, humility can quickly vanish instead of expanding the soul and helping it serve God. It takes courage to live with oneself, one's failings and cowardliness in the face of the demands of life. Love also needs courage because true love often demands that we take risks, the very surrender of love is a frightening risk between humans, but when that love is directed exclusively to a divine being in a culture such as ours—which at best can be described as agnostic, and lacking the pervasive support systems Teresa enjoyed in her day—such a lifetime commitment truly demands courage. Even the faith context in which Teresa lived did not project her from years of aridity and doubt, so that is why fortitude or perseverance then as now remains crucial. Yet Teresa sincerely believed and taught that mystical experience, infused contemplation, was within the reach of all her nuns or any Christian for that matter. She considered herself living proof, for she was neither a learned theologian nor an overly penitential person, but she had a great capacity for love. It is no wonder then that in her day people already referred to her as a mystical doctor of the Church, although in her dying words she was content simply to declare herself a "daughter of the Church."[104]

For Teresa the whole spiritual life is structured in terms of prayer. To advance in prayer, God, not we, must suspend the understanding. If we suspend it, we'll stay stupid and achieve nothing. When God suspends it, he gives it something which both amazes it and keeps it busy so we understand more in a short space of time than with many years of effort. Lack of confidence and self-love are the usual reasons for a lack of progress. The only purpose of prayer is to help Christ bear the Cross. In this regard, Teresa reflects sound biblical theology and stands squarely in the tradition of ancient Israel whose concern was not with accumulating merit for the next life but simply the privilege of being able to worship God. In W she says her whole desire is the "hallowing of his Name."[105] Prayer is a challenge as any relationship is. Prayer and comfortable living are incompatible. To think of other things while speaking with God amounts to not knowing what mental prayer is.[106] Prayer is the gate of entry into the mystery of God.[107] But, in the final analysis for spiritual growth what matters is not to think much but to love much.[108] Failure to grow is a very bad sign because love is never idle.[109].

Teresa offered her contemporaries a spirituality grounded in a Bible that the Church had placed off limits to her, because as a woman she lacked knowledge of Latin. Today we live in an age that is rediscovering the riches of the Bible, but we are not denied access to it: in fact, our very access to its sacred pages can prove an inhibiting factor in a feminist's prayer life—either because we stumble over its patriarchal sexism or because we discover Christ's liberating message and then look in vain in our ecclesiastical structures for its implementation. Teresa did not hesitate to launch a reform which began with herself, nor should we. She is striking proof that even in unfavorable social and ecclesial circumstances, prayer can flourish; for true prayer is thwarted by nothing, not even the Inquisition, and the latter was a very real threat to her existence and reform. At least four times accusations against Teresa or her L were made to the inquisitors.[110]

Women always have to have the last word, and in Teresa's case that includes the last laugh. Having endured so much hostility and obstructionism from ecclesiastical circles it is amusing to note at least one ecclesiastic whose words must have come back to haunt him. I refer to the Papal Nuncio who referred to Teresa as a "restless gadabout . . . who teaches theology as though she were a doctor of the Church." But evening the score was not her prime concern. Prayer was.

Fidelity to a life of prayer is not easy, prayer ultimately is a gift and this gift which may be long in coming may also have a high price tag in terms of both human and spiritual suffering. In short, her teaching on prayer is very sobering; the stark realism of it, however, is balanced by an amazing enthusiasm which suggests no matter what the price, it is indeed worth it. Surrender remains the hallmark of true prayer; for true prayer is an intimate sharing between friends—not mental gymnastics or dramatic monologues.

True progress comes, she is told, not from trying to enjoy God more, but by trying to do God's will. Jesus' words: "Don't try to hold me within yourself but try to hold yourself within me,"[111] would seem an explicit divine endorsement of the "womb" image we have tried to develop earlier. Moreover, Teresa has left us God's own definition of the nature of union. This is the real challenge and a fitting word on which to conclude:

Union does not lie in being very close to me. For those, too, who offend me are close, although they may not want to be. (Union) consists in the spirit being pure and raised above all earthly things so that there is nothing in the soul that wants to turn aside from God's will . . . no thought of love of self or of any creature.[112]

NOTES

1. Richard Gagnon, "Middle Age for the Christian: Simply a Decline or a Transfiguration?", *Sisters Today,* 52 (1980), 25 and 23. He also notes that Paul was about 47 when he wrote 2 Cor 4:7—11, 16: "the outer man decays . . . the inner is renewed day-by-day."

2. Marcelle Auclair, *Teresa of Avila* (Garden City: Doubleday Image Books, 1959), pp. 77 and 84.

Unless otherwise indicated, references to the works of Teresa will be from the I.C.S. ed., and the Peers ed. for the *Letters* and the *Book of the Foundations.* See L, 7, 11-17.

3. E. Allison Peers, *Mother of Carmel* (New York: Morehouse-Gorham Co., 1946), p. 8: "Servile fear more than love urged her to enter religion." V. Sackville-West, *The Eagle and the Dove* (Garden City: Doubleday, 1944), p. 23 says that at first she was against religious life, then saw it as safest and best. The love of God was not a factor.

4. Auclair, *Teresa,* p. 123. See L, 31, 13 and 32, 10: "I was so perfectly content in the house in which I was because it was very much to my liking and the cell in which I lived was just what I wanted." Although she had thought of going to a stricter convent, she remained undecided until urged by God.

5. Auclair, *Teresa,* p. 387. Teresa blames 400% inflation in part on the Spanish taste for gold and ostentation. Inflation had even ruined Teresa's father (who died in 1543). See Teófanes Egido, "Historical Setting of St Teresa's Life," *Carmelite Studies,* 1 (1980), 148.

6. The I.C.S. ed. loses somewhat the flavor of the older Peers ed. In L, 19, 2 "filthy mud" was "filthy slime"; "wings fall off" replaces "wings droop" in L, 10, 8; and in L, 20, 7 "befouled body" is now "body . . . made of such foul clay."

7. Joann Conn, "Horizons on Contemporary Spirituality," *Horizons,* 9 (1982), 60-73; Ann Carr, "On Feminist Spirituality," *Horizons,* 9 (1982), 96-103; Elizabeth Fiorenza, "Why not the Category Friend/Friendship?", *Horizons,* 2 (1975), 117-118; Ann Whittmann, "Spirituality: A New Force in Feminism," *Sisters Today,* 53 (1981), 83-91; Carol Christ, *Diving Deep and Surfacing* (Boston: Beacon Press, 1980); and Ann Ulanov, *The*

Feminist in jungian Psychology and Christian Tradition (Chicago: Northwestern U. Press, 1971).

8. Carr, *Feminist Spirituality,* p. 101.

9. Ibid., p. 100.

10. Letter to Mother Mary of St Joseph, July 2, 1576 (Stanbrook ed.). At the time Teresa was under investigation by the Inquisition.

11. Sackville-West, *Eagle and Dove,* p. 70 and Auclair, *Teresa,* p. 304.

12. Letter to Gratian, May 24, 1581.

13. Letter to Gratian, September 1, 1582. In the same letter she confesses to Gratian, who went on before she arrived, that " . . . I have felt your absence at such a time so keenly that I've lost all desire of writing to (you) . . . " [both quotations taken from the Stanbrook ed.]

14. Benedict Zimmerman, "Introduction," *The Book of the Foundations of St Teresa of Jesus,* trans. David Lewis (New York: Benziger Brothers, 1912), p. xvi.

15. Auclair, *Teresa,* pp. 392, 393 and 394.

16. Letter to Lawrence, January 17, 1570. See Letter to Joan de Ahumada, December 1569 in which she asks one thing of her sister: " . . . not to love me because I look after your worldly interests, but because I pray for you."

17. Letter to Alonso Ramirez, February 5, 1571.

18. E.g., in Letter to Doña Mary de Mendoza, October 1571 she notes that Father Provincial never answers her letters.

19. Sackville-West, *Eagle and Dove,* p. 69 and Auclair, *Teresa,* p. 266.

20. Auclair, *Teresa,* p. 27.

21. Ibid., p. 40.

22. L 4 7.

23. L, 7, 4 and W, 11,3.

24. Auclair, *Teresa,* p. 43.

25. Ernest Larkin, "St Teresa of Avila and Women's Liberation," *Sisters Today,* 45 (1974), 565.

26. Egido, *Historical Setting,* p. 154.

27. Letter to Gratian, July 14, 1581.

28. L, 19, 4.

29. Otger Steggink, "Teresa of Avila, Woman and Mystic," *Carmel in the World,* 15 (1976), 58,

30. Bernadette Lorenzo, "Le statut corporel de la femme mystique et la relation à Marie chez Thérèse d'Avila," unpublished paper delivered at Eighth International Mariological Congress, Zaragoza Spain, 1979, pp. 5-6. See Spiritual Testimony, 12, 6; the vision occurred in April 1571.

Lorenzo explores the paternal image in Teresa in detail. Teresa goes to school, gets sick, father gets her, takes her home; same sequence occurs in convent, twice! Finally, she returns to the convent, he comes, she teaches him to pray, he dies, she takes his confessor. (Over the years she has sixty or so male advisors and confessors.) Only at sixty-six does she no longer need to run to theologians, she is at peace—see Spiritual Testimony, 65. But Teresa is only partially cured of her dependence on her father, e.g., she took Gratian as confessor while she was sixty-two and he thirty-two, and she bound herself to him by vow of obedience. She admitted it upset her, because she "could not discern the secret dynamism behind the resolution." She associated the pain of this act with that of leaving her father's house for the convent—see Spiritual Testimonies 35 and 36, especially 36, 6.

31. J. Ruth Aldrich, "Teresa, A Self-Actualized Woman," *Carmelite Studies,* 2 (1982), 81.

For a comprehensive survey of psychological assessments of Teresa, see Angel L. Cilveti, *Introductión a la mistica española* (Madrid: Catedra, 1974).

32. L, 36, 12-14.

33. Aldrich, *Teresa, Self-actualized,* p. 88. According to Auclair, *Teresa,* p. 197, Teresa used the great and the powerful but never ceded an inch of her independence or judgment; but God taught her it is sometimes necessary to use a grain of diplomacy—see Letter to Discalced Nuns of Seville, January 31, 1579.

34. Auclair, *Teresa,* p. 208.

35. W, 3, 7.

36. Spiritual Testimony, 11.

37. Auclair, *Teresa,* pp. 305-06 (quoting Letter to Ambrose Marian, October 21, 1576).

38. L, 23, 11.

39. L, 38, 16-17.

40. Sackville-West, *Eagle and Dove,* p. 64. Teresa had a low opinion of woman's intellectual endowments.

41. *Constitutions,* Peers ed., 3, p. 230.

42. Letter to Doña Mary de Mendoza, March 7, 1572.

43. Auclair, *Teresa,* p. 195.

44. Spiritual Testimony, 15.

45. See Kieran Kavanaugh, *Introduction to W,* p. 23ff.

46. Ibid., p. 26.

47. See Kavanaugh, W, note 1, p. 461.

48. Fragment of Letter to Gratian, August 1577 [?]. In her Letter to Anthony Gaytan, March 28, 1581 she refers to Teresita, Casilda and Isabel.

49. Letter to Gratian, September 9, 1576.

50. See Fragment of Letter to Gratian, August 1577 [?].

51. Auclair, *Teresa,* p. 120ff.

52. F, 31, 46.

53. Letter to Mary of St Joseph, April 3 [18?], 1580.

54. He ate some, lest they incriminate people involved in the Reform, as the Carmelites of the Mitigated Observance battered down the doors prior to kidnapping him and holding him prisoner for six months. Later in life he realized his attachment to a bundle of her letters that he still possessed and burned them.

55. Letter to Don Hernando de Pantoja, January 31, 1579.

56. Letter to Mary of St Joseph, November 19, 1576.

57. See Letter to Ambrose Marian, December 12, 1576 and Letter to Lawrence de

Cepeda, February 10, 1577.

58. Letter to Don Peter Castro y Nero, November 19, 1581.

59. Spiritual Testimony, 65, 2, 3, 5, 6 and 7.

60. Letter to Mary of St Joseph, early January 1580.

61. Letter to Elizabeth of St Jerome and Mary of St Joseph, May 3, 1579; also Letters to Mary of St Joseph, dated July 4 and October 25, 1580 respectively.

62. Letter to Discalced Carmelite Nuns of Seville, January 13, 1580.

63. L, 22, 10.

64. W, 4, 5 and 6, 7.

65. Auclair, *Teresa,* p. 163.

66. L, 11, 2.

67. W, 32, 7.

68. Larkin, *Teresa and Women's Liberation,* p. 567.

69. See quotations of Osuna by Kavanaugh, *Introduction to W,* p. 23: " . . . lock the door or break your wife's leg if she's visiting churches and pretending to be a saint."

70. Kavanaugh, *Introduction to W,* p. 23. The series of *Indexes* of Valdés in question appeared in 1551, 1554 and 1559. The editors quote a notation by the censor regarding W, 21 : " . . . it seems she is reprimanding the Inquisitors for prohibiting books on prayer."

She maintained it was wrong to prevent women from enjoying the riches contained in God's words and works. See *Meditations on the Song of Songs,* 1, 8 and Kavanaugh's *Introduction to Song of Songs,* p. 207.

71. Kavanaugh, *Introduction to Song of Songs,* p. 209. In her commentary on the Song of Songs she concentrates on love between Jesus and the soul. Later, about 1580, a confessor ordered her to burn it because it was not right for a woman to write on the Song of Songs.

72. W, 7, 8.

73. Letter to Don Jerome Reinoso, May 20, 1582.

74. Kavanaugh, *Introduction to W,* p. 28.

75. Pierluigi Pertusi, "Spiritual Direction in the Major Works of St Teresa," *Carmelite Studies,* 1 (1980), 53.

76. L, 19, 9. "Serve me and don't bother about such things" was what she perceived in her first locution (which frightened her).

77. John Welch, "Jungian Readings of Symbols in the *Interior Castle,*" talk given at Washington, D.C. in February 1982. See his work *Spiritual Pilgrims: Carl Jung and Teresa of Avila* (New York: Paulist Press, 1982).

78. W, 28, 10.

79. Sonya Quitslund, "In the Image of Christ," *Women Priests* ed. Leonard and Arlene Swidler (New York: Paulist Press, 1977), p. 262.

80. Sonya Quitslund, "Putting the Finger on the Sore Spot: Sexuality," paper given at College Theology Society Annual Meeting, June 3, 1977. See also Walter Bedard, "Symbolism of the Baptismal Font in Early Christian Thought," Ph.D. Dissertation submitted to Catholic University of America, 1951.

81. Julian of Norwich, *Revelations of Divine Love* (Baltimore: Penguin Books, 1966),

p. 165: "God all-wise our kindly Mother . . . The Second Person . . . is our Mother, Brother and Savior"; and p. 169: "What does Jesus, our true Mother, do? Why, he . . . bears us to joy and eternal life!"

82. Gershom Scholem, *Major Trends in Jewish Mysticism*. (New York: Schocken Books, 1941), pp. 49-54:

The idea of the seven heavens through which the soul ascends to its original home, either after death or in a state of ecstasy while the body is still alive, is certainly very old. In an obscure and somewhat distorted form it is already to be found in old apocrypha such as the Fourth Book of Ezra or the Ascension of Isaiah, which is based on a Jewish text. In the same way, the ancient Talmudic account of the seven heavens, their names and their contents, although apparently purely cosmological, surely presupposes an ascent of the soul to the throne in the seventh heaven. Such descriptions of the seven heavens plus a list of the names of their archons, have also come down to us from the school of the Merkabah mystics of the post-Mishnaic period.

Jewish mysticism was almost exclusively masculine, with perhaps the exception of the maid of Ludmir.

Stephen Clissold, *Wisdom of Spanish Mystics* (New York: New Direction Books, 1977), p. 6f. says there is no question of any interaction of Jews on Catholic mysticism, but the high percentage of Spanish mystics with Jewish blood remains a remarkable fact.

83. Kavanaugh, *Introduction to C,* p. 278.

84. There is some exceptions: saints like Catherine of Genoa claim that it occurred at the moment of her conversion and continued for the rest of her life. In the fourth dwelling place Teresa is very explicit: God is not obliged to give the gift and nothing we can do will produce the gift. See C, 4, 2, 9.

85. W, 31, 9.

86. See Elmer O'Brien, *Varieties of Mystic Experience* (New York: New American Library, 1964), p. 33f.

87. C, 4, 3, 5.

88. Ibid., 5, 3, 5.

89. Ibid., 5, 4, 1-2. We might also recall how in the Bible, the dove functions as a symbol for God or the divine presence.

90. Sonya Quitslund, "Women of the Covenant," *Sign Magazine,* May (1981), 13.

91. C, 6, 6, 4. She would give a thousand lives—if she had that many—if one soul were to praise God a little more through her.

92. Kavanaugh, *Introduction to W,* p. 20.

93. Peers, *Mother of Carmel,* p. 82.

94. Larkin, *Teresa and Women's Liberation,* p. 567.

95. Auclair, *Teresa,* p. 59 and C, 5, 3, 8.

96. W, 32, 7.

97. Ibid., 13, 1.

98. C, 2, 1, 3.

99. L, 23, 6-7 and 10.

100. Ibid., 24, 1-2.

101. Michael Griffin, "The Dying Teresa of Avila," *Spiritual Life,* 22 (1976), 190.

102. Auclair, *Teresa,* p. 337.

103. F, 5, 2.

104. Auclair, *Teresa,* pp. 383, 435 and 443. The University of Salamanca has the honor of first officially recognizing her as a Mystical Doctor, well before the Vatican.

105. W, 31, 3 as found in Peers ed., p. 128.

106. Ibid., 4, 2 and 22, 8.

107. Kavanaugh, *Introduction to C,* p. 270.

108. C, 4, 1, 7.

109. Ibid., 5, 4, 10.

110. These occurred in 1576, twice in 1578 and in 1579.

111. Spiritual Testimony, 14.

112. Spiritual Testimony, 25, 1-2.

Teresa and Her Times

St Teresa of Avila and the Avila of St Teresa

◆ ◆ ◆

Jodi Bilinkoff, Ph.D.

Jodi Bilinkoff earned her doctorate in history from Princeton University by presenting a dissertation on "The Avila of St Teresa: Religious Reform and Urban Development, 1480-1620." She now teaches history at the University of North Carolina at Greensboro.

INTRODUCTION[1]

St Teresa is closely associated with the city of her birth. She is commonly referred to as "St Teresa *of Avila*" rather than by her name in religion, Teresa of Jesus. Yet studies generally emphasize purely literary or theological features of the saint's experience, and, modern, critical research on the city of Avila hardly exists at all. The purpose of this study is to examine the social and religious history of Avila in the early sixteenth century, and to suggest ways in which its people and institutions influenced the content and character of St Teresa's reform movement.

AVILAN LIFE UNTIL THE 1540S

In the Middle Ages Avila existed as a frontier fortress-city. Located on strategic mountain passes between the Duero and Tajo valleys, it was the site of fierce and continual warfare between Christians and Muslims during Spain's centuries-long Reconquest. The Christians finally gained definitive control of the region in 1083 and began to repopulate the city. The city's cathedral and famous massive walls date from the early twelfth century.[2]

In this "Society Organized for War,"[3] military strength and prowess were set at a premium. A class of noble warriors quickly came to dominate residents dependent upon them for protection. The city was known as "Avila de los Caballeros," "Avila of the Knights."

By the end of the fifteenth century, during a period of relative political stability and economic prosperity, descendants of these knights, and of men more recently enobled through service to the Castilian crown, strove to consolidate their hold on the city's political institutions. Aristocrats controlled Avila's City Council, possessing public offices for life and then bequeathing them to sons or nephews. Municipal documents record how members of certain families held positions in city government for four or five consecutive generations, as elites sought power and influence for themselves and their heirs.[4]

These concerns were reflected in their control of many features of the city's religious life as well. Between 1450 and 1510 members of Avila's upper class families established or restored monasteries, convents and churches, and actively endowed *capellanías,* or chaplaincies. This institution perhaps best illustrates the concern for dynastic consolidation and continuity held by noble donors.

Typically a patron would donate an annual income to a religious house or church in exchange for burial in a particular chapel. He would mandate prayers for his soul and for those of his heirs in perpetuity, and often, for his parents as well. In the case of Dōna María de Herrera's 1512 endowment at the chapel of Mosén Rubí, this entailed moving remains from one location to another.[5] By 1623 Don Diego de Guzmán gained the right not only to bury members of his family at the new Jesuit college of San Ignacio, but also to disinter the bodies already there![6]

The regular and secular clergy of Avila's religious institutions, especially its monastic houses, practiced a style of spirituality appropriate to the dynastic concerns of their benefactors, and of the class from which, in fact, most monks and nuns derived. Anniversary masses and other commemorative and intercessory prayers chanted for the souls of patrons, their kin and clients made up a considerable portion of their liturgical program.

These prayers were vocal prayers. Because of this benefactors or their descendants could ascertain if the religious fulfilled the terms of their endowments or not. And it was extremely important that they know, because prayers helped an individual toward salvation, and proclaimed the power and continuity of his dynasty as surely as the family coat-of-arms he had carved upon the chapel walls.[7]

In the decades between 1510 and 1550 Avila experienced remarkable growth and development. Its population, of under 10,000 inhabitants in 1530 reached 15,000 by 1561.[8] Economic expansion, especially in the flourishing Castilian wool trade attracted migrants of all different social ranks. Noble landowners left their estates in the care of stewards and moved to the city, constructing elegant urban *palacios* within Avila's walls. Outlying poor and artisanal neighborhoods swelled with incoming rural dwellers, seeking opportunities in the textile and leather trades, as domestic servants to the rich, or as beggars, thieves or prostitutes. By the late 1550s Avila's city councilors banned further construction in one of the city's two main marketplaces, the Mercado Chico, claiming that it was already so crowded that "gentlemen cannot turn their horses."[9]

Urban growth brought urban problems. The sheer concentration of people often stretched the city's resources to the limit. Food, water and shelter were often in short supply, especially for the poor.

These problems in turn strained already existing tensions between social groups within the city. As early as 1502 the royal official Anthony Pérez noted the resentments which arose from the unequal distribution of power in a city in which a small social elite dominated municipal administration. He recommended that the citizens of Avila assemble each year to elect two representatives, one for the nobles, and one for the mass of tax-paying commoners, a policy he felt would avoid "muchas discordias," "many conflicts."[10]

Demographic expansion and urban development brought noteworthy changes to Avila in the first half of the sixteenth century, which affected the character of relations between social groups. Economic opportunity attracted large numbers of rural immigrants. The city's poor and artisans were particularly vulnerable to shortages of food and water, overcrowding and unsanitary conditions. Often frustrated in their expectations of material gain, they occasionally resorted to vocal, or even violent forms of protest, much feared by local elites.

In this period the spiritual climate within Avila underwent important changes as well. Religious reform movements, originating outside as well as inside the city addressed personal and social problems brought into focus by accelerated urban growth. Traditionally, effecting religious reform consisted of providing sufficient endowments for a decorous and numerous clergy, which prayed continuously for the souls of departed benefactors and their clients.[11] This system satisfied the spiritual, economic and dynastic needs of a hereditary aristocracy.

Beginning in the 1540s, new religious movements articulated an alternative definition of reform, which emphasized the importance of a personal experience of conversion and penitence and reflected the concern among many to relieve the condition of the poor. It featured a clergy committed to the active apostolate among a large community of believers, and the development of methods of internalized mental prayer which afforded the individual a more immediate and direct experience of God. In Avila the ideals of service to the community on the one hand, and of the spiritual formation of the individual on the other appealed to an important group of concerned clerics and laymen. Members of this group patronized the Children of Christian Doctrine, the Jesuit College of San Gil, the Seminary of San Millán, the holy woman Mari Díaz, and eventually, Teresa of Jesus and her reform of the Carmelite Order. The saint, in turn, took many of her ideas concerning religious practice, practical administration and prayer from the religious movements and institutions which emerged in Avila in the mid-sixteenth century. They fostered an atmosphere in which her own ideas could develop.

EMERGING NEW MOVEMENTS

The famous preacher, writer and clerical reformer, John of Avila (1499?-1569), played a critical role in the spiritual revitalization and administrative reorganization of the Church in Spain in the sixteenth century.[12] He was not from the city of Avila, but rather from La Mancha, and spent most of his life in southern Spain, where he gained fame as the "Apostle of Andalucía." Although he never set foot in Avila, his writings and programs greatly influenced a group of followers there, as in other parts of Spain, Italy and France. "Maestro Avila," as he was known, corresponded with many religious reformers in Avila, including the nun Teresa de Ahumada.[13]

John of Avila began his apostolate as a young priest in the late 1520s. He stayed in towns in Andalucía, preaching, hearing confessions, organizing aid to the numerous poor and educating children and unlearned adults in the fundamentals of Christian doctrine. He felt that the responsibility for remedying the problems of the Church lay in the hands of its clergy. He would eventually write "It is ordained by God that the harm or benefit of the people depends upon the diligence and care of the ecclesiastical estate as the land depends upon the influences of the heavens."[14]

Armed with this high conception of the priestly vocation, Maestro Avila and his followers began to redefine the character and function of the secular clergy. He proposed restricting ordination to a small, but select group of men who felt a genuine calling, rather than merely to anyone who wanted to enjoy the material comforts of a benefice. Potential priests must receive theological and moral training from the earliest age. Only careful formation, not the threat of punishment, would alter men's behavior. By the time of his death in 1569, John of Avila had established fifteen schools for young men, in addition to several schools specifically for the education of priests.

He espoused, and exercised, an active apostolate. He urged priests to imitate Christ in their pastoral work, preaching, hearing confessions, engaging in works of charity and education and living simple, virtuous lives. John of Avila himself had remarkable success as a popular preacher and spiritual director in many Andalucían towns.

The Maestro urged priests to maintain a commitment to preaching the Word to a large audience, regardless of social distinction, and relieving, where possible, the wretched condition of the poor. His writings contain implicit criticisms of chaplaincies and benefices, which bound ecclesiastical organization and religious practice to the needs of a privileged elite, and an ingrained system of patronage and clientage. He condemned the situation in which young men could become priests merely "by virtue of the chaplaincies of their lineages," then neglect their parishioners.[15] John of Avila's uniqueness, and his major importance for reform in Avila lay in his emphasis on religious education, especially for the poor. Humanist interest in education of course, well predated Maestro Avila. But John of Avila succeeded in institutionalizing and popularizing humanist concepts of education, by composing catechisms, establishing a system of schools for both children and adults and developing methods of pedagogy later utilized and expanded by the Society of Jesus and the teaching orders of the seventeenth century.[16]

The concept of the clergy formulated by John of Avila, which emphasized an active apostolate of preaching, confessing, ministering to the poor and educating the young, provided an important model for a group of clerics and devout laymen living in Avila in the 1540s and '50s. This coterie centered around the figure of Gaspar Daza, a major exponent of the ideas and methods of John of Avila. Daza and his "sacerdotal team" became involved in virtually every reform movement in mid-sixteenth century Avila, including that of Teresa of Jesus.[17]

Daza, a prebendary in Avila's Cathedral Chapter, gained fame as a learned and effective preacher. In the 1530s and '40s Daza, like the Maestro, preached to audiences both in the city and in rural villages. The Cathedral Chapter of Avila commissioned him several times to deliver the cycle of Lenten sermons. In addition, Daza heard confessions, lodged students in his home and personally cared for the poor and the sick.

Gradually, Gaspar Daza, like John of Avila, "collected and gathered around him" a group of disciples, natives of Avila who formed the core of a "reform party."[18] These included Francis Salcedo, the "holy gentleman" who figured prominently (with Daza) in the spiritual direction of Teresa de Ahumada, Gonzalo de Aranda, another early supporter of Carmelite reform and Francis de Guzmán. Daza particularly influenced the young Julian of Avila, the future chaplain and biographer of St Teresa.

In 1547 the devout Hernando Alvarez del Aguila, related through marriage to several members of Daza's circle, endowed a new educational and charitable institution called the "Niños de la Doctrina Cristiana," the Children of Christian Doctrine, which resembled in both name and character the schools established by Maestro Avila in Andalucía. Here poor boys would be given food and lodging at the church of San Millán and instructed in the basics of Christian dogma.[19]

Alvarez del Aguila and his associates envisioned a foundation which would form character, not merely distribute alms like traditional relief institutions. Their hope was that the house would produce candidates for the priesthood, young men perhaps without funds or status, but imbued with a sense of Christian purpose and morality, who would go on to serve the community. The foundation, in fact, graduated some of the city's earliest Jesuits, and students at the Seminary of San Millán, Avila's first Tridentine seminary.

The goals and methods of John of Avila and his sacerdotal school were adopted and expanded by the Society of Jesus, the most important of the orders of priests founded in the sixteenth century. Ignatius of Loyola, who greatly admired and often corresponded with the Maestro, developed a similar, but much more tightly organized program of clerical reform, which centered around the formation of active priests engaged in public preaching, missionary work, education and poor relief.[20]

Jesuits also responded to deeper problems of urban life. In Avila, a period of rapid growth and unresolved conflicts had alienated individuals and strained relations between social groups. The Jesuits, especially in their elaboration of confessional techniques, addressed the needs of individual laymen as well as clerics. Their organizational structure, which featured a hierarchy bound by a sense of commitment and obedience, offered an alternative to a larger, societal hierarchy based upon birth and privilege. The Society institutionalized periods of mental prayer and examination of conscience, which virtually abolished choral, intercessory prayer, and emphasized service to the individual and to a community of believers, rather than to particular families. Ignatian spirituality and institutional organization would make a profound impression upon St Teresa, who counted Jesuits among her most trusted confessors.

Ignatius of Loyola felt that Jesuits must, as far as possible, "be left free to accept the missions from the Apostolic See and other works for the service of God and the help of souls."[21] For this reason Loyola departed from a traditional system which bound religious spiritually and economically to particular families. He left the members of his Society free to serve the needs of a wider community of believers, especially the poor. Jesuits normally did not accept obligations to celebrate masses, positions as parish priests or prelates, or gratuities for spiritual duties. In the early years of the Society, they charged no tuition fees at their schools. Their interpretation of the vow of poverty and desire for autonomy precluded this.[22]

At the College of San Gil in Avila, founded in 1553, one of the most generous of a consortium of backers was John Vázquez de Medina, Dean of the Cathedral Chapter and uncle of one of the college's founders, the Jesuit Louis de Medina. Don John, in his 1566 will, left money for the house, and a substantial donation for the upkeep of deserving students. He, however, made no mention of anniversary masses, chaplains, tombs, coats-of-arms or any of the usual stipulations contained in chaplaincies.[23] San Gil was a different kind of foundation, and its supporters shared the humanist ideals of education and moral foundation, and the concern for an educated and committed clergy then being articulated at the Council of Trent.

The ideas and program of the Society of Jesus found acceptance with the reforming party associated with Gasper Daza. Hernando Alvarez del Aguila, the founder of the Children of Christian Doctrine, became a Jesuit around 1550. After several years of negotiations, Alvarez gained papal permission to apply his ecclesiastical benefices toward the establishment of a Jesuit college in Avila. In 1553 Bishop Diego de Alava y Esquivel, a participant at the Council of Trent and generous supporter of the Jesuits, offered them the old parish church of San Gil as a college for young men.[24]

The reforms initiated by the sacerdotal school of John of Avila and the Society of Jesus concentrated on the role of trained, virtuous and committed priests who would serve a community of believers through education, poor relief, preaching and spiritual direction. Paralleling these developments was the emergence of a form of spirituality which featured the practice of extreme asceticism and the reception of a direct experience of God on the part of extraordinary and largely autonomous individuals. In Avila, this trend was represented by the *beata*, or charismatic holy woman, Mari Díaz.[25] This illiterate peasant woman became the most revered religious figure in mid-sixteenth century Avila. Through her holy example and talent as advisor, consoler and mediator of conflicts, she too succeeded in serving the urban community. A person who deeply influenced St Teresa by her willingness to suffer, and unquestioning faith in God's providence, Mari Díaz lent her spiritual prestige to the Jesuits, and to the project which symbolized the culmination of the apostolic program of Gaspar Daza and his circle, the foundation of Avila's first Tridentine seminary in 1568.

Mari Díaz was born to prosperous peasants in the village of Vita, in the province of Avila, probably around 1490. She moved to Avila, like so many rural dwellers, in the 1530s, when she was about 40 years old. In this case, the immigrant moved to the city, not in search of work in the wool trade, but "Because she had heard it said that there were sermons in the city of Avila."[26]

Mari Díaz lived at first in the working district of *las Vacas:* She quickly gain recognition for her life of extreme austerity and prayer. She had made a vow of chastity back in the village. Once in Avila, she vowed also to live in complete poverty, giving her few possessions to the needy around her.

She sought spiritual directors, exhausting, as one writer claimed "several monasteries with her pleas that they might confess her."[27] The foundation of San Gil in 1553 changed her life. The enthusiastic young Jesuits, committed to developing programs of systematic prayer and mortification, and indifferent to the social status and potential for donations of their penitents, agreed to direct the holy woman. On the orders of her confessors, she went to live at the palace of the pious widow, Doña Guiomar de Ulloa.

Here her humility was put to the test. Taken from her poor, but free and respected life in the neighborhood, she now worked as a domestic servant. But her six-year stay at this house had several important consequences. Through Doña Guiomar the holy life and edifying words of Mari Díaz became familiar to members of Avila's aristocracy. Her neighborhood reputation grew to city-wide recognition and respect. And it was here in the late 1550s that Mari Díaz met St Peter of Alcántara, the renowned Franciscan reformer, and Teresa de Ahumada.

In 1564 or '65 Bishop Alvaro de Mendoza gave Mari Diáz permission to move from the house of Doña Guiomar to a side chamber of the church of San Millán. She lived there until her death in 1572. Her decision to remain cloistered in a tiny room, subsisting on one meal a day, wearing rags, sleeping on a board with a stone for a pillow and spending hours in prayer before the Blessed Sacrament recalls the heroic asceticism of the stylite saints and desert hermits of late antiquity.[28] The early Christian monks built a city in the desert, and Mari Díaz, by living like a hermit, but in a church located right off Avila's main marketplace, succeeded in bringing the desert to the city. Her presence sacralized this corner of worldly bustle and activity.

The *beata* played an integral part in the city's social life. The "Mother" Mari Díaz interacted with the people who continually came to talk with her, offering words of consolation, homely advice and spiritual counsel, settling disputes and interceding for her suppliants with her prayers. A villager who had come to the city, a woman hostile to the vanities of dress and good looks, an old person who involved herself with the problems of the young and a peasant who had lived in the palace of an aristocrat, Mari Díaz occupied a social category all her own, sexless, ageless and classless. Her success in expressing a generalized, urban spirituality lay in her ability to reconcile disparate elements of the city's population.

Mari Díaz could not exercise the forms of spiritual leadership open only to men. She could not preach, celebrate Mass, hear confessions or absolve sins. She could, however, set an example, expressing in a less formal way the virtues of penitence and mortification emphasized by the Jesuits. Not surprisingly, many held the holy woman, with her piety, patience and humility, as a model for female behavior. Interestingly, she also influenced male behavior, in particular, male clerical behavior, which, as we have seen, in this period was undergoing careful scrutiny and redefinition.[29]

Although well-advanced in years during her period of cloister at San Millán, Mari Díaz maintained a special relationship with young people. Like John of Avila, she taught the city's children their basic prayers. Years after her death, many of Avila's priests would recall the uplifting conversations they had had with Mari Díaz during their years as seminarians. She also gathered around her a group of young women who came to the *beata* for their moral education and formed the core of a network of female spiritual support and communication which spanned two generations.

In 1568 the trio consisting of Gaspar Daza, Julian of Avila and Mari

Díaz approached the Bishop of Avila with a plan. As the Children of Christian Doctrine occupied only a small part of the building complex at San Millán, they proposed converting the remainder to a seminary for the training of the bishopric's priests, as mandated by the recently-ended Council of Trent. The bishop, Don Alvaro de Mendoza, enthusiastically supported the project, and directed certain funds for this purpose. By 1572, although still awaiting papal approval, the Seminary of San Millán operated with a rector and six poor boys.[30]

Daza and Julian of Avila, involved many years in educational and clerical reform measures, probably conceived the Seminary of San Millán. But in order for their project to succeed, they needed the prestige, the popular appeal and the connections with the city's aristocracy which only their illiterate penitent could provide. By 1568 the *beata* who spoke familiarly with God from her little room at San Millán distinguished the church as the site of direct religious experience. The involvement of a figure widely known and identified with youth, education and clerical formation added legitimacy to an enterprise precisely designed to further these ends. Mari Díaz, mystic and holy woman, played a fundamental role in the creation of the first Tridentine seminary in Avila, and one of the first in all of Spain, completing the drive for formalized clerical education begun some forty years earlier by Maestro John of Avila.

ST TERESA AND THE REFORM PARTY

The period between 1540 and 1570 saw religious innovation and experimentation in Avila, as new ideas, some external, some indigenous, affected the spiritual atmosphere within the city. Urban growth and social change over several decades precipitated the emergence of an alternative vision of the religious life, which developed alongside an older view linking religious patronage and liturgical practice to the consolidation and perpetuation of the city's great dynasties. The institutions fostered by Gaspar Daza and members of his circle, namely, the Children

of Christian Doctrine, the Jesuit College of San Gil and the Seminary
of San Millán emphasized the role of a secular clergy dedicated to the
ideals of service to a wide community through public preaching, poor
relief and the education of youth. The Society of Jesus in particular also
stressed the spiritual formation of the individual through confession,
penitence and a program of systematic mental prayer. The charismatic
holy woman, Mari Díaz, lent her spiritual prestige and authority to the
articulation of these apostolic goals as well.

When, on August 24, 1562, Teresa de Ahumada and four other
women officially established the Convent of St Joseph as nuns of the
primitive Carmelite *Rule,* Gaspar Daza presided over the ceremony,
reserving the Blessed Sacrament in the convent and bestowing upon
the nuns their habits of coarse woolen material. Present also were other
members of Avila's "reform party" who had helped to realize this foundation, Julian of Avila, Gonzalo de Aranda and Francis Salcedo.[31]

It was entirely fitting that these people, some of whom had supported local reform institutions for the preceding fifteen years, would
have been in attendance at the birth of a monastic order which emphasized many of their goals and values. St Teresa was deeply affected
by the reform movements of the mid-sixteenth century in Avila. She
attempted to adapt the features of apostolic service, religious autonomy,
mental prayer, asceticism and the reception of direct religious experience to a female, monastic and contemplative context. Her ability to
reconcile the structure and discipline of institutional reform with the
emotional, experience-based spirituality of the holy woman resulted in
the reform of the Carmelite Order, one of the great achievements of the
Counter-Reformation, and Avila's most enduring legacy.

NOTES

1. Because of the use of archival materials throughout this article I will use the following abbreviations:

ADA   Archivo Diocesano, Avila
AGS   Archivo General del Estado, Simancas

AHN   Archivo Histórico Nacional, Avila
AHPA   Archivo Histórico Provincial, Avila
ASA   Archivo del Seminario, Avila
BAH   Boletín de la Real Acadmia de la Historia
CODOIN   Colección de Documentos Inéditos de la Historia de España

2. For the early history of Avila see general works such as Juan Martín Carramo-lino, *Historia de Avila, suprovinciay obispado* I (Madrid, 1872), pp. 5-136; José María Quadrado, *Salamanca, Avila y Segovia* (Barcelona: Ed. Daniel Cortezo y Cia., 1884), pp. 302-03; Enrique Ballesteros, *Estudio histórico de Avila y su territorio* (Avila, 1896), pp. 16-21; and Luis Ariz, *Historia de las grandezas de la Ciudad de Avila* (Alcalá de Henares: Luys Martinez Grande, 1607), I^r-7^r (not always reliable).

3. Elena Lourie, "A Society Organized for War: Medieval Spain," *Past and Present,* 35 (1966), 54-76.

4. This information comes from an analysis of the Actas Consistoriales, AHPA, and genealogical material provided in Ariz and other sources.

See also Luis Suárez Fernández, *Nobleza y monarquía: Puntos de vista sobre la historia política castellana del siglo XV* (Valladolid: U. de Valladolid, Fac. de Filosofia y Letras, 1975), pp. 9-17. Coll. "Estudios y Documentos," 15; Salvador de Moxo, "De la nobleza vieja a la nobleza nueva: La transformación nobiliaria castellana en la baja Edad Media," *Cuadernos de Historia,* 3 (1969); and Marie-Claude Gerbert, "Les guerres et l'accès à la noblesse en Espagne de 1465 à 1592," *Mélanges de la Casa de Velázquez,* 8 (1978), 295-325.

5. The will of Doña Maria de Herrera was published by Manuel de Foronda, "Mosén-Rubín: su capilla en Avila y su escritura de fundación," BAH, 63 (1913), 332-50.

6. AHN, sección Jesuitas, legajo 489-1.

7. See, for example, the busy calendar of anniversary Masses in the cathedral's "Libro de pitanzas, sepelios y aniversarios," AHN, Codices 914-b; and Nicolas González y Gonzalez, *El monasterio de la Encarnación de Avila* I (Avila. Caja Central, 1976), pp. 177-95.

8. Felipe Ruíz Martín, "La población española al comienzo de los tiempos modernos," *Cuadernos de Historia,* 1 (1967), 189-202; Ramon Carande Thobar, *Carlos V y sus banqueros* (Madrid: Soc. de Estudios y Publicaciones, 1965), pp. 57-71; and "Vecindad de la Ciudad y Arrabales de Avila," May 17, 1561, AGS, Expedientes de Hacienda, seg. serie, leg. 50-3.

9. Actas, AHPA, 1588 and 1562. The "Ordanazas" of Avila of 1485 ordered the churches of San Juan and la Magdalena to keep the Mercado Chico and Mercado Grande, respectively, free of objects during public use of these spaces, such as bullfights, jousts, etc.: BAH, 72 (1918), 313-16.

10. "Copia de carta o memorial del licenciado Antonio Pérez," April 24, 1502, CODOIN, vol. 36, pp. 447-54. I owe this valuable reference to Prof. Charles Gibson.

11. Marcel Bataillon, *Erasmo y España,* trans. Antonio Alatorre (Mexico City: Fondo de Cultura Económica, 1950), pp. 1-10.

12. John of Avila, long neglected by historians and theologians, finally began receiving scholarly attention in *the* years surrounding his canonization in 1970. The best

study of his life and work is the six volume *Obras completas del Santo Maestro Juan de Avila* ed. Luis Sala Balust and—continued after Sala's death by—Francisco Martin Hernandez (Madrid: La Editorial Catholica, 1970). Coll. "Biblioteca de Autores Cristianos," 313-15.

13. For correspondence with Gaspar Daza, Francisco de Guzmán, Mari Díaz, and St Teresa see José Vicente Rodriguez, "Cinco cartas ineditas de San Juan de Avila," *Revista de Espiritualidad,* 34 (1975), 366-71.

See, also, *Obras* V, pp. 573-76; 655-56; and 660-61.

14. "Memorial segundo al Concilio de Trento, 1561" (Causas y remedios de las herejías), *Obras* VI, p. 86.

See also the valuable work of Carlos Maria Nannei, *La "Doctrina Christiana" de San Juan de Avila* (Pamplona: Eds. U. de Navarra, 1977).

15. See, for example, *Obras* VI, pp. 40, 55 and 222-25.

16. *Obras* VI, p. 36; and Jean Pierre Dedieu, "'Christianisation' en Nouvelle Castille: Catéchisme, Communion, Messe et Confirmation dans l'Archevêché de Tolède, 1540-1650," *Mélanges de la Casa de Velazquez,* 15 (1979), 264.

17. Rodriguez refers to the "equipo sacerdotal" in *Cinco cartas,* p. 369.

For Daza see Efrén Montalva and Otger Steggink, *Tiempo y Vida de Santa Teresa* (Madrid: La Editorial Catolica, 1968), pp. 149-54. Coll. "Biblioteca de Autores Cristianos," 283; Silverio de Santa Teresa, *Historia del Carmen Descalzo en Espana, Portugal y America* I (Burgos: Ed. El Monte Carmelo, 1935), pp. 369-75; and Victoriano Larranaga, *La espiritualidad de San Ignacio de Loyola: Estudio comparativo con la de Santa Teresa de Jesús* (Madrid: Casa de San Pablo, 1944), pp. 56-62.

18. Luis de la Puente, *Vida del Padre Baltazar Alvarez* (Madrid, 1958), p. 57.

19. Ferreol Hernández Hernández, "El convento cisterciense de Santa Ana en Avila," *Cistercium,* 11 (1959), 136-44; Carramolino, *Historia de Avila,* 553; ASA, leg. 2, no. 10; and AHN, Clero, leg. 245, 529.

20. For relations between Loyola and Maestro Avila and efforts to amalgamate the two systems of schools see Juan de Avila, *Obras* I, pp. 108-185.

21. *The Constitutions of the Society of Jesus,* trans. George E. Ganss (St Louis, 1970), pp. 94, 174-76 and 281.

22. Ibid., pp. 262-64.

23. AHN, Jesuitas, leg. 491, no. 3.

24. For the origins of the Jesuit college in Avila see *Monumenta Historica Societatis Jesu* II, pp. 108-09, 132 and 141; III, pp. 311 and 366; IV, pp. 584-87; and V, pp. 442-444; also Antonio Astrain, *Historia de la Compania de Jesús en la asistencia de Espana* I, pp. 419-22; Larrañaga, *La espiritualidad,* pp. 62-68; and AHN, Jesuitas, leg. 491, no. 30.

25. Most information concerning Mari Díaz comes from the "Informatión de la vida, muerte y milagros de la Venerable María Díaz," a series of testimonies by people who remembered the holy woman, commissioned by the bishops of Avila between 1600 and 1623. The manuscript is located in ADA, cod. 3.345.

See also De la Puente, *Baltazar Alvarez,* pp. 60-64; Ariz, *Historia,* 50^{v}-51r; Gerardo de San Juan de la Cruz, "María Díaz, llamada La Esposa del Santísimo Sacramento," *El*

Monte Carmelo, 16 (1915), 174-77, 380-82, 414-18; 17 (1915), 102-05, 166-70, 224-29, 300-04, 410-16; (1916), 56-59; Jodi Bilinkoff, "The Holy Woman and the Urban Community in Sixteenth-Century Avila." Paper presented at the Fifth Berkshire Conference on the History of Women, Vassar College, June 1981; and Gerardo de San Juan de la Cruz, *Vida del Maestro Julián de Avila* (Toledo: Impr. de la Viuda e Hijos de J. Peláez, 1915), pp. 183-204.

26. "Information," testimony of Ana Reyes.

27. Ibid., testimony of Bartolomé Dáaz de Luján.

28. Peter Brown, "The Rise and Function of the Holy Man in Late Antiquity," *Journal of Roman Studies,* 61 (1971), 80-101.

29. De la Puente, *Baltazar Alvarez,* p. 60.

30. Hernández, *El convento cisterciense,* pp. 136-44; AHN, Clero, leg. 245; and ASA, leg. 8, no. 6.

31. L, 36.

Teresa of Jesus:
Daughter of the Church and
Woman of the Reformation

◆ ◆ ◆

Keith J. Egan, Ph.D.

*Keith Egan is now Professor and Chairperson of the
Department of Religious Studies at St Mary's College
in South Bend, Indiana. His doctoral dissertation was
completed at Cambridge University and it concerned the
English Medieval Carmelites.*

INTRODUCTION

Some months before her death in 1897, St Thérèse of Lisieux echoed
the dying sentiments of her patroness, St Teresa of Avila. Thérèse wrote:
"Finally, I want to be a daughter of the Church as our holy Mother
St Teresa was . . . "[1] The young French Carmelite thus demonstrated
the power of this image of the Church as mother, a heritage passed on
to her by Teresa of Jesus, for on her deathbed Teresa said many times:
"Finally, Lord, I am a daughter of the Church."[2]

If this study were an inquiry into the psychological implications of
Teresa's devotion to the Church, one could easily show, I expect, that
Teresa's relationship with the Church was not only on the elementary
level of birth, nourishment and a call to loyalty, but was, moreover, a

transforming relationship involving risk and growth, terminology borrowed from John Welch's study of Jung and Teresa of Jesus.[3] I must leave the psychological inquires to others. My task here is to offer some historical reflections upon Teresa's filial kinship with the Church as we learn about this relationship from her life and writings and as it expressed itself in the reform of her Order. Is such filial devotion strained by the impulse to reform? How does a reformer remain a loyal daughter of the Church? What kind of a daughter of the Church is also a woman of the reformation?

MATERNAL IMAGE

Since the theme of this essay concerns the imagery of mother and daughter, it is pertinent to begin with Teresa's own appreciation of the worth of being a daughter. First of all, one may note that Teresa pays special attention to her own role as a daughter and to the impact on her of her parents when she selects material from her childhood for the story of her life.[4] Moreover, she is critical of a family who registered disappointment at the birth of a fifth daughter.

> It is certainly a matter for deep regret that mortals, not knowing what is best for them, and being wholly ignorant of the judgments of God, do not realize what great blessings can come from having daughters or what great harm can come from having sons, and, unwilling, apparently, to leave the matter to him who understands everything and is the Creator of us all, worry themselves to death about what ought to make them glad . . . And how many fathers will find themselves going to hell because they have had sons, and how many mothers, through the help of their daughters, will find themselves going to heaven![5]

Teresa, moreover, uses maternal imagery for her relationship with the Carmelite nuns for whom she writes. She regularly calls them "daughters,"[6] or "my daughters."[7] At other times she addresses them as "sisters"[8] or "my sisters."[9] Teresa as a prioress was "Mother" to her nuns.[10] John of the Cross writes of " . . . the blessed Teresa of Jesus our Mother . . . "[11] As foundress she has ever since been known to her progeny as *La santa Madre,* our holy Mother.

Yet, there is a problem in Teresa's attitude toward women. Her deprecating remarks about them are well known by her readers, such as her comment that " . . . everything can be harmful to those as weak as we women are,"[12] or stronger still: *"I* would not want you, my daughters, to be womanish in anything, nor would I want you to be like women but like strong men."[13] She tells a correspondent that she would not want him " . . . to pay any heed to what we silly women say . . . "[14] The place of women in society and the Church at her time, the lack of education on the part of Teresa and her nuns account for this impoverished attitude toward women that troubles us moderns. Yet, Teresa sees beyond this time-bound outlook. She affirms the worth of women very emphatically in words omitted from the second redaction of W at the insistence of the Dominican García de Toledo who obviously thought Teresa's statement too bold. The omission is the bracketed section of the following quotation:

> Nor did you, Lord, when you walked in the world, despise women; rather, you always, with great compassion, helped them. [And you found as much love and more faith in them than you did in men. Among them was your most blessed mother., and through her merits—and because we wear her habit—we merit what, because of our offenses, we do not deserve. Is it not enough, Lord, that the world has intimidated us . . . so that we may not do anything worthwhile for you in public or dare speak some truths that we lament over in secret, without your also failing to hear so just a petition? I do not believe, Lord, that this could be true of your goodness and justice, for you are a just judge and not like those of the world. Since the world's judges are sons of Adam and all of them men, there is no

virtue in women that they do not hold suspect. Yes, indeed, the day will come, my king, when everyone will be known for what he is. I do not speak for myself, because the world already knows my wickedness—and I have rejoiced that this wickedness is known publicly—but because I see that these are times in which it would be wrong to undervalue virtuous and strong souls, even though they are women.][15]

Teresa is backed up by a dear friend in her estimate that more women than men receive mystical gifts:

There are many more women than men to whom the Lord grants these favors. This I heard from the saintly Friar Peter of Alcantara— and I too have observed it—who said that women make much more progress along this path than men do. He gave excellent reasons for this, all in favor of women; but there's no need to mention them here.[16]

The best affirmation of women by Teresa is her own personality, character and achievements as author, foundress and reformer, and her growth in holiness. Her derogatory remarks about women pale alongside the splendidly independent and mature woman she becomes. Melveena McKendrick knows the names of only four women of Spain's Golden Era who qualify as truly seeking intellectual and creative excellence. She counts Teresa of Jesus as not only one of these four but as " . . . the only outstanding woman writer of the Golden Age . . . " According to McKendrick, Teresa's " . . . works rank with the greatest of her religious contemporaries."[17]

THE CHURCH

The point at issue, however, is Teresa's devotion to the Church. To document this devotion for readers of St Teresa is redundant. What

is more, Teresa surely would consider it an exercise in the obvious.
However, to ground this exploration in some specifics, allow me to indicate broadly Teresa's attitude toward the Church. First of all, affiliation
with the Church began for her soon after her birth in 1515 when she
received the sacrament of Baptism at the parish church of St John in
Avila.[18] At this ceremony she was named for her maternal grandmother,
Doña Teresa de las Cuevas, but the name Teresa caused her biographers
some embarrassment because it did not appear in the church's martyrol-
ogy. Later her friend, Jerome Gratian, would tease her about not having
a saint's name. Never left without a retort, Teresa practiced some home-
spun philology by replying that the name Teresa comes from that of St
Dorothy *(Dorotea)*.[19]

It is in her writings that St Teresa reveals the intensity of her attachment to the Church for whose growth she is always concerned. The
signs of love, Teresa says, consist " . . . in desiring with strong determination to please God in everything, in striving, insofar as possible, not to
offend him, and in asking him for the advancement of the honor and
glory of his Son and the increase of the Catholic Church."[20] Elsewhere
Teresa reports that she " . . . always persuaded the sisters . . . to be zealous for the good of souls and the increase of his Church."[21]

Teresa's classic statement about the Church occurs at the outset of
W where she elaborates the reasons for her first foundation of St Joseph
in Avila, the prototype of her reformed monasteries of nuns. News of
the trouble which the heretics in France, called by her Lutherans, were
causing the church greatly "distressed" Teresa.[22] These "traitors,"[23] she
claims "want to ravage his Church . . . ;"[24] in fact, the "world is all in
flames."[25] As a woman, Teresa cannot do the "useful things" she desires
"to do in the service of the Lord."[26] She resolves, nonetheless, to make
sure that the Lord's "few friends be good ones."[27] Teresa's initial foundation is a response to the needs of the Church as she knows them.
She and her sisters are "to pray for the Church,"[28] and for its captains,
the preachers and the theologians.[29] Teresa's first foundation, that of St
Joseph in Avila, has its origins as a house of "unceasing prayer"[30] estab-

lished to serve a troubled Church which she cannot serve more directly. Teresa is explicit about this intention. Her heading for chapter 1 of W is "the reason I founded this monastery with such strict observance." This chapter, the next two chapters and the first two paragraphs of chapter 4 articulate the troubles and the needs of the Church and Teresa's response to them. Teresa of Jesus, as she calls herself from the time of this first foundation,[31] and the women who follow her are daughters of the Church whose very raison d'être is to meet the needs of the Church. Teresa spends the rest of her life and all her energy extending this ecclesial commitment by means of her subsequent foundations.

Teresa feels no reluctance in submitting her writings to the judgment of this Church to which she is so devoted; in fact, she is even more eager to seek advice and clearance for her writings from learned men and theologians. However, she makes quite formal submissions of her writings to the Church. With a late addition to W she states in a section that has been called a Foreword to this book: "In all that I say in this book I submit to what our Mother the Holy Roman Church holds."[32] A similar statement appears in the Prologue to the F: "In everything I submit to the doctrine of my Mother, the Holy Roman Church, and I have resolved that before this reaches your hands, my sisters and daughters, it shall be seen by learned and spiritual men."[33] These declarations are worth hearing in full as they reveal on the part of Teresa a precise and detailed exposition of submission. There are several others that accumulatively convey just how precise Teresa is about her announcements of submission to the authority of the Church. Teresa both opens and closes her masterpiece, C, written in 1577 with further nuances to the submission of her writings to the Church. In the Prologue of this work she writes:

If I should say something that isn't in conformity with what the Holy Roman Catholic Church holds, it will be through ignorance and not through malice. This can be held as certain, and also that through the goodness of God I always am, and will be, and have been subject to her.[34]

The Epilogue of C has the following concise statement of submission:

> If anything is erroneous it is so because I didn't know otherwise; and
> I submit in everything to what the holy Roman Catholic Church
> holds, for in this Church I live, declare my faith, and promise to live
> and die.[35]

Finally, Teresa makes another kind of submission, this time an overall
declaration of identification with the Church in one of her *Spiritual
Testimonies,* that was written in 1576 for the Inquisitor of Seville:

> She ever was and ever is subject to all that the holy Catholic faith
> holds, and all her prayer and the prayer in the houses she has
> founded is for the increase in the faith. She used to say that if any of
> her experiences were to induce her to turn against the Catholic faith
> or the law of God, she would have no need to go in search of proof,
> for then she would see it was the devil.[36]

While these submissions, except for the last, sound much like the
statements later to appear on the back of the title pages or in the pref-
aces of books published by Roman Catholics, there is no indication by
Teresa of any irritability or impatience with what she must feel to be a
requirement of the contemporary ecclesiastical atmosphere in Spain. In
this age. of the Spanish Inquisition and the *Index,* Teresa is more than
willing to comply in order to achieve her goals. In this regard as in others Teresa is a pragmatist. She yields easily on nonessentials.

THE INQUISITION

Although Teresa's *Vida* was delated to the Inquisition,[37] she is not
intimidated by this formidable and, in Spain, politically controlled ecclesiastical office. She takes the Inquisition very much in stride. It is not
clear to what extent her use of pseudonyms in her letters is a concern

for the Inquisition, the "Calced" Friars, or merely in some cases a matter of Teresa's playfulness.[38] Moreover, in the so-called *Judgment* document, Teresa is playful and speaks of the Inquisition with tongue-in-cheek.[39] On another occasion she is quite happy to hear that the Grand Inquisitor himself is reading her *Vida*.[40] When friends warn her that she may be accused to the Inquisition, Teresa lightheartedly remarks:

> This amused me and made me laugh, for I never had any fear of such a possibility . . . And I said they shouldn't be afraid about these possible accusations; that it would be pretty bad for my soul if there were something in it of the sort that I should have to fear the Inquisition; that I thought that if I did have something to fear I'd go myself to seek out the Inquisitors; and that if I were accused, the Lord would free me, and I would be the one to gain.[41]

Teresa must take the Inquisition into account, but she works quite easily within a system that even for the times must be reckoned oppressive.[42] Yet, in Teresa it arouses no rancor. The Inquisition may be an arm of ecclesiastical polity, but for Teresa it is obviously not at the heart of what it means to be Church.[43]

THE ROMAN CHURCH, THE COUNCIL OF TRENT

It is the climate in the post-Tridentine church that accounts for Teresa's use of the qualifier "Roman" in writing of the Church. Its use occurs only later in Teresa's life and only when she makes a specific and precise submission of her writings to the Church. The qualifier "Roman" she adds herself, sometime after its composition, in the margin of the submission that appears in the Prologue to the F.[44] The words "Holy Roman Church" appear in the Foreward that is an addition to W.[45] She also adds the words "the holy Roman Church" in a revision of a statement of submission that appears in one of the chapters of the same work.[46] The phrase "Roman Catholic Church" in the Prologue and the

Epilogue of C comes from a work written in 1577, only five years before her death.[47] *Ecclesia Romana* is a traditional phrase that had appeared in the documents of the Fourth Council of the Lateran in 1215, in a listing of opinions of John Wyclif from the Council of Constance, 1414-1417, and at the Seventh Session of the Council of Trent (3 March 1547).[48] It is in the years following Trent that this qualifier becomes more popularly used in order to distinguish the Roman Church or Roman Catholicism from the Protestant Churches.[49] Teresa's later years witness in her writings and precisely in her notes of submission to the judgment of the Church this growing popularization of the qualifier "Roman" for the Church.

The climate created in the Church by the Council of Trent affects the whole of Catholic life from the sixteenth century onwards. However, this council which ended in 1563, the year after Teresa's first foundation, has specific relevance for Teresa as a result of its twenty-fifth and last session in December 1563 with its decree on religious men and nuns.[50] The council's regulations on endowments, enclosure, episcopal licenses for making new foundations, and the minimum age for taking the habit are all issues that concern Teresa as she goes about making her foundations. Teresa's attitude to the Church in council is the same as her attitude to the Church's authority in general. She is deferential and obedient with acquiescence taken for granted. Teresa refers to the Council of Trent only in the F and in her letters.[51] In the former she uses the phrase "Holy Council" except once when it is only "the Council."[52] In her letters she refers merely to "the Council."[53] In regard to the Council of Trent it may even be said that Teresa of Jesus in her choice of strict enclosure at the first foundation of St Joseph at Avila in 1562[54] anticipates the Council's insistence on enclosure for nuns in its Decree on Religious Men and Women enacted on 3-4 December 1563.[55]

CHURCHMEN

Teresa of Jesus leaves us no reflections on the papacy or the popes of her time. She requests and receives a brief from Pius IV in order to make her first foundation.[56] However, the Council of Trent decrees that religious are to seek the permission of the local bishop for new foundations, thus making further recourse to the papacy for this purpose unnecessary for Teresa.[57] The papacy plays so indirect a role in the ambiguities about authority and jurisdiction during the troubled days of the reform that no comments are elicited from Teresa that would reveal anything significant about the papacy in relationship to the Church. Teresa quite naturally acknowledges the authority of the papacy.[58] However, unlike some other women mystics, such as Catherine of Siena, Teresa has no messages to be passed on to popes.[59] Teresa treats with bishops in a businesslike manner and with some of them she is on very friendly terms, for example, Álvaro de Mendoza and Teutonius de Braganza.[60] She takes it for granted that her sisters pray for the bishop[61] and she obviously respects the authority of the bishop.[62] Teresa of Jesus also has great affection for John Baptist Rossi (Rubeo), Vicar General of the Carmelite Order from 1562 and Prior General from 1564 until his death in 1578.[63] When Teresa hears of Rossi's death, she says that she "wept and wept."[64] This Prior General admires Teresa greatly. On the 8th of January 1569 he writes to the Discalced nuns of Medina del Campo:

> I give infinite thanks to the divine majesty for so great a favor bestowed on this order by the diligence and goodness of our reverend Teresa of Jesus. She has done more for the Order than all the friars of Spain. May God grant her long years of life.[65]

Teresa's reputation with Philip Sega, Papal Nuncio in Spain,[66] is not on so warm a note. He speaks of Teresa as a "restless, disobedient and contumacious gadabout, who, under the guise of devoutness invented false doctrines, leaving the enclosure against the orders of the Council of Trent and her own superiors, and teaching as though she were a Master, contrarily to the instructions of St Paul, who had ordered that women were not to teach."[67]

One would trivialize Teresa's relationship with the Church if one

were to hint that her vision of the Church depends upon her dealings
with churchmen or ecclesiastical organizations. Neither, on their own,
constitute the Church. On the other hand, it is no easy task to determine
with exactness what Teresa's notion of the Church is. She is no academi-
cian and has no technical theology of the Church. Yet, we can be more
precise than we have been thus far about her idea of the Church. Like
her Spanish co-religionists in that era, Teresa considers the Church and
Christianity to be identical, a point made by Kieran Kavanaugh in his
Introduction to W.[68] Teresa herself prays: " . . . my God . . . help your
Church. Don't allow any more harm to come to Christianity, Lord."[69]
Those whom she calls Lutherans, in reality Protestants in France, perhaps
Huguenots,[70] " . . . were through Baptism members of the Church."[71]
Now they are "heretics,"[72] a "miserable sect."[73] Yet, she asks her sisters,
each time they read C, to pray "for light for the Lutherans."[74] It would
be anachronistic to expect of Teresa a modern ecumenical appreciation
of Protestant participation in the life of the Church. Nor ought much,
if anything, be made of Teresa's claim to a divinely inspired message that
Christians ought not to follow the Lutherans in discarding externals that
awaken love: "My Christians, daughter, must now more than ever do the
opposite of what they do."[75] In such instances Teresa is not making any
theological precisions; nor does she allege them of God.

Teresa of Jesus' ecclesiology is direct and unsophisticated. For
Teresa the Church is "God's Church."[76] More specifically, the Church
is Christ. In the beginning of W, where she takes up the relationship of
her first foundation to the Church, Teresa writes: "The world is all in
flames, they want to sentence Christ again, so to speak, since they raise
a thousand false witnesses against him . . . "[77] It is Teresa's view that
those who ravage "his Church"[78] are attacking Christ.

CHURCH AS MOTHER

Because Teresa makes no pretense at a theology of the Church,
one may turn to several of her images of the Church. She writes, for

instance, of the Church as bark or ship. Taking her cue from the story in Mt 8:25-26, Teresa prays: "Now Lord, make the sea calm! May this ship, which is the Church, not always have to journey in a tempest like this. Save us, Lord, for we are perishing."[79]

The Church as Mother is Teresa's central image for the Church, not because she used this image often but because she chose this image to express the meaning of her life just before she died. This sentiment, "Finally, Lord, I am a daughter of the Church,"[80] is reported by various witnesses to her last days.[81] In her writings Teresa does not use this image frequently. When she does, with one exception, it is in connection with a submission to what the Church believes.[82] Thus in the F she writes: "In everything I submit to the doctrine of my Mother, the Holy Roman Church . . ."[83] The Foreword she adds to W has this statement: "In all that I say in this book I submit to what our Mother the Holy Roman Church holds . . ."[84]

This image of the Church as Mother is used in 1547 by the Council of Trent which speaks of the " . . . Roman Church which is the Mother and Teacher of all churches . . . ,"[85] and Trent's usage is reminiscent of the words of the Fourth Council of the Lateran (1215) where references is made to the "Roman Church" as " . . . the Mother and Teacher of all the faithful of Christ . . . "[86] Teresa's contemporaries use the image very much as she does. Her collaborator St John of the Cross (d. 1591) in his Prologue to A affirms his intention in this work not " . . . to deviate from the true meaning of Sacred Scripture or from the doctrine of our Holy Mother the Catholic Church."[87] An elder contemporary of Teresa, St Ignatius of Loyola (d. 1556) in the *Spiritual Exercises* also uses the image of the Church as Mother in a like vein. There we hear:

All matters in which we wish to make a choice must be either indifferent or good in themselves. They must meet with the approbation of our Holy Mother, the hierarchical Church, and not be bad or repugnant to her.[88]

In his "Rules for Thinking with the Church," Ignatius also mentions " . . . our Holy Mother, the hierarchical Church." Among the same rules, Ignatius says that scholastic doctors " . . . are helped by the Councils, Canons, and Constitutions of our Holy Mother Church," and that " . . . the same Spirit and Lord, who gave us the Ten Commandments, guides and governs our Holy Mother Church."[89] The image of the Church as Mother had become somewhat formalized in sixteenth-century Spain. On the other hand, the image has a long, rich heritage. It dates back to the second century of the Christian era[90] and in addition has biblical roots in the Old Testament and the New.[91] The image is connected with the Virgin Mary as type of the Church.[92] The Church is both virgin and mother as is Mary of Nazareth. Both are spiritual mothers of Christians. However, in her writings Teresa does not use this imagery with this fullness. Yet, Teresa has a fulsome image of motherhood. The death of her mother is traumatic for Teresa. This event in the *Vida* wherein she sets about trying to understand God's activity in her life (which is what I think she is doing in the *Vida*) is one of the key incidents which she recalls. She writes:

> I remember that when my mother died I was twelve years old or
> a little less. When I began to understand what I had lost, I went,
> afflicted, before an image of Our Lady and besought her with many
> tears to be my mother. It seems to me that although I did this in
> simplicity it helped me. For I have found favor with this sovereign
> Virgin in everything I have asked of her, and in the end she has
> drawn me to herself.[93]

Teresa becomes a member of Our Lady's Order[94] and wears Our Lady's habit.[95] As we have seen above from our discussion of the place that the new foundation of Carmelite nuns at St Joseph in Avila had in Teresa's mind, the renewal of Carmelite life is what we would call an ecclesial event.[96] Teresa had taken a new mother and she now belongs to her new mother's Order. She speaks of her new mother with a warmth that reminds one of the affection she had for the mother who died when she was a teenager.[97]

In her writings Teresa has a sensitivity for the tenderness of a mother's care. Here are some remarks on this theme as she discusses God's activity in prayer: "And notice carefully this comparison [for the Lord put it in my mind while I was at prayer]; it seems to me very appropriate: the soul is like an infant that still nurses when at its mother's breast; and the mother without her babe's effort to suckle puts the milk in its mouth in order to give it delight."[98]

As she faces death, Teresa's lifelong affection for the Church and her appreciation of motherhood make it possible for her to sum up the meaning of her life with the words: "Finally, Lord, I am a daughter of the Church."[99]

TERESA AS REFORMER

Teresa is many things in her life: a lively child, a vivacious young woman, a good nun, an intensely converted nun at midlife, the recipient of special graces in prayer, a foundress of monasteries for nuns, one who fosters a new way of life for friars, a writer with a gift for understanding her own experiences and with a gift for sharing that understanding, and a friend to many contemporaries. Since her time, she has been appreciated for these gifts and more. Consistently, however, history looks back and calls her a reformer. In 1622 Pope Gregory XV in the Bull of Canonization mentions her initiation of the reform of the Carmelite Order.[100] In a letter issued in May of 1982, Pope John Paul II, writing to the Discalced Carmelite nuns of the world calls St Teresa "your reformer,"[101] and "the Reformer of Carmel" in his homily of November 1, 1982, at Avila.[102] The venerable Protestant scholar of the Reformation, Roland H. Bainton, published during the 1970s three volumes on *Women of the Reformation*. In one of these he offers a vivid sketch of the life of St Teresa.[103] However, Teresa is not only a woman from the time of the Reformation. She is a reformer and she is remembered as a reformer from an age when reform is on everybody's mind and when there are numerous reformers. She is a reformer who feels that she best sums up her life by expressing to those who bid her farewell her filial kinship with the Church.

The late medieval Church talks much about reform and tries its hand at numerous reforming ventures. For the most part these attempts at reform are successful on only the local or regional levels. Outram Evennett sketches the futility of these late medieval efforts in a striking way: "The essential sterility and ephemerality—in the long view—of all reform movements between the Council of Constance and the pontificate of Paul III proceeded in the last analysis from the tiredness of generations which seemed to have lost the art of creation, or recreation, in so many spheres of human activity; which could produce neither a Loyola nor a Luther . . ."[104] To Evennett's list of creative reformers I add Teresa of Jesus. There had been reforms in the Carmelite Order during the fifteenth and early sixteenth centuries that produced distinctively holy persons, to name but a few, the Blesseds Bartholomew Fanti, Baptist of Mantua, Angelus Mazzinghi, John Soreth, Aloysius Rabatá, Frances d'Amboise, Archangela Girlani, and Joan Scopelli.[105] Yet, the reforms, out of which these blesseds came, remained largely on the level of the restoration of observance. Moreover, during nearly all of Teresa's lifetime the Carmelite Order had two priors general who both sympathized with and fostered reform.[106] Yet, a creative and far-reaching reform of the Carmelite Order would have to await the unlikely reformer, the lady from Avila, Doña Teresa de Ahumada.

The notion and the word reform are very much in the air in sixteenth-century Europe. The decree opening the Council of Trent asks the Fathers of the Council if they are ready to begin their work of which the "reformation of the clergy and the Christian people" is a principal item on the agenda.[107] Yet, Teresa of Jesus nowhere refers to herself as a reformer. She never uses the word *reforma* or *reformar* in any of her major works. Outside of her correspondence, Teresa uses *reformar* only once and that is late in 1575 in one of her *Spiritual Testimonies:* "I was once thinking about whether they were going to send me to reform a certain monastery [that of the "Calced" Nuns at Paterna], and this troubled me. I heard: 'What do you fear? I shall help you.' It happened on a certain occasion in such a way that my soul was much satisfied."[108]

Interestingly, all the other uses of this word reform by Teresa in her correspondence, twenty-two times in fifteen letters, occur between January 1575 and October 1578.[109] In an era, when the word is on the tongue and pen of numerous churchmen and politicians, this sparse and late use of the word by Teresa is significant. Her first reformed monastery (1562) is inaugurated thirteen years before she ever uses the word. When everyone else is beguiled by the idea of reform, Teresa remains unselfconscious. Only gradually and for a brief time does she use a word that others would later use to classify her mission in the Church and in her Order. It may not cross her mind to speak of reform for a long time after she begins to reform her Order because the idea might well strike her as grandiose and not something women do in the sixteenth-century Church, not the work of a daughter of the Church.

DAUGHTER AND REFORMER OF THE CHURCH

However, Teresa of Jesus is not only a reformer but the creative reformer that Outram Evennett laments the absence of in the late medieval Church. Genuine renewal in the Church is always the work of the Spirit. Vatican II's Pastoral Constitution on the Church in the Modern World, *Gaudium et Spes,* speaks of the " . . . Holy Spirit who renews and purifies her [the Church] ceaselessly."[110] It is the Spirit who brings new life, or "a new Pentecost," as Pope John XXIII has called it.[111] Life is what Teresa searches for, a new life for herself and the nuns who are her daughters. Just before she tells us the story of her conversion, Teresa pauses to say: "I wanted to live (for I well understood that I was not living but was struggling with a shadow of death), but I had no one to give me life, and I was unable to catch hold of it."[112] When Teresa resumes the story of her life after sharing with us her "Treatise on Prayer" in

chapters 11 to 22 of the *Vida,* she rejoices in the discovery of the gift
of new life:

> I now want to return to where I left off about my life, for I think
> I delayed more than I should have so that what follows would be
> better understood. This is another book from here on—I mean
> another, new life. The life dealt with up to this point was mine;
> the one I lived from the point where I began to explain these things
> about prayer is the one God lived in me . . . [113]

Reform is genuine renewal and regeneration, when it brings new life.
Teresa of Jesus knows that her new life comes from the God active in her
and it is this Spirit-filled life that she shares with others by means of her
reform. Yet, the Holy Spirit works through human intermediaries. The
manner in which this creativity in Teresa of Avila is manifested is hinted
at by Louis Gognet, the much missed historian of Christian spirituality, who notes of Teresa: "All her historians are struck by the exceptional
richness of her temperament where so many apparent contradictions are
resolved: she was at the same time a contemplative and a realist, an idealist
and a firmly practical person rigorous and at the same time very humane,
essentially feminine but with certain masculine characteristics."[114] Teresa,
as do all creative and rich personalities, keeps in tension the polarities of
her paradoxes which give birth to new life.

Teresa also knows and speaks of the ideal of "the primitive
Church."[115] It is to primitive Carmelite life that she looks for inspiration. Though she understandably mistakes the revised *Rule* of Innocent
IV for the original *Rule* of St Albert,[116] her instincts are right on target. Her intuitive rather than academic memory take her back to the
Carmelite hermitage near the spring of Elijah on Mount Carmel. Her
memory is vivid:

> Let us remember our holy fathers of the past, those hermits whose
> lives we aim to imitate. What sufferings they endured! What soli-

tude, cold, and hunger, and what sun and heat, without anyone to complain to but God![117]

Teresa looks back for inspiration. She wants to restore primitive Carmelite solitude, not merely reestablish observances. Yet, Teresa, is no antiquarian, no *laudator temporis acti.* She not only wants to re-create the original life of the Carmelite Order, she also knows how to read the signs of the times. From her almost twenty years at the Incarnation she knows what may impede the activity of the Spirit in her life and that of others. Moreover, from the way she tells the story of her life in the *Vida,* it is clear that her reform, the establishment of the new monastery at St Joseph of Avila, is born of her experience of spiritual rebirth at the age of thirty-nine and as a result of the "favors" that she has received in prayer.[118] Teresa both "remembers" the primitive experience of the first Carmelites and at the same time addresses the critical issues that face the Carmelite nuns and friars of the sixteenth century. Her reform is, indeed, a paradigm for the wisdom shared with modern religious in Vatican II's Decree, *Perfectae caritatis:* "The appropriate renewal of religious life involves two simultaneous process: (1) a continuous return to the sources of all Christian life and to the original inspiration behind a given community and (2) an adjustment of the community to the changed conditions of the times."[119]

CONCLUSION

Teresa's reform is creative and successful because she is unwilling to opt for facile solutions to the contradictions and paradoxes of her life. The easiest way out of such dilemmas is to invest all one's energies in one pole or the other of the paradox. Here Emerson's aphorism, "consistency is the hobgoblin of mediocre minds," applies. Despite all the conflict she had with ecclesiastical authorities and the grief she had endured from fellow Carmelites and the many painful ambiguities of the work of reform, Teresa of Jesus confidently faces death as a daughter of the Church. In a unique and renewed way she restates the meaning, which had become formalized in her time, of the ancient image of the Church as Mother. Just as T.S. Eliot at the end of the *Four Quartets* realizes that "The Fire and the Rose are One," so Teresa of Jesus at the end of her life realizes that as a woman of reform her relationship to the Church can rightly be expressed through her filial kinship with the Church.

Recognized as an especially blessed member of the Church in the ceremonies of beatification in 1614 and as a saint of the Church in 1622, Teresa of Jesus waited until 1970 to be declared by the Church as a daughter who is also a doctor of the Church.[120] That may all seem like an orderly progression from hindsight, four hundred years after her death. Yet, only a graced vision of the Church and a marvelous capacity to live with paradox make it possible for Teresa of Jesus, who receives in her last days the Eucharist and the Last Anointing of the Church,[121] to recapitulate then the many diverse elements of her sixty-seven years in a confession to her sisters and daughters: "Finally, Lord," I am a daughter of the Church."[122] She who had said she " . . . would die a thousand deaths for the faith or for any truth of Sacred Scripture,"[123] and that she " . . . would have given a thousand lives to save one soul . . . ,"[124] discovers at death the meaning of her life through the image of the Church as Mother.

NOTES

1. *The Story of A Soul: The Autobiography of St Thérèse of Lisieux,* 2nd ed. trans. John Clarke (Washington: ICS Publications, 1976), pp. 253-54. See p. 42 on Teresa of Jesus as patroness of Thérèse of Lisieux.

2. Efrén Montalva and Otger Steggink, *Tiempo y Vida de Santa Teresa,* 2nd ed. (Madrid: La Editorial Catolica, 1977), pp. 983-84. Coll. "Biblioteca de Autores Cristianos," 283.

3. John Welch, *Spiritual Pilgrims: Carl Jung and Teresa of Avila* (New York: Paulist Press, 1982), pp. 188-89.

4. L, 1-7. The works of Teresa are cited from the I.C.S. ed. unless indicated otherwise.

5. F, 20, 3. Peers ed., p. 98.

6. W, 4, 1; 9, 3 and passim in Teresa's writings addressed to her nuns. See W, 4, 4: "my friends and daughters."

7. W, 2, 5 and 9 and passim.

8. W, 2, 1 and 3, 6, 4 and passim.

9. W, 1, 5; 2, 1 and passim.

10. *Constitutions,* Peers ed., 3, p. 229.

11. St John, C, 13, 7.

12. W, Prologue, 3.

13. Ibid., 7, 8.

14. Letter to Teutonius de Braganza, January 6, 1575.

15. W, 3, 7.

16. L, 40, 8.

17. Melveena McKendrick, *Woman and Society in the Spanish Drama of the Golden Age: A Study of the Mujer Varonil* (Cambridge: University Press, 1974), p. 22.

18. Montalva and Steggink, *Tiempo y Vida,* pp. 24-25.

19. Ibid., p. 25.

20. C, 4, 1, 7.

21. F, 1,6.

22. W, 1, 2.

23. Ibid.

24. W, 1, 5.

25. Ibid.

26. W, 1, 2.

27. Ibid.

28. W, 4, 1 and 1-3. See L, 40, 12 and C, Epilogue, 4.

29. W, 3, 2. See W, 1, 2.

30. Ibid., 4, 1.

31. Montalva and Steggink, *Tiempo y Vida,* p. 237.

32. W, Foreword.

33. F, Foreword.

34. C, Prologue, 3.

35. Ibid, Epilogue, 4.

36. Spiritual Testimony, 58, 10. See also L, 25, 12 and 33, 5; W, 21, 10 and 30, 4; Meditations on the Song of Songs, 1, 8; and Letter to Lawrence de Cepeda, February 27-28, 1577.

37. Kavanaugh, *Introduction to L,* p. 27.

38. For an index of the pseudonyms see Peers ed. of *Letters,* 2, pp. 1003-04 and also 1, pp. 4-5.

39. Peers ed., 3, pp. 266-68.

40. Letter to Lawrence de Cepeda, February 27-28, 1577.

41. L, 33, 5.

42. Yet, according to John W. O'Malley, "Catholic Reform," *Reformation Europe: A Guide to Research,* ed. Steven Ozment (St Louis: Center for Reformation Research, 1982), pp. 305-06 recent "scholarship shows the Inquisition to have been fairer and more moderate than its critics have maintained . . . "

43. For what may have been a wry remark by Teresa about the Inquisition, see C, 6, 8, 9 (and Kavanaugh's note 11).

44. See Peers ed., 3, p. xxiii.

45. W, Foreword.

46. Kavanaugh's note 3 for W, 30, 4.

47. C, Prologue, 3 and Epilogue, 4.

48. *Conciliorum Oecumenicorum Decreta,* 2nd ed. (Barcelona: Herder, 1962), pp. 212, 389 and 661.

49. *The Oxford Dictionary of the Christian Church,* 2nd ed., eds. F. L. Cross and E. A. Livingstone (New York: Oxford U. Press, 1974), p. 1194.

50. *Conciliorum Decreta,* pp. 752-60.

51. *Concordancias de las Obras y Escritos de Santa Teresa de Jesús,* ed. Luis de San José (Burgos: Editorial de Monte Carmelo, 1965), p. 312 and my research.

52. F, 9, 3; 17, 8 and 16; and 24, 15. "Council" only at 31, 3.

53. Letters passim.

54. L, 40, 21: " . . . in this little corner so enclosed . . . " See also L, 33, 2; 36, 5, 8 and 10; and 39, 10.

55. *Conciliorum Decreta,* pp. 753-54.

56. *Tiempo y Vida,* p. 212. This brief is received in Avila in July 1562. Pius IV issued a bull of confirmation on July 17, 1565.

57. *Conciliontm Decreta,* p. 753.

58. Letters to Mo. Mary Baptist, December 30, 1575 and to Jerome Gratian, April 15, 1578.

59. Tomas Alvarez, "Santa Teresa de Avila, Hija de la Iglesia," *Ephemerides Carmeliticae,* 17 (1966), 305-06. See, also, Kavanaugh, *Introduction to W,* p. 20.

60. E. Allison Peers, *Handbook to the Life and Times of St Teresa and St John of the Cross* (Westminster, MD: Newman Press, 1954), pp. 203-04 and 131-32.

61. W, 3, 10.

62. L, 33, 16 and 36, 2.

63. Peers, *Handbook,* pp. 218-19.

64. Letter to Jerome Gratian, October 15, 1578.

65. Otger Steggink, *La Reforma del Carmelo Español: la visita canónica del general Rubeo y su encuentro con Santa Teresa (1566-1567),* (Roma: Institutum Carmelitanum, 1965), p. 488..

66. Peers, *Handbook,* p. 222 and Montalva-Steggink, *Tiempo y Vida,* p. 1019 (index).

67. Note 2 for Letter to Paul Hernandez, October 4, 1578 (Peers ed., 2, p. 611).

68. Kavanaugh, *Introduction to W,* p. 20.

69. W, 3, 9.

70. Kavanaugh, *Introduction to W,* p. 20.

71. L, 32, 6.

72. W, 3, 1 and 8.

73. Ibid., 1, 2.

74. C, Epilogue, 4.

75. Spiritual Testimony, 26.

76. C, 4, 3, 10 and 5, 3, 3. See also 5, 2, 3.

77. W, 1, 5.

78. Ibid.

79. W, 35, 5 (Spanish original "esta nave de la Iglesia").

80. Montalva and Steggink, *Tiempo y Vida,* p. 983.

81. Ibid., pp. 983-84.

82. The exception is a qualified one where Teresa writes of what people say about paying to much attention to venial sins. See *Meditations on the Song of Songs,* 2, 20.

83. F, Foreword.

84. W, Foreword.

85. *Conciliorum Decreta,* p. 661.

86. Ibid., p. 212.

87. St John, A, Prologue, 2.

88. *The Spiritual Exercises of St Ignatius,* trans. Anthony Mottola (Garden City, NY: Doubleday Image Books, 1964), p. 83 and *Ejercicios espirituales, Directorio y Documentas de S. Ignacio de Loyola,* 2nd ed., ed. José Calveras (Barcelona: Balmes, 1958), p. 125: "la santa madre Iglesia hierárquica."

89. *Spiritual Exercises,* pp. 139, 140 and 141; Calveras ed., pp. 217, 220 and 221: "La nuestra sancta madre Iglesia hierárquica"; "nuestra sancta madre Iglesia"; "nuestra sancta madre Iglesia." The Spanish text has *"sancta."*

90. Karl Delahaye, *Ecclesia Mater chez les Pères des trois premeiers siècles,* trans. P. Vergriete and E. Bouis (Paris: Editions du Cerf, 1964), pp. 73-80. Coll. "Unam Sanctam," 46.

91. Ibid., pp. 53-65.

92. R. E. Brown, K. P. Donfried, J. A. Fitzmeyer and J. Reumann eds., *Mary in the New Testament* (Philadelphia: Fortress Press/New York: Paulist Press, 1978), p. 216.

93. L, 1, 7. See also 1, 1.

94. F, 10, 1; 22, 20; 27, 2, 6 and 11; and 28, 38.

95. Ibid., Prologue, 5; 16, 5; 23, 3 and 6; 28, 31, 36 and 39; L, 36, 6; W, 3, 7; 13, 3; and C, 3, 1, 3.

96. See p. 73 *supra.*

97. C, 3, 1, 3.

98. W, 31, 9. See also *Meditations on the Song of Songs,* 4, 4; C, 4, 3, 10 and 7, 2,6.

99. Montalva and Steggink, *Tiempo y Vida,* pp. 983-84.

100. *Acta Sanctorum,* Octobris (VII, 1) (Paris/Rome, 1869), p. 418.

101. Letter "Con vivissima gioia," *A.A.S.,*74 (1982), 840.

102. See *Origins,* 12 (November 11, 1982), 360.

103. R. H. Bainton, "Teresa of Avila," *Women of the Reformation, from Spain to Scandinavia* (Minneapolis: Augsburg, 1977), pp. 47-64.

104. H. Outram Evennett, *The Spirit of the Counter-Reformation,* ed. John Bossy (Cambridge: University Press, 1968), p. 25.

105. Joachim F. Smet, "The History of Reform in the Carmelite Order"(Unpublished mimeographed essay, n.d.), p. 4. See Benedict Zimmerman, "Les réformes dans l'Ordre de Notre-Dame du Mont Carmél," Etudes Carmélitaines, 19 (1934, 2), 155-95.

106. They were Nicholas Audet (1481-1562) and John Baptist Rossi/Rubeo (1507-1578).

107. *Conciliorum Decreta,* p. 636.

108. Spiritual Testimony 45.

109. *Concordancias,* pp. 1138-39. Add letters to Teutonius de Braganza, January 6, 1575; to Ambrose Marian, February 6, 1577; and to Jerome Gratian, April 15, 1578.

110. *The Documents of Vatican II,* ed. Walter Abbott (New York: America Press, 1966), p. 219, no. 21.

111. "Prayer of Pope John XXIII . . . for the Success of the Ecumenical Council," ibid., p. 793.

112. L, 8, 12.

113. Ibid., 23, 1.

114. Louis Cognet, *La Spiritualité Moderne I: L'Essor, 1500-1650* (Paris: Aubier, 1966), p. 81. Coll. "Histoire de la Spiritualité Chrétienne," 3.

115. F, 29, 27: (Spanish original) "Es verdad que me parecía cosa la primitiva iglesia— al menos no muy usada ahora en el mundo . . . "

116. Ludovico Saggi, "Santa Teresa 'Carmelitana,'" *Carmelus,* 18 (1971), 53ff; and "Questioni connesse con la Riforma Teresiana," *Carmelus,* 11 (1964), 169ff.

117. W, 11, 4. See also 4, 4.

118. L, 9-10.

119. *Documents of Vatican II,* p. 468, no. 2.

120. Montalva and Steggink, *Tiempo y Vida,* p. 996.

On Teresa's doctorate see Keith J. Egan, "The Significance for Theology of the Doctor of the Church: Teresa of Avila," *The Pedagogy of God's Image: Essays on Symbol and the Religions Imagination,* ed. R. Masson (Chico, CA: Scholars Press, 1982), pp. 153-71.

121. Montalva and Steggink, *Tiempo y Vida,* pp. 981-84.

122. Ibid., pp. 983-84.

123. L, 33, 5.

124. W, 1, 2.

◆

*Teresa and
Her Culture*

◆

"I Will Give You a Living Book": Spiritual Currents at Work at the Time of St Teresa of Jesus

◆ ◆ ◆

Ciriaco Moron-Arroyo, Ph.D.

Fabled Pastrana near Madrid is the birthplace of Dr Morón-Arroyo. Now that he has settled in the U.S. and has raised a family, he still studies about and comments on his native land as the Emerson Hinchliff Professor of Humanities and Hispanic Studies at Cornell University.

INTRODUCTION

In chapter 26 of St Teresa's autobiography we find the following text, which for a proper interpretation must be quoted both in the English translation and in the Spanish original:

Spanish

"Cuando se quitaron muchos libros de romance que no se leyesen, yo sentí mucho, porque algunos me daba recreación leerlos, y yo no podia ya por dejarlos en latin, me dijo el Señor: "no tengas pena, que yo te daré libro vivo." Yo no podia entender por qué se me havía dicho esto, porque aun no tenía visiones; después, desde a bien pocos días lo entendí muy bien, porque he tenido tanto en qué pensar y recogerme en lo que vía presente y ha tenido tanto amor el Señor conmigo para enseñarme de muchas maneras, que muy poca u casi ninguna necesidad he tenido de libros. Su Majestad ha sido el libro verdadero a donde he visto las verdades."

English

When they forbade the reading of many books in the vernacular, I felt the prohibition very much because reading some of them was an enjoyment for me, and I could no longer do so since only the Latin editions were allowed. The Lord said to me: "Don't be sad, for I shall give you a living book." I was unable to understand why this was said to me, since I had not yet experienced any visions. Afterward, within only a few days, I understood very clearly, because I received so much to think about and such recollection in the presence of what I saw, and the Lord showed so much love for me by teaching me in many ways, that I had very little or almost no need for books. His Majesty had become the true book in which I saw the truths.[1]

This text suggests three questions: first, is St Teresa erasing the trace of her sources or suffering the illusion of a nonexistent originality? This question is legitimate, but can be disposed of immediately; the sincere attitude of search and the creative power revealed by her texts defy any suspicion as to her credibility and mental lucidity. Secondly, is it possible to determine the specific books to which she refers? Finally, taking the text as a stimulus for the comparison between St Teresa's writings and the spiritual literature available to her, can we verify her claim for originality? And if so, what are the parameters of continuity and discontinuity between her and her circumstances?

The English translation, while being faithful to the letter, has introduced an element of precision which cannot be found in the Spanish text; "libros de romance" is well translated by "books in the vernacular," and there seems to be nothing wrong in translating "dejarlos en latin" by "only the Latin editions were allowed." However, the contrast that is established between "vernacular" and "Latin editions" suggests that St Teresa refers to many books existing in both Spanish and Latin, that the Spanish editions were prohibited, and the Latin were allowed to circulate. A perusal of the *Index* proves that this is not the case. Only fourteen foreign books and eighteen written by Spanish authors, plus the works of Constantino Ponce de La Fuente, were included in the *Index*.[2] Some of them were prohibited *both* in the vernacular *and* in Latin, and most of the other were available only in the vernacular.

This reflection indicates that, when St Teresa mentions the permission to read spiritual books in Latin, she is not referring to the Latin editions of specific titles, but to the impression that any spiritual book in Spanish was suspicious in the eyes of the Inquisition. More than specific books, the Index in fact condemned the very practice of reading on the part of "idiots"—those who did not know Latin—and "little women," as the expression goes in the inquisitorial trials.

But, however imaginative and honest the research in this direction may be, it would not carry us beyond plausible conjectures about bibliographical details; and what St Teresa tells us is that her system should be understood from within itself. As a result, a comparison of her works with other spiritual treatises should emphasize the differences rather than the similarities between them. I am prepared to heed her advice, in principle because respect for a text requires that all comparative literature end up being contrastive literature, and historically because her claim of originality is fully substantiated by the massive documentation at our disposal.

THE SETTING

St Teresa was born in 1515. Two years later, the partners, themes and conditions of the dialogue we are going to recount appear on the scene. In 1517 Erasmus' translation of the *New Testament* and the Alcalá *Polyglot Bible* are both published; Charles I, soon to become emperor

Charles V, inherits the thrones of his grandparents the Catholic Kings, effectively uniting them as the kingdom of Spain (Charles will be the main adversary of Luther who on October 31 of the same year proposes his 95 theses). Finally, Cardinal Cisneros died in 1517.

Erasmus' *New Testament,* the *Alcalá Polyglot* and Luther's theses were manifestations of a new way of thinking, in fact, of a historical revolution brought about by the Italian humanist Lorenzo Valla (1407-1457). Valla approached the Bible from a purely historical point of view, trying to ascertain the meaning of the words when they were written and denouncing the deviations introduced by the Scholastics during the Middle Ages. Valla attacks the Scholastics on all fronts, and from the epistemological point of view, Erasmus and Luther are only followers of Valla. But the Italian humanist is not a parasite who lives from the body he is destroying; his attack on Scholasticism is an epoch-making feat in European thought: he introduces the historical sense, historical semantics, the esthetic sense for his attention to stylistic detail, and finally an empirical attitude which will eventually reflect itself in the observation of nature and in the rise of modern science.[3]

Valla produces this innovation as a grammarian who dares to challenge the theologians. These were divided in different schools: Thomists, Scotists, Augustinians, etc., usually in accordance with the religious order to which they belonged. As a matter of fact each of the three orders mentioned had an official doctor: St Thomas Aquinas, Duns Scotus and Giles of Rome respectively, whose doctrine had to be followed by the teachers of the order. But whatever their differences all Scholastics coincided in a common frame of thought, the Scholastic method.

The Scholastic method is the reading of the Bible within the context of Aristotelian metaphysics and cosmology. The Bible narrates the relations between God and humankind as two persons in dialogue. According to the Bible, there is only one God; according to the Scholastics, God is the One, the highest and most simple concept our mind can reach. According to the Bible, God is a mysterious Trinity;

the Scholastics codify that revelation in analogy to the powers of the soul and fix the differences between the divine persons with terms such as *substance* and *supposition,* taken from the Aristotelian tradition. According to the book of Genesis, God created us in his image and likeness; Hebraists know that "image and likeness" is a means to emphasize the fact that humankind, in contrast to all other creatures, can speak and listen to God. The Scholastics codified the words of Genesis in accordance with the Aristotelian hierarchy of beings. All creatures coincide in participating in the being, truth and goodness of God; they are his footprints (*Vestigium*). Humankind, on the other hand, participates in God's intellect and will, this makes us the image *(imago)* of God, and finally grace makes us similar to God; thus the Hebrew idiom that emphasizes the closeness of us to God becomes a codified hierarchy on the basis of Greek cosmology: *vestigium, imago, similitudo.*

The concept of grace is perhaps the best example of the fusion between Greek categories and Biblical history which constitutes the Scholastic way of thinking. Grace in the Bible is God's mercy toward us: creation, conservation, and help in the moments of joy and distress. For the Scholastics it is also that, but in a derivative sense: primarily grace is a supernatural entity which is infused by God into our soul, bringing about the inhabitation of God in it, and acting as the seed that blossoms in virtues and bears fruit in acts of merit toward salvation. The interpretation of grace with categories such as entity, habits and acts is a good example of the fusion whose outline we are tracing.

The result of this way of thinking is a structuralism—and I shun the temptation of reading contemporary concerns into ancient questions—which directs the mind toward correspondence and symmetry rather than toward an innocent observation of nature or reading of texts. Hence the Scholastic tendency to classify the world according to numerical patterns: seven ages of the Old, and seven of the New Testament, seven planets, seven virtues and vices, seven sacraments and seven petitions in the Lord's prayer. The most striking example of how this pattern of thought can enslave the mind is the number of the "gifts of the Holy Spirit." The Hebrew text of Isaiah 11:2, mentions only six gifts, but the Vulgate version translated in one case "pietas" and in the following "timor Domini" thus making two out of one and completing the number seven which matched beautifully the rest of the septenaries.

Valla's and Erasmus' attack on Scholasticism is a systematic dismantling of all the structures of medieval thought and of the practical consequences of that thought. The Scholastics reacted with all theoretical and political means in their power in order to sustain what were, in their opinion, the unchangeable pillars of the Church. Thus a struggle ensued which in Spain is the cornerstone of intellectual life throughout the sixteenth century.

The most important manifestations of the struggle between Scholasticism and humanism during St Teresa's lifetime were: (1) the rise of mysticism as a cultural force and the inquisitorial trials against the "dexados" in favor of the "recogidos" (the "abandoned" versus the "recollected" mystics); (2) the prestige and decline of Erasmus (1517-1533); (3) the popularization of contemplative spirituality by John of Avila, Fr Louis of Granada and the early Jesuits; (4) the crisis produced by the *Index* of 1559, and St Teresa's original response to it. This response saved mysticism as a way of life, and the Spanish language as a legitimate vehicle for spiritual literature.

The "dexados" or followers of the total abandonment of the soul into the hands of God were some laymen and women who, following the doctrine of the Franciscans, purported to reach perfection without fighting against the powers of the soul. They muster a remarkable psychological realism in that perfection is an attitude toward God and the world, not a series of acts. But they were trapped in the insidious consequences of their position. If one has a sexual temptation, should he fight it or not? The traditional doctrine says yes and the result could be an attempt to eradicate the image from our mind; but the more we fight the image the more intense it may become, whereas a realistic attitude would let it pass and take it for a sign of weakness. At that point these mystics were accused of indulging in dirty thoughts. This is but one example of the complex situation which, complicated by the spread of Lutheranism, brought the pious "dexados" into conflict with the Inquisition beginning in 1525.[4]

ST TERESA'S TEACHING AND OSUNA

St Teresa's doctrine is far removed from this spiritual trend. It coincides with them in stressing the need for the soul to abandon itself to God's mercy, while stressing at the same time that perfection is not withdrawal from, but work in the world.

Since the "dexados" were in fact disciples of the Franciscans, and in particular of the most prestigious one, Francis of Osuna (1492?-1541), this mystic tried to take his distance from them in his book *Third Spiritual Alphabet* (1527).[5] In it Osuna describes a way of perfection based on recollection, hence the name "recogidos" for the followers of his doctrine. "Recollection" is an attempt to ascend to the highest degree of contemplation by renouncing the objects of the senses, the images of fantasy, and the ideas of the intellect in order to rest in the pure love of the divinity. Unlike the "dexados," Osuna stresses the need for fighting against anything in our mind that is material or figurative with the aim of reaching a point which is nothing for the intellect and everything for the will: pure love without thought.

This book is typical of the Scholastic formulation of mysticism. The love between God and his creatures was expressed by means of an erotic allegory in the *Song of Songs,* and by a realistic and demanding analysis in the Gospel of St John: "This is my commandment, that you love one another, as I have loved you. Greater love than this no one hath, that one lay down his life for his friends" (Jn 13:12-13). I call this expression of love "realistic" because it is applicable to situations of commitment which have nothing erotic in them; and "demanding" because that commitment may require us to put our life in danger for the defense of certain persons or values.

To the two biblical formulations of love the medieval mystics added a third: the neo-Platonic one. The resulting synthesis described the Christian way of perfection as an ascension in three stages: purification, illumination, union. Purification from what? from matter. Matter is the origin of obscurity, pluralism and evil. Rununciation of matter brings about illumination, contemplation in simplicity and perfection. The three religious vows: poverty, chastity and obedience sanction the renunciation of external, internal and "supernal" goods (riches, body, intellect), thus placing the religious person in an objective state of perfection. Recollection is the method by which the individual realizes in himself the rejection of matter.

In addition to the neurotic struggle within the individual that this method could produce, it had a bizarre consequence. If everything that is material and figurative must be abandoned in favor of spiritual contemplation and love, the image of Christ as man and love for the humanity of Christ must be considered an imperfect stage on the spiritual journey.

St Teresa read Osuna's book in 1538 and, according to her own testimony, she resolved to follow it with all her strength.[6] This testimony led to the persistent legend that St Teresa's system derives from Osuna. In my opinion this idea should be abandoned; in fact, the effort she made to proceed in Osuna's steps, left in her a suspicion against the system of the Franciscan which is the most recurrent motif of all her works. For one thing St Teresa, the mystic par excellence, ignores the most basic terminology of traditional mysticism: "In some books written on prayer it is said that even though the soul cannot reach this state of prayer by itself, since the work is an entirely supernatural one that the Lord effects in the soul, it will be able to help itself by lifting the spirit above all creatures and humbly raising it up, and that the soul can do this after having passed many years in the purgative life while it is advancing in the illuminative. (I don't really know why they say illuminative. I understand it to refer to those who are advancing)" (L, 22, 1).

The substitution of the popular term "advancing" for the technical 'illuminative" illustrates St Teresa's independence from the Scholastic formulation. With regard to the contemplation of, and love for, the humanity of Christ, she is not only independent but combative:

> I had no master and was reading these books in which I thought I was gradually coming to understand something . . . It seemed to me that I felt the presence of God, as was so, and I strove to recollect myself in his presence. This is a pleasing prayer, if God helps in it, and the delight is great. Since I felt that benefit and consolation, there was no one who could have made me return to the humanity of Christ; as a matter of fact, I thought the humanity was an impediment. O Lord of my soul and my good, Jesus Christ crucified! At no time do I recall this opinion I had without feeling pain; it seems to me I become a dreadful traitor —although in ignorance (L, 22, 7).

These words could not be more clear: she embraced Osuna's system for a while, she then realized that it was wrong; whenever she remembers her previous attitude she considers herself a traitor and, as a result, she considers it a wrong path. In chapter 7 of the sixth dwelling places she returns to the point on a sarcastic tone: "It will seem to you that anyone who enjoys such lofty things will no longer meditate on the mysteries of the most Sacred Humanity of our Lord Jesus Christ. Such a person would now be engaged entirely in loving . . . They will not make me admit that such a road is a good one" (C, 6, 7, 5).

We could ask with the Scholastics: why is this not a good road? Is the divinity not higher than the humanity in Christ? St Teresa does not reject any thesis of the Scholastics, she simply does not think with their categories. At the same time, by presenting a mystical system which is independent from Scholasticism, she is undermining the way of thinking that enjoyed greatest authority in the Church.

After Osuna, John of Avila, Louis of Granada and Ignatius of Loyola wrote spiritual books with which the saint was undoubtedly familiar. Several Jesuits were her spiritual directors in Avila and at one point she declares that the spirituality of the Discalced Carmelites is all inspired by the Jesuits.[7] John of Avila's *book Audi, filia* (1556) and Fr Louis of Granada's *Treatise on Prayer* (1554) and the *Guide of Sinners* (1556-57), were included in the *Index of Prohibited Books* in 1559. They are orthodox in every respect and basically Scholastic, but the fear of Protestantism caused the Inquisitors to uproot any seed of potential danger.

The potential danger lay in the fact that they seemed to propose contemplative life for all Christians, even for "the wives of carpenters," as Inquisitor Valdés told Fr Louis of Granada in person.[8] In addition to the popularization of mysticism, those books emphasized the action of grace over the personal work of the soul, thus bordering on Luther's denial of free will; and by recommending the communication of the soul with God, they seemed to dispense with the Church and its ceremonies as the intermediary between God and man—another Lutheran tenet. The orthodox and pious intentions of John of Avila and Fr Louis of Granada were never put in doubt, but their wisdom was questioned especially for writing about those subjects in the vernacular, thus making esoteric doctrines available to laymen. In order to measure the impact of the *Index* one must recall that none other than the Archbishop of Toledo, the Dominican Fr Bartholomew de Carranza had his *Cathecismo Christiano* (1558) condemned by the Inquisitor, and he himself was imprisoned by the Inquisition for the rest of his life.[9]

ST TERESA'S ORIGINALITY

It is against this background and in response to the panic surrounding mysticism and its vernacular expression that St Teresa begins to write her works. Bereft of Scholastic learning, she describes her experience, shows respect for official learning, but she refrains from teaching any general truths. The interpretation of her experience is left to the authorities of the Church which, in turn, must respect her veracity.

In a previously quoted text she reproduced some Scholastic terms such as "lifting the spirit above all creatures and humbly raising it up."

She confessed that with that terminology she would not be able to express her mind. But at the end of the C we find words that sound similar to those ignored in her autobiography: "I really believe that in rapture he (God) unites it (the soul) with himself . . . But it doesn't seem to the soul that it is called to enter into its center, as it is here in this dwelling place, but called to the superior part" (C, 7, 1, 5). The similarity of the expression should not deceive us; she is not reflecting the Franciscan theory of the "illumination" or "acies mentis," she is describing the difference between the experience of rapture and the complete self-possession of oneself when the soul reaches God. Dwelling with God and in God is the perfect conquest of the self, the center of the soul. Nevertheless, it must be said that in the description of the powers of the soul St Teresa basically coincides with the Scholastics who were very empirical on this point.

She does not agree with the Scholastic writers on spirituality in the very conception of Christian perfection or sainthood. In the neo-Platonic process of immaterialization, contemplative life should be superior to the active one and sainthood would imply the mystical process. Not so in St Teresa. She considers the mystical experiences a special grace of God, but not necessary for sanctification. The only sure criterion of sainthood is love shown to our neighbor, which is an indication of love for God. For the nuns, her sisters, the criterion of sainthood is not contemplation, but to conform their will to the will of God as expressed in the rules of the Order. This idea of sainthood, which sounds so natural, collides with the Scholastic concept of mysticism. If grace is a vital principle which blossoms and bears fruit through purification and illumination, mysticism is the natural development of grace. For St Teresa on the contrary, mysticism is just a special mercy on the part of God. Nobody can lay claim to it and it does not guarantee greater spiritual perfection. At the same time, mystical experience helps the soul become more perfect; it is not simply a sign of the divine power for the benefit of others. The Scholastics called "sanctifying grace" the supernatural entity that brought about the inhabitation of God in the soul; the mercies that were granted for the benefit of others, such as the capacity to perform miracles, were called "gratuitous grace" *(gratia gratis data)*. St Teresa explodes this distinction by introducing a grace—the mystical experience—which is both sanctifying and gratuitous.

Equally unorthodox is her use of the term "supernatural." For the Scholastics, the "supernatural" in contrast to the "natural" was a formal as opposed to an "exemplary" participation on the part of creatures in the being of God. All created beings, including the angels, are natural, while grace is supernatural. For St Teresa, assuming that the mystical experience presupposes God's grace, most mercies are momentary gifts which cannot be attained through any effort on our part. These mercies she calls "supernatural."

The following seems to me the most unorthodox text in all of St Teresa's works:

> I know a person who hadn't learned that God was in all things by presence, power and essence, and through a favor of this kind that God granted her she came to believe it. After asking a half-learned man—he knew as little as she had known before God enlightened her—she was told that God was present only by grace. Such was her own conviction that even after this she didn't believe him and asked others who told her the truth, with which she was greatly consoled (C, 5, 1, 10).

The saint seems to have experienced a presence of God in the soul that she considers deeper than the presence by grace. Far from dwelling upon the scholarly distinction of the natural and the supernatural, for her the mystical union of the soul with God is the return to its natural roots. The rediscovery of its creator is the attainment of its own natural identity. For the Scholastics on the other hand, God's presence in the soul through grace, or "supernatural" presence, would be "essentially" superior to his natural presence as creator.

The Scholastic way of thinking intended to defend the tradition of the Church against Luther's upheaval; but in Spain, where Lutheranism did not pose a danger, the target of the Scholastic attacks was Erasmus, who was accused of laying the theoretical foundations of Lutheranism. Erasmus, following Valla's lead, expanded the historico-philological method throughout Europe. Without formally denying his allegiance to ecclesiastical institutions, he knew how to put them in perspective; hence the simplification he advocated in external ceremonies in favor of true Christianity; and finally, as a result of his creative position, he enjoyed perhaps excessively in mocking those who were unable to distinguish what was permanent from what was transitory in the Church.

In Spain the philological method had been imported by Nebrija (1444-1522), who studied in Bologna from 1460 to 1470. The Alcalá *Polyglot* was the work of Spanish humanists without the inspiration of Erasmus; on the contrary, this interest in the study of the Bible paved the way for the influence of the humanist. In the 1520's, when Pope Clement VII allied himself with France against the Spanish King, Erasmus' doctrine provided the intellectual justification for fighting the Pope while remaining Catholic, thus a political situation reinforced the reception of Erasmus' works in Spain. But even with these favorable conditions his influence is much smaller than we have been led to believe by Marcel Bataillon's book *Erasme et l'Espagne.*[10]

As far as mysticism is concerned, even the translator of Erasmus' *Enchiridion militis christiani* into Spanish proves unfaithful to the humanist's text. The father of the classical formulation of the three mystical stages: purification, illumination, union, was a certain Dionysius, believed for many centuries to be the Athenian judge converted to Christianity by St Paul's sermon. Valla proved that the writings attributed to Dionysius could not belong to the disciple of St Paul. As a result, Erasmus calls him "Dionysius quidam" ("a certain Dionysius"). For the spiritual writers, on the other hand, Dionysius was an authority respected by the greatest theologians. The translator of the *Enchiridion* into Spanish simply translates "Dionysius quidam" by "San Dionisio" (Saint Dionysius), thus veiling Erasmus' intention and text.

The same happens in a more sensitive passage. As we said before, in the logic of the Scholastics, the official renunciation of matter declared in the three religious vows, placed the religious individual in an objective state of perfection. Erasmus did not even need to refute this claim, Valla had already done it in the dialogue *De professione religiosorum;* he simply repeats his conviction in the famous sentence: "monachatus non est pietas sed vitae genus." The friars' attack on Erasmus, in turn, was not elicited by the humanist's ironical remarks about them. The attack was directed against a doctrine that destroyed the traditional theory of religious life altogether: the theory of the objective state of perfection. The Spanish translator obviates the difficulties by means of the non-committal proverb: "the cassock doesn't make the monk."

The spirituality derived from Erasmus' theology was world oriented, behavioristic rather than contemplative, respectful of the ceremonies of the Church as long as the ceremonies were conducive to essential piety, and sarcastic when they became ridiculous or superstitious. With regard to the vows in particular Erasmus warned against an immature commitment and defended the right of the layman to play an active role in the Church.

St Teresa was as removed from the principles of Erasmus as one can be. She did not know Latin, she would never claim the right to teach in the Church: "just being a woman is enough to have my wings fall off—how much more being both a woman and wretched as well" (L, 10, 8). However, her realism allowed her to discover many questionable things within the ecclesiastical institutions. At times she sounds like Erasmus in her demand for perfection in religious life: "Believe me, the whole affair doesn't lie in whether or not we wear the religious habit but in striving to practice the virtues, in surrendering our will to God in everything" (C, 3, 2, 6). But it would be wrong to interpret this statement in the light of Erasmus. For St Teresa, the call to religious life is already a special mercy of God; the sacrifice inherent in the renunciation of the world is an act of merit; religious life in particular is a sign of election, not because it is an objective state of perfection, but because it demands and nurtures a yearning for it. In this sense, although she does not coincide with the Scholastics in their theory of religious life, she considers it more conducive to perfection than the layman's life in the world. Christ told her in a vision "that even though religious orders were mitigated one shouldn't think he was little served in them" (L, 32, 11). And even when she criticizes harshly the excesses of certain monasteries, she doesn't do it with Erasmus' irony, she bleeds because God is offended and the souls miss their goal.[11]

However, if her respect for the Church would prevent her from talking and acting, when Christ, the living book, dictates a different course, she will obey the Lord without losing her respect for others. This happened quite often during the foundations when she had to prove herself prudent like a serpent and guileless like a dove. She believed, like most philosophers and theologians of her time, that woman was inherently inferior to man in intellect and will, that is, in the spiritual powers of the soul. When the Papal Nuncio Sega found out about her moves, he dismissed her with the remark that she was a *femina inquieta e andariega* (a restless and wandering female). The clergyman did not know that her only intent was to help others find the rest and center she had already found.

Hearing these criticisms and accepting them, she expressed her doubts to the Lord reminding him of St Paul's injunction: "let the woman learn in silence, with all subjection. But I suffer not a woman to teach, nor to use authority over the man; but to be in silence" (1 Tm 2:11-12). Christ answered: "Tell them they shouldn't follow just one part of Scripture but that they should look at other parts, and ask them if they can by chance tie my hands" (Spiritual Testimony 15, July 1571). I do not think I am inferring too much if I point out the explosive potential of this text. The theological basis for the silent position of woman in the Church is challenged by Christ, God himself. Who are those who pretend to tie God's hands? If this is true, how many "eternal" injunctions issued by them are not ephemeral regulations? Would St Teresa condemn an equal participation of women in the ministries of the Church?

We have now outlined the fundamental principles of the systems in struggle during the formative years of St Teresa. As is well known, the Erasmian trend was dealt a deadly blow in the *Index of Prohibited Books,* which prohibited most of Erasmus' works in any language. One of the most influential theologians of the time, who contributed to the *Index,* Dominic Soto, had written in 1547 that the study of languages and concupiscence had been the cause of the tragedy the Church was suffering.

St Teresa began to write in 1562, three years after the *Index* had been published. Writing was for her an act of obedience; she never purported to teach, but to illuminate herself and present her experience as a possible analogy for souls in similar circumstances. Instead of a system, she writes autobiography. The facts may come from the devil, this is up to the learned to decide, but nobody will be able to doubt the facts themselves. In this way she is able to circumvent the difficulties of the "dexados" who involved themselves in snares by using abstract concepts without proper definitions.

In the matter of contemplation versus action, St Teresa diffuses the question by ignoring it: the contemplative nuns are the elite soldiers who help the Church by praying while the Catholic armies fight and the missionaries preach. The mystical experience cannot be codified as a system; the only permanent trait in the way of perfection is to fulfill one's duties with love for God and neighbor. The seven dwelling places of the interior castle, are not seven, but a million. This is extremely important, for, by affirming that the soul does not remain permanently at a certain level of spirituality, she once more dismantles the traditional system of the purgative, illuminative and unitive states. The mystical experience is never a state, it is only a history of mercies from the Lord. In this she also disagrees with St John of the Cross.[12]

With regard to the superiority of mental over oral prayer, she is not only ironic, but even sarcastic. W, in its first version, contains several passages which were suppressed in the definitive edition. These passages concern precisely that question. She advises her sisters to pray orally the Our Father. A small amount of courtesy requires that they pay attention to what they are reciting; that is already mental prayer, that is, oral prayer with respect and courtesy for God. In the Our Father all the secrets of contemplative life can be enjoyed. And in a clear reference to the *Index,* she remarks: "Hold fast, daughters, for they cannot take from you the Our Father and the Hail Mary."[13]

Her work in that moment of profound disarray for authors of spiritual literature opened a new, original way which, in fact, saved mysticism from suspicion. The Dominican Melchior Cano (1509-1560) had been instrumental in condemning the books of the Dominicans Carranza and Fr Louis de Granada; the two disciples of Melchior Cano, Bartholomew de Medina and Dominic Báñez, both professors of theology at Salamanca, became staunch defenders of St Teresa; thus she contributed to the harmony of theology and mysticism among the Dominicans.

The theologian Bartholomew de Medina was a bitter enemy of Fr Louis de Leon because of the philological approach to the Bible defended by the latter. Medina, the admirer of St Teresa, died in 1580; in 1588 Fr Louis became the first editor of the writings of the saint. Two enemies who coincided in their admiration for St Teresa —she would have succeeded in straightening out their differences.

And when we approach her text today, we may as literary historians admire her vitality and originality as a writer; as Catholics, her example of commitment; but beyond any particular interest, as human beings, we are captivated by the humble attitude of search that permeates her writings, epitomized in that sentence: "to walk in the truth," which sounds even better in Spanish, "andar en verdad."

NOTES

1. L., 26, 5.

2. Heinrich Reusch, *Die Indices libronan prohibitorum des sechzehnten Jahrhunderts* (Tübingen: Litterarisch Verein, 1886), pp. 209-42.

For an identification of the books include in the *Index* see Melquíades Andrés, *La teologia española en el siglo XVI,* II (Madrid: La Editorial Gatolica, 1977), pp. 615-23. Coll. "Biblioteca de Autores Cristianos," Serie Maior, 4.

3. This is the conclusion of my article: "A Historical Revolution: Lorenzo Valla's

Attack on Scholasticism," given as a lecture at S.U.N. Y. Binghamton on April 2, 1981 and soon to appear in *ACTA*(Binghamton, NY: Center for Medieval and Early Renaissance Studies).

4. Antonio Marquez, *Los alumbrados: Oríagenes y filosofía,* 2nd ed. (Madrid: Taurus, 1980), pp. 229-93.

5. Francis of Osuna, *The Third Spiritual Alphabet* trans. Mary E. Giles (New York: Paulist Press, 1981). Coll. "The Classics of Western Spirituality."

6. L, 4, 7: "That uncle of mine . . . gave me a book. It is called *The Third Spiritual Alphabet* . . . I was very happy with this book and resolved to follow that path with all my strength."

7. Letter to Christopher Rodriguez de Moya, June 28, 1568, listed as Letter no. 11 in the Spanish ed. of Montalva/Steggink of the *Obras Completas* (5th ed., 1976) and cited here in the original because Peers did not include it in his ed.: "Porque no todas las personas espirituales me contentan para nuestros monasterios, si no son las que estos padres [Jesuitas] confiesan, y ansí casi todas las que están en ellos, y no me acuerdo ahora estar ninguna de las que he tornado que no sea hija suya, porque son las que nos convienen; que como ellos havían criado mi alma, hame hecho el Señor merced que en estos monasterios se haya plantado su espíritu."

8. Letter of Fr Louis of Granada to Archbishop Bartholomew de Carranza in J. Cuervo "Fray Luis de Granada y la Inquisición," Homenaje a Menendez Pelayo I (Madrid: V. Suarez, 1899), p. 738: "Con todo esto habrá un pedaço de trabajo, por estar el arzobispo tan contrario a cosas (como él llama) de contemplatión para mugeres de carpinteros."

See Alvaro Huerga, "La vida cristiana en los siglos XV-XVI," *Historia de la espiritualidad* I (Barcelona: Juan Flors, 1969), p. 103.

9. See Bartholomew Carranza de Miranda, *Comentarios sobre el Catecismo Cristiano,* ed. J. I. Tellechea Idígoras (Madrid: La Editorial Catolica, 1972), 2 vols. Coll. "Biblioteca de Autores Cristianos," Serie Maior, 1-2. In the introduction Professor Tellechea studies the condemnation of the book by the Inquisition and the conditions surrounding it.

For the text of Melchior Cano's "Censure" on which the condemnation is based see José Sanz y Sanz, *Mechor Cano: Cuestiones fondamentales de critica histórica sobre su vida y sus escritos* (Madrid: Editorial Santa Rita, 1959), pp. 581-83.

10. Originally published in French in 1937, I refer to the Spanish translation of Antonio Alatorre, *Erasmo y España,* 2nd ed. (Mexico City: Fondo de Cultura Económica, 1966).

11. See L, 7, 4. Also L, 38, 31.

12. This is the obvious sense of St Teresa's remarks on St John's response to a "Vejamen" in 1577: "It would be a bad business for us if we could not seek God until we were dead to the world. Neither the Magdalen, nor the woman of Samaria, nor the Canaanitish woman was dead to the world when she found him"— Peers ed., 3, p. 267.

13. W, 21, 8.

The Vernacular Mind
of St Teresa

◆ ◆ ◆

Elias Rivers, Ph.D.

*Professor Elias Rivers is a leader in the field of Spanish
literature studies in our country and he is invited often to
lecture in Spain on the subject. He is a distinguished faculty
member of the S.U.N. Y. system at its Long Island campus
at Stonybrook.*

PREFACE

I am not a specialist in Santa Teresa or in Spanish mysticism: my spe-
cialty is secular Renaissance poetry of sixteenth-century Spain. My
paper reflects this non-specialized approach. Since writing it, I have
had some more time to read recent studies by specialists, and I discover that I coincide closely with one of them in my point of entry into
Santa Teresa's way of writing, which is through the eyes of the great
Renaissance poet Friar Louis of Leon. This specialist is Víctor García
de la Concha, the author of an important book entitled *El arte literario
de Santa Teresa.*[1] I have also read with fascination some passages in the
book by Dr Enrique Llamas Martinez, of the Pontifical University of
Salamanca, a book published in 1972 on Saint Teresa and the Spanish
Inquisition;[2] this work documents fully the ferocious attack by a certain
group of Scholastic Dominicans upon the writings of Mother Teresa of

114

Jesus. They, no doubt sincerely, considered her very dangerous to the Church, not so much because her paternal grandfather was a convert from Judaism as because she was a woman who presumed to teach men (and we all remember St Paul's unfortunate phrase "mulieres in ecclesia taceant"), a woman who in her claims of direct communication with God coincided, according to them, with dangerous heretics. Not long after her works were published posthumously, an Inquisitor named Friar Alonso de la Fuente, in August of 1589, led the attack with these words, among others:

> The author of the said book passes if off and recommends it as doc-
> trine revealed by God and inspired by the Holy Spirit; but if in fact
> the author was that nun whose name is on the title-page, it is a mat-
> ter *praeter naturam* for her to have written something taught by an
> angel, because it exceeds a woman's capacity. In any case it could not
> have been a good angel, but a bad one, the same one that deceived
> Mohammed and Luther and the other leaders of heretics. This being
> the case, the so-called miracle of the nun Teresa of Jesus, that her
> body is today intact and un-corrupted, is a fabulous business, either
> the work of Satan or the invention of heretics.[3]

I think we should keep it in mind that Santa Teresa lived, and orga-
nized convents, and wrote books in this violent atmosphere of *odium theologicum,* and that she knew that, as the descendent of a convert, as a woman, and as a radical reformer, she was vulnerable to attack at any time. She refers frequently to her vulnerability, or to the danger of unwitting heresy; she fearlessly protected herself by frequent acts of submission to the authority of the Church.

FUNCTIONS OF LANGUAGE

As a writer trying to convey to readers her experiences of God, St Teresa was involved in a basic mystery of human existence: the peculiar way in which language mediates between reality and a community of minds. How is it possible for one person to use words in such a way as to convey to other people a unique experience? Before trying to answer this question, we should first meditate upon the nature of the human race and its peculiar dependence upon language. Oral language seems to be, in fact, the one fundamental social institution to which all normal human beings belong; when a child begins to learn to understand words and to talk, that is, to use sounds systematically as symbols and to join them together in grammatical sequences, that child begins to participate actively as a member of the human family, responding to questions and asking for objects by name. The evolution of language must have accompanied the evolution of the human body and the evolution of human communities. Sexually, we know that human beings are different from other mammals; and no other mammal has a taboo against incest, a taboo which seems related to being able to give names to relationships and to invent rules for exchanging spouses, with all the sociopolitical ramifications that result from such rules. Language does not seem to have functioned primarily as a technological instrument for economic production: the complexity of human language was not needed for the planting of wheat or the invention of the wheel or the smelting and forging of metals. If we examine closely the pragmatic functions of language, its peculiar complexities seem to have developed to cope, not with production, but with the distribution of social prestige, power and wealth. The sociolinguistic rules of courtesy, which make possible orderly verbal transactions and peaceful reconciliations of conflicting interests, are a universal aspect of human life everywhere.

The human child, according to Noam Chomsky, is born with an innate capacity for assimilating rapidly the highly complex phonological, morphological and syntactic rules which give specific structure to the language of his/her immediate community, normally that of the mother. When the child, in dialogue with his/her mother, learns to use the two basic personal pronouns "I" and "you," he/she acquires, according to the great French linguist Emile Benveniste, our specifically human subjectivity: the alternating use of the shifters "you" and "I" in dialogue is the linguistic source of the individual subject and of social intersubjectivity. These two pronouns exist in all natural languages. But this simple grammatical confrontation between two pronouns, between mother and child, becomes complicated by the differing forms of polite address: in Spanish, for example, as the child grows up, he learns that he can't call everyone "tú"; he learns another pronoun, "usted," and with it the complex rules governing who uses it to address whom. This is one of the Spanish child's first important sociolinguistic lessons, the lesson entitled by Professors Brown and Gilman "the pronouns of power and solidarity";[4] later he learns all the sociolinguistic rules as to how one should address other people ("uncle," "mister," "Jack") and how to greet them and make them promises, petitions, threats, commands, blessings and curses, all the speech acts which go to make up the complex transactions of his immediate social group and related groups and social classes.

Since prehistoric times sociolinguistic rules for oral discourse and dialogue have been, and continue to be today, fundamental for all human communities. The great revolution in linguistic media began only about 5,000 years ago, with the invention of writing, and especially, about 2,500 years ago, with the invention of the Greek alphabet. This invention affected the foundations of the sociolinguistic system. Soon, it wasn't enough to make simple oral promises, face to face, in the physical presence of another individual: the written contract was invented, converting social commitment into a piece of paper, a material object, functioning in the absence, or after the death, of the individuals involved. And with the invention of writing, historiography and grammatical treatises and logical analysis became possible. A new segregation of human language came in with the differentiation between informal oral discourse and formal written documents. This sort of differentiation, two sets of different linguistic registers with different social functions, has been given the name of diglossia by sociolinguists; acute forms of diglossia are found today in German-Switzerland and Haiti, for example, where one mother-tongue or local dialect is learned for talking at home, and another quite different standard metropolitan language is learned for reading and writing in school, and for formal discourse in public.

In our Western tradition a certain form of diglossia first became important with the establishment of Classical (written) Latin by authors such as Cicero and Virgil. These writers were bilingual: they knew Greek as well as Latin, and Greek had the prestige of an already established literary tradition. When these Roman authors began to write Latin, they translated and imitated Greek texts as models, borrowing and inventing new words and phrases in Latin. The result was a written style quite different from the language of the man in the street; this standard Classical Latin was clearly differentiated from the various Vulgar Latin dialects spoken by most inhabitants of the Italian peninsula and of Roman colonies in Gaul, Iberia, North Africa and elsewhere. The stability of Classical Latin depended upon the military and political stability of the Roman state; with the decline and fall of the Roman Empire, the social subversion fomented by Christianity radically changed the quality of written Latin. The Fathers of the Western Church deliberately created a new style of writing based upon a special Christian variety of Vulgar Latin, spoken by a lower-class secret society of believers, with their own monotheistic and anti-aristocratic community, and their own semi-Greek jargon. St Jerome translated the Bible for this social group; he saw Cicero's elegant Classical Latin as the enemy of Christianity and deliberately tried to convey in the common language of the Roman people the religious sense of sacred texts originally written in Hebrew and in vulgar Greek. Similarly, St Augustine invented in his *Confessions* and his sermons a new colloquial eloquence reminiscent of the Hebrew Psalms. And, as a convert from the political rhetoric of pagan schools, he records his amazement at seeing Ambrose, Bishop of Milan, silently reading to himself, in intimate Christian alienation from society (*Confessions*, iii, 3): "Sed cum legebat, oculi ducebantur per paginas et cor intellectum rimabatur, vox autem et lingua quiescebant"— "But as he read, his eyes traveled over the pages and his heart dug out the meaning, and yet his voice and tongue were motionless." (St Teresa read a Spanish version of St Augustine's *Confessions;* it was the most influential model for her *Libro de la vida,* the L.)

With the social rise of Christianity within the Roman Empire, the constant liturgical use of patristic Latin, derived originally from a particular lower-class dialect, gradually raised the new style from the gutter and gave it a peculiar dignity and sanctity as the primary written language of medieval Europe. But then, as is the case with all stable written styles, a more and more noticeable new gap began to grow between the written language of the Western Church and the spoken language, or rather the innumerable dialects, of illiterate peasants and landowners. The decline of trade and the disappearance of an urban reading public tended to restrict reading and writing to the clergy alone. Gradually during the European Middle Ages the Latin language ceased being anybody's mother tongue; it was taught to a few boys, who were separated from their mothers and sisters and were destined for a life of celibacy. (Fr Walter J. Ong, of St Louis University, has called this process a male puberty rite,[5] the linguistic hazing of new young leaders for Church and University.) Thus the only literate class, the clergy, was cut off from much of the rising secular society. A radical new diglossia had come into existence throughout medieval Europe.

The socially restricted nature of the clerical reading public was an important factor in the rise of a new vernacular literature toward the end of the eleventh or beginning of the twelfth century. Troubadour poets began using the alphabet to record, compose and copy love lyrics; the alphabet was also used to transcribe and compose long epic poems. Even though at first these texts were sung or chanted aloud more often than they were read silently, their mere existence soon gave rise to a new courtly reading public, made up largely of ladies, demanding literature written, not in Latin, but in Provençal and Anglo-Norman. The medieval culmination of this new vernacular literature took place in Italy, with Dante's *Divine Comedy.* And it was in Italy, shortly afterwards, that Renaissance humanists successfully revived the Classical style of written

Latin; the mutual reinforcement of Latin and the vernaculars was the point of departure for modern European, and world-wide, literature.

The situation was somewhat different in the Iberian peninsula, where Latin had been permanently weakened by the eighth-century Islamic invasion; in the south, particularly in the region around the caliphate of Cordoba, Classical (written) Arabic, rather than Latin, became the principal language of literate culture. Hebrew and Visigothic Latin did exist, but primarily as liturgical languages; if a rabbi or a Christian priest wanted to write a message, he normally used Arabic, the written language generally taught in the local grammar schools. Yet at home and in the streets the predominant spoken language was a Romance dialect, called Mozarabic, with lots of Semitic loan-words. This was the spoken language, the *lingua franca,* commonly used by Moslems, Jews and Christians alike. The French-inspired Christian Reconquest of the Iberian peninsula brought in Carolingian Latin, the new *Roman Missal,* and vernacular literature; and already by the thirteenth century the king of Castile decided to develop a new written version of spoken Spanish, instead of Latin, for official documents, law codes, historiography and scientific treatises. Devout Christians and Jews, who could not read the Bible in Church Latin or in Synagogue Hebrew, commissioned translations into this written Spanish in order to be able to study the Bible at home. Spanish was the first European vernacular to have a full-scale written grammar published; this grammar book appeared in the fateful year of 1492, in which the last Moslem kingdom in Spain was conquered, all practicing Jews were expelled, and a new European frontier was established in the Caribbean, under the Catholic monarchs Ferdinand of Aragon and Isabel of Castile.

Latin humanism was weak in sixteenth-century Spain, but vernacular literature continued to develop brilliantly. In the 1530s two friends and members of Charles V's international court, Juan Boscán from Barcelona and Garcilaso de la Vega from Toledo, wrote the first secular masterpieces of Renaissance classical Spanish prose and poetry, strongly influenced by Latin and Italian models. In exactly the same years and within the same Italo-Hispanic cultural world, at its major center in Naples, John de Valdés wrote his *Diálogo de la lengua* (or *Dialogue about Language)*, in which we can see the close relationship between religious reform and the use of the Spanish vernacular. "Vox populi vox Dei" ("The voice of the people is the voice of God"): this was in practice the motto of Luther (whose translation of the Bible was the foundation of German prose) and of the Anglicans (we all know how important an influence the King James version of the Bible had upon writers in English); its influence is also present in such Spanish religious writers as Louis of Granada (born 1504), John de Valdés (1510?), and Teresa of Jesus (1515).

Each of these three writers has a different Spanish style. Louis of Granada was a polyglot Renaissance Dominican, writing in Latin, in Spanish and in Portuguese; in his Spanish sermons and theological writings he was one of the founders of the new Ciceronian or rhetorical style. John de Valdés had a university education, which means that he did read Latin; but he was influenced by Protestant ideas and by Erasmus's anti-Ciceronianism. Valdés wrote Spanish only, and in an elegantly courtly, but informally colloquial, style. Teresa of Jesus knew very little Latin, and she deliberately refused to imitate the new style of classical Spanish prose; in a true patristic spirit, she invented her own vulgar style of substandard written Spanish, a style that is clearly anti-academic and even anti-rational. I would now like to explore some of the possible implications of her more or less self-conscious attitude toward language.

ST TERESA AND LANGUAGE

I don't think that St Teresa's rather remotely Jewish family background has much to do with her ignorance of Latin. The fact that she was a woman, however, is important. Queen Isabel had studied humanistic Latin in a Renaissance court setting. But Teresa's world was quite different, not courtly, but middle-class: she learned to read Spanish fluently as a young girl and knew that she had an advantage there that she could never have in the official Scholastic language of the Western Church, with its exclusively male priesthood. Her oral use of Spanish was not structured, as Louis of Granada's and John de Valdés's was, by a familiarity with written Latin, whether ecclesiastical or neo-classical. And when she wrote, she neglected, or perhaps deliberately avoided, the normal spelling and syntax of the Spanish texts that she had voraciously read. She seems to have wanted to transcribe her experiences as directly as possible into the Spanish sounds and the rapid, but irregular, flow of speech that an intelligent woman would come out with spontaneously, with no thought of constructing a well-written text. Teresa's written Spanish is in fact hard for us to read and understand in a wholly rational way; it is comparable, within an American context, to something composed by a writer of Black English, who deliberately tries to avoid the academic sound of white bourgeois correctness. Her style was rooted in her intimate mystical experiences as a woman who had been brought up in a close-knit family of readers and who was living within an intensely personal religious community of the sort that she had brought into existence by her reform of the Carmelites.

Teresa herself makes some revealing comments about the close relationship between her experiences and her ability to tell about them. She writes these words in the L, 17, 5:

> One favor is for the Lord to give that favor, and it's another to understand what favor it is and what grace; and yet another is to know how to tell it and explain what it's like.
>
> Una merced es dar el Señor la merced, y otra es en tender qué merced es, y que gracia; otra es saber decirla y dar a entender cómo es.

In another passage she attributes directly to God her linguistic communication:

> I see clearly that I'm not the person who says it, for I neither arrange

it with my understanding nor do I know later on how I've managed
to say it.

Veo claro no soy yo quien lo dice, que ni lo ordeno con el entendimiento ni sé después cómo lo acerté a decir.

For St Teresa, her peculiar use of language is in itself a gift from God.
I suspect that as she wrote, remembering her experiences, she relived
them and wrote in a state of semi-trance.

In order to gain new insight into St Teresa's way of writing, I now
propose to approach what I have called her vernacular mind through the
eyes of her first editor, the Augustinian friar and professor of Hebrew
scriptures at Salamanca, Louis of Leon, who was twelve years her junior.
They both belonged to that peculiar Spanish social group known as
the New Christians, that is they belonged to families converted from
Judaism in the fifteenth century. Both of them were radically critical of
the spiritual stagnation of Spain's Old Christian majority, largely made
up of illiterate peasants. But these two New Christians had very different educational backgrounds. Fray Louis could read, not only Spanish,
but Italian, Latin, Greek and Hebrew; he was a professional theologian
and, as such, thought and wrote professionally in Latin. Even when he
wrote Spanish, he usually had a model, or subtext, in Latin. His poems,
for example, were normally Horatian odes: translations, imitations or
adaptations to Spanish of poems written in Latin by the great pagan
poet Quintus Horatius Flaccus. Fray Louis's prose also followed classical models, especially the elaborate rhetoric of Cicero, St Jerome's *bête
noire*. Although flexible and varied, Louis of León's prose is always consistent and coherent on all levels: grammatical, rhetorical and logical.
He explains his stylistic ideal in the dedication to the third book of
his great work *De los nombres de Cristo* (*On the Names of Christ*), as he
defends his theological and artistic use of the Spanish vernacular:

And to this ignorant group belong those who say that I do not speak
the vernacular because I do not speak in a disjointed and disorderly

way, and because I harmonize my words and select them and put
each one in its place; for they think that to speak the vernacular is
to speak as the man in the street speaks, and they do not realize that
good speech is not common, but the result of individual judgment,
both in what one says and in the way one says it, a judgment which,
from among the words that everyone speaks, chooses those that are
suitable, and considers how they sound, and sometimes even counts
their syllables and weighs them and measures them and arranges
them so that they say what one is trying to say not only with precision, but with sweetness and harmony.[6]

When he wrote these words, Louis of Leon was not only explaining
his own theory of style but at the same time was giving an example of
the elegant intellectual prose that he was reinventing in Spanish, on the
basis of classical Ciceronian models.

On St John of the Cross's recommendation, the Carmelite Order
commissioned Louis of Leon, as a leading Augustinian friar who sympathized with reforming movements, to publish the first edition of the
works of Mother Teresa of Jesus, after her death in 1582, but before
her canonization. He published them in 1588 with a dedicatory letter
addressed to the Prioress Ann of Jesus and her sisters, who belonged to
the Discalced Carmelite convent in Madrid. In this letter we are immediately struck by Louis of León's great admiration, and even reverence,
for the future St Teresa. He says that he had never met her personally
while she was alive, but that he knows her now through her daughters
and through her writings. He emphasizes the difference between himself and her when he says that God, in order to fight the devil, had
decided "to set against him, not a brave man fortified with great learning, but a poor solitary woman to challenge him and to raise up an army
against him" and thus to restore the holiness of the primitive Church in
Spain. (Louis of Leon had spent five years in the Spanish Inquisition's
dungeons because of his reforming activities; Teresa's L, in manuscript,
had spent twelve years in the hands of suspicious inquisitors.) According

to Louis of Leon, the reformed Carmelite nuns had helped him understand the works of Teresa that he was publishing; in his opinion there was a curious similarity of tone between their voices and her writings, such that to hear them talk was to read her, and vice versa:

> I believe that your reverences are important witnesses, for you are quite similar models of excellence: I never recall reading her works that I do not seem to be hearing your reverences talk, nor, conversely, do I ever hear you talk without imagining that I am reading Mother Teresa . . . [there is] the same illumination and profound understanding of matters of the spirit that are subtle and difficult . . . the same fire from God . . . [7]

Thus the oral tradition of a community's spoken style helped Louis of Leon to understand and appreciate the written texts that he was editing.

Later on this editor explains the scholarship that he has had to devote to establishing Teresa of Avila's authentic texts: "I have worked," he says " . . . by comparing them with her own manuscripts, which were in my hands for many days, in order to reestablish their original integrity . . . " Louis of Leon had the attitude of the authentic textual critic belonging to the humanistic tradition: he knew that many corruptions had seeped in, as he says, "either because of scribes' carelessness, or because of erroneous presumption." This is the way in which he criticizes the presumptuous people who have pretended to correct St Teresa's style:

> To change things written by a heart in which God lived, and which he apparently moved to write them, was a great act of presumption, and it was a terrible error to try to correct her words, because if they really understood Spanish, they would realize that Mother Teresa's Spanish is elegance itself; for even though, in certain passage of what she writes, before she completes the sentence that she has begun, she contaminates it with other sentences and breaks the train of

thought, often beginning anew with interpolations, nevertheless she interpolates so dexterously and commits such delightful contaminations that the defect itself is a source of beauty, like a mole on a lovely face.[8]

I think we could use Louis of León's observations to help us develop a whole theory of the relationship between experience, speech and writing. Fray Louis was undoubtedly drawing upon traditional ideas deriving from Plato and St Augustine, but he was applying them to a concrete Spanish situation, that of Teresa of Jesus, who had been requested to describe her mystical experiences in writing. We have to imagine her as a person raised within an intensely oral culture; but, influenced by a family tradition of reading and writing, this person, while still very young, had learned to read Spanish with great fluency. In the first two or three chapters of L she gives us a few details that allow us to imagine the intensity of her youthful readings: her father and her mother were great readers; she was her father's favorite daughter; with one of her brothers of about the same age she read saints' lives, and together they dreamed of going off to Africa and seeking martyrs' deaths in order to go straight to heaven; with her mother she read romances of chivalry, secretly, hiding from her father; when she was sixteen, she apparently became romantically involved, and her father, without accusations, put her secretly in a convent; though not eager to become a nun, under the influence of her father's brother she began to read, with the same voracity, books of devotion, meditation and mystical theology. It was in these circumstances, complicated by severe illness, that her religious vocation developed. When, later on, her confessors urged her to write about her experiences, she wrote with a similar intensity and fluency.

About forty years ago a great Spanish scholar named Ramon Menéndez Pidal began to analyze Teresa's written style. He cited a fascinating passage from her family correspondence, a letter addressed to her younger brother Lawrence. (I find it curious that she addresses him very formally as "vuestra merced," the equivalent of modern "usted," instead of the more familiar "tú" or "vos.") Commenting on the letters that they write to one another, Teresa writes the following to her brother:

> I don't know if I've answered everything; I always re-read your letter, I'm lucky to have the time to, and now hastily I've re-read it in fragments. Don't you waste your time re-reading the letters you write me: I never do so. If there are words with letters missing, put them in at your end, for that's what I do with yours at my end: then we understand what it means, otherwise it's a useless waste of time.
>
> No sé si he respondido a todo, que siempre torno otra vez a leer su carta, que no es poco tener tiempo, y ahora no sino a remiendos la he tornado a leer. Ni vuestra merced tome ese trabajo en tornar a leer las que me escribe: yo jamás lo hago. Si faltaren letras, póngalas alla, que ansí haré yo acá a las suyas—que luego se entiende lo que quiere decir—que es perdido tiempo sin propósito.[9]

She lets us see, in this passage, her writing and reading as intuitive processes taking place rapidly under the pressure of time. According to her, she doesn't want to waste time with the mechanics of writing: missing letters don't matter, because the reader is concerned with making sense of the text and can make any necessary adjustments. For her, it seems to me, writing is an inferior substitute for talking. Ellipsis, for example, which is perfectly normal in oral conversation, appears constantly in her writing, which is difficult for us to read precisely because she expects us to be able to read between the lines. This is exactly the opposite of what Louis of León did when he wrote his own artistic prose: he did not want to speak "in a disjointed and disorderly way," but to put each word and each letter "in its place," listening to its sound and counting syllables, trying always to achieve clarity and precision as well as sweetness and harmony.

I find it significant that Louis of León could appreciate Teresa's written style only by applying to it criteria that are quite different from his own humanistic ones. It seems to me that this is what he is driving at when he talks of hearing the reformed Carmelites speak when he reads Teresa's works, and vice versa. He is referring to a community's way of speaking that is always the same, whether oral or transcribed graphically. Louis says that he recognizes the same person Teresa, whether through conversation with her spiritual daughters or through her written works, because both modes of linguistic communication convey the same illumination stemming from God.

It is this divine source, preserved in the nun's speech and in Teresa's writings, that inspires Louis of León's great respect for her "ipsissima verba," which he tries to reestablish on the basis of her autograph manuscripts: God lived in her heart and moved her to write words that no one should dare to change in the smallest detail. For him, her ellipses and anacolutha are paradoxical "beauty-spots": that is, these apparent imperfections in fact constitute the essential elegance of Teresa's style. Her sentences are syntactically incomplete: she sacrifices grammatical coherence to precision of reference, the beauty of Reality.

In his 1941 essay on "St Teresa's Style," Menéndez Pidal was actually following Louis of León's lead when he commented on her "incessant elipses; confused grammatical agreements; enormous parentheses, which cause the reader to lose the train of thought; lines of reasoning that are never completed because of interruptions; verbless sentences." And he added that "St Teresa does not really write, but speaks through writing; thus the excitement of her emotional syntax constantly overflows the restrictions of ordinary grammar."[10] Menéndez Pidal simply makes more explicit what Louis of León has already observed with spiritual appreciation, in his 1588 dedicatory letter. She used grammatical fragmentation as a linguistic metaphor to convey prelinguistic communications that her soul had received directly from God. (In similar, but postlinguistic terms, the Argentine Borges refers in the twentieth century to "a purely ideographic writing: the direct communication of experiences, not of sounds.") And St Teresa's own references to writing as a problem show how fully aware she was of her stylistic peculiarities. At one point she says: "I wish I could write with many hands, so that some of them would supply the lack of others." (Her Spanish isn't all that clear: what she actually says is "Ojalá pudiera yo escribir con muchas manos, para que unas por otras no se olvidaran,"—"so that some are not forgotten because of the others.")[11] I think this statement points in the same direction as her ellipses and incomplete sentences: she refuses to accept the analytical or linear sequentiality of linguistic discourse, and she strives for simultaneity, for saying everything all at once, as it actually happens, "writing with many hands."

To conclude, I would like to draw one final example from Teresa of Jesus' text of her L, section 8 of chapter 27, translated as literally as possible. (Incidentally, everything that I've written here indicates how very difficult it is to translate St Teresa's writings: first, as reader, the translator must have the spiritual intuition necessary to follow her elliptical train of thought, and then, as writer, he must be able to produce in another language a similar degree of ellipsis, requiring a similar level or spiritual intuition on the part of the reader of the translation.)

In the conversation that has been referred to before, God makes one's understanding pay attention, even against one's will, so as to understand what's being said; in that case the soul seems to have other ears to hear with, and this makes it listen and not be distracted; like someone who could hear well and wasn't allowed to stop up his ears and was being talked at loudly from up close: he would hear even if he didn't want to. Anyhow, he must be doing something, because he's paying attention to understand what's being said to him. But in this other case, nothing: even that little bit of just listening, which it did in the past, is all gone. One finds everything already cooked and eaten; there's nothing to do but enjoy, like someone who without learning or working to know how to read, or even studying at all, would suddenly find all knowledge already known in itself, without knowing how or where, for he hadn't even ever worked even to learn the ABC's.

En la habla que hemos dicho antes, hace Dios al entendimiento que advierta, aunque le pese, a entender lo que se dice; que alla parece tiene el alma otros oídos con que oye, y que la hace escuchar, y que no se divierte; como a uno que oyese bien y no le consintiesen atapar los oídos y le hablasen junto a voces, aunque no quisiese lo oiría. Y, en fin, algo hace, pues está atento a entender lo que le hablan. Acá, ninguna cosa; que aun este poco que es solo escuchar, que hacía en lo pasado, se le quita. Todo lo halla guisado y comido; no hay mas que hacer de gozar, como uno que sin deprender ni haber trabajado nada para saber leer ni tampoco hubiese estudiado nada, hallase toda la ciencia sabida ya en sí, sin saber cómo ni dónde, pues aun nunca había trabajado aun para deprender el abecé.

I would like briefly to interpret this passage. What Teresa here says is that the divine, or subconscious, messages came to her as a sort of oral speech penetrating her ears, even against her will, violently taking over her attention and understanding. She doesn't even have to make the effort of listening: God's language simply invades her. Then Teresa briefly changes her metaphor: the divine invasion takes the form of baby food, already fully prepared and chewed up in advance, to be absorbed and enjoyed with no effort at all, like mother's milk in a baby's mouth. Teresa now returns to the linguistic, but not unrelated, metaphor, based on her own experience as a voracious reader: the alphabet has been internalized to such an extent that writing itself becomes mystic knowledge. The alphabet actually disappears, and all that's left is the direct experience of Reality, expressed in a completely non-humanistic prose, which revels in its ungrammatical carelessness as it makes us readers play an active role, for we can understand Teresa's intuitive prose only if we make an effort to comprehend its subtle inner coherence, a coherence which exists beyond words.

NOTES

1. Victor Garcia de la Concha, *El arte literario de Santa Teresa* (Barcelona: Ariel, 1978.)

2. Enrique Llamas Martinez, *Santa Teresa de Jesus y la Inquisitiín española* (Madrid:

C.S.I.C., 1972).

3. Ibid., pp. 396-97.

4. R. Brown and A. Gilman, "The Pronouns of Power and Solidarity," in T. A. Sebeok ed., *Style in Language* (Cambridge, MA: M.I.T., 1960), pp. 253-76.

5. Walter J. Ong, "Latin Language as a Renaissance Puberty Rite," *Studies in Philology*, 56 (1959), 103-24.

6. Luis de León, *Obras completas castellanas*, ed. Félix Garcia (Madrid: La Editorial Catolica, 1944), p. 674, Coll. "Biblioteca de Autores Cristianos," 3.

7. See Peers ed., 3, pp. 368-78 for full text of the dedicatory letter.

8. See ibid, p. 373 for Peers' freer translation.

9. Letter to Lawrence Cepeda, January 17, 1577.

10. Ramón Menéndez Pidal, "El estilo de Santa Teresa," first published in *Escorial* (October, 1941) and then in *La lengua de Cristóbal Colon* (Buenos Aires: Espasa, 1942), p. 135. Coll. "Austral," 280.

11. W, 20, 6.

*Teresa and
Her Church*

The Saving Role of the Human Christ for St Teresa

◆ ◆ ◆

Eamon R. Carroll, S.T.D.

Fr Eamon R. Carroll has many academic posts and distinctions to his credit, along with the Presidency of the Catholic Theological Society of America and the Mariological Society of America. Currently he is Professor of Theology in his hometown university of Loyola, Chicago.

INTRODUCTION

Christianity has lived on the conviction that there is no true Christian prayer without Christ. The Letter to the Hebrews 3:1 reads: "Fix your eyes on Jesus the apostle and high priest whom we acknowledge in faith," and the *Carmelite Rule* says we are to live "in allegiance to Jesus Christ." One of the all-time greatest defenders of this tradition is St Teresa of Avila, in her typically forthright style. The theology of this doctor of the Church was also her experience, in the deepest and most ancient sense of the word "theology" as God-centeredness, but also theology as a human science that fully involves the human person, specifically Teresa's own polyvalent and rich human personality. The Jesus whose name became attached to Teresa's when she chose to be known as Teresa of Jesus at her first foundation of St Joseph is the triumphant victorious Christ of the Holy Scriptures and the Holy Eucharist.

In this study I offer reflections on St Teresa's extraordinarily accurate christology; I say "extraordinary," for, as she was the first to say, Teresa had no theological training as such. A contemporary French Carmelite has written of her "learned lack of learning." Yet along the road of prayer, on the pilgrimage of faith, through all her progress on the "way of perfection" toward the throne room of the King at the center of the many dwelling places of the spiritual life, Teresa learned from the master teacher, Jesus himself. It is another depth to Teresa's christology that she saw the achievement of full human potential in union with Christ. We become most properly human beings when in the inmost center of our selves Christ is enthroned, the human Jesus who is the very Son of God, the revelation of God's kindness to us in the power of the Spirit. Moreover, this wise woman constantly sought advice from theologians. It is almost embarrassing to me as a theologian to read her words of confidence in their judgment, even when they had not themselves experienced ways of prayer about which their advice was being sought and concerning which they were in fact able to give good advice.[1] She also had the experience of confessors who held her back along the ways of prayer because of their ignorance, but, if anything, that sharpened her sense of the importance of learning. And, as is well known, the necessity of good instruction spurred Teresa to write her own great books on prayer. Along the same lines of seeking advice from experts was Teresa's respect for Church authorities, such as the bishops with whom she had to deal in making her many foundations, and the religious superiors to whom she was in various ways subject.

We recall from her description of the fourth dwelling place how for a bleak period Teresa tried to follow the advice of certain books about prayer—that the humanity of Christ was a hindrance to higher forms of prayer. Her subsequent reaction was "high treason, though done in ignorance." Through the experience of the mystical marriage, again as described in C, she realized that the "soul never ceases to walk with Christ," even if no longer through analytic thought and the incessant use of the imagination, factors rightly regarded as keeping the soul from attaining full enlightenment. It is also well-known that when Teresa herself experienced the culminating blessings of the seventh dwelling place, the mystical nuptials, she was granted a special vision of the humanity of Christ, which must be regarded as the formal confirmation of her spiritual marriage.

LIFE STORY

The Spanish "golden age" of the sixteenth century had its dark side in "alumbradismo," with its exaggerated spiritualism, while from beyond the borders of Spain came the challenge of Protestant rejection of many old forms of devotion.

In all her visions and locutions Teresa experienced reference to Jesus Christ. The words to Philip at the Last Supper, "who sees me sees the Father" (Jn 14:9), were axiomatic in Teresa's life. In her existential openness to the Absolute she kept her balance only in identifying this Absolute with Jesus Christ. The abstract distant God was gradually "concretized" for her in Jesus. She did not simply "put on" Christ, she was transformed into him, a development not from without but from within, Jesus acting in her, at the heart of the interior castle of her personality. The progressive degrees of prayer in her life were stages in grasping Christ, or better, being seized by him.

Pivots of Teresian christology are the humanity and divinity of Jesus, the Cross and Resurrection, not excluding the other mysteries of his earthly life, and then a remarkable set of "presences" of the Risen Lord—in his Church, in the Eucharist, in the community and in one's innermost self. For centuries we have limited the words, "real presence," to the special presence of the Risen Savior in the Eucharist, under the signs of bread and wine. But recent theology, supported by the Second Vatican Council, has stressed other presences of the Risen Christ that are no less "real presences," albeit of a different kind than the sacramental presence of the Holy Eucharist. Teresa was sensitive to these other real presences: in the gospel words of Jesus, in the Church, in the community, and profoundly in the inner self of the follower of Christ.

Christ is the place of our encounter with God. For Teresa, the humanity of Jesus, or "the most Sacred Humanity" (her preferred phrase), is no abstraction: the man Jesus of Nazareth is indispensable to the spiritual life at every stage, mystical as well as ascetical. With St John's Gospel Teresa writes frequently that Jesus is "the way, the truth and the life"; no stage of the spiritual life, no matter how advanced, can do without these roles of Jesus. Teresa's quest for the Lord began in her childhood. Even as a small girl she sought solitude for prayer, and loved the rosary which her mother had taught her. Devotion to the mother of Jesus was to remain a strong part of her spirituality, even into the highest stages of her union with God.

When she was an adolescent boarder at the Augustinian convent of Our Lady of Grace, thanks to the good influence of one of the sisters, Teresa began to meditate on Jesus in the Garden of Olives, and to consider a vocation to the religious life. Her pious Uncle Peter gave Teresa some of St Jerome's letters, and from Jerome's love for Jesus she came to appreciate the demands of her own vocation as the call of Christ. In the first years of her religious life at the Incarnation in Avila Teresa regarded her profession as "espousals" with Christ, but a long road still lay ahead. She was already fond of the gospel story of the Samaritan Woman at the well seeking the water of life and she had learned to pray "Lord, give me always this water." Osuna's book, *The Third Spiritual Alphabet* exercised a strong influence on her; through reading Osuna she discovered the true vocation of prayer. She experienced the prayer of quiet and of union. For Teresa, that infused contemplation was the work of Christ dwelling in her. Her advice to beginners was to start with the life of Christ.

At her father's death the Dominican Vincent Barron, who had been her father's confessor, was also, she writes, "of the very greatest help" to her and under his guidance she took up again the way of prayer, never again to abandon it. A third and famous "conversion" in her life occurred in Lent, 1554, before an image of Christ in his Passion (most likely an *Ecce Homo),* as she describes wonderfully in chapter 9 of her L.

It can be said that from her first visions of Christ Teresa enjoyed his presence almost constantly; she writes (of the sixth dwelling place) of the Lord walking by her side, not in any sensible way, but in her words, "this vision comes in another unexplainable, more delicate way" that "is so certain and leaves much certitude . . . an intellectual vision." The locutions of Teresa were also strongly christological; they often came prior to the visions and prepared the way for them. She experienced these for the first time in the years 1554-1556 and they continued almost without interruption for the rest of her life.

Throughout her life the words of Jesus strengthened Teresa. The incident in chapter 25 of her L is familiar. She was in a state of exhaustion when she heard words that brought total tranquility: "Be not afraid, daughter, it is I and I will not forsake thee; fear not." The effect was instantaneous; she received fortitude and courage, and conviction and tranquility and light, so that in a moment she found her "soul transformed and . . . would have maintained against the whole world that this was the work of God . . . What a powerful Lord! He gives not only counsel but solace. His words are deeds. See how he strengthens our faith and how our love increases." She recalled how the command of Christ stilled the waves.

Later in L, 38 she recalls how when she was at prayer the Lord sometimes spoke to her of her faults but also of the favors he had already given her. On one such occasion she saw the Sacred Humanity in far greater glory than ever before, "a most clear and wonderful representation of the Sacred Humanity in the bosom of the Father," a good example of how even in her visions of the Trinity she did not lose the sense of the humanity of Jesus.

For Teresa the words of Jesus were also "deeds"; having said this, she added, "See how he strengthens our faith and how our love increases!" She saw all the enterprises to which the words of Jesus directed her as bearing the seal of Christ. In the convents she founded she saw the mysteries of Christ renewed, from the Holy Family at Bethlehem to the apostolic community in the Cenacle. When Teresa speaks of the "humanity" of Jesus she intends the whole Jesus Christ, including all aspects of his human life, crowned by the Resurrection.

The heart of Teresa's teaching is prayer: this is her role as "Doctor of the Church." We might note Pope Paul VI's words on September 27, 1970, at the ceremony proclaiming her first woman Doctor of the Church: "We have conferred—rather, We have acknowledged—St Teresa of Jesus' title of Doctor of the Church." In the same homily the Pope spoke of Teresa's "human vitality and spiritual vivacity."[2] The title of a modern study about her, *I Want to See God* (by Fr Marie-Eugène, O.C.D.) describes well her life of prayer and her teaching about it. For Teresa to be recollected meant to be immersed in Christ; to pray meant to be transformed in Jesus the Lord, the whole human personality caught up in Christ.

DWELLING PLACES

Even in the first dwelling place of C Teresa is conscious of the presence of Jesus; already, in L, 40 she had written of Jesus as a present in the innermost recesses of the soul. In the first dwelling place the fountain of water is symbolic of Christ: "the streams that flow from a crystal-clear fount . . . this fount of life, in which the soul is planted like a tree." Throughout her writings water symbolism is associated with Jesus—in W but frequently elsewhere also, often in connection with the Samaritan Woman who unknowingly was thirsting for the living water. Light is another favorite symbol for Christ; he is the water that satisfies, the light that illuminates. Self-understanding, dominant note of the first dwelling place, is achieved through Christ; he is the mirror. We note again the strong anthropology of Teresa's christology. She would have cheered the statement for the Second Vatican Council, "Only in the mystery of the incarnate Word does the mystery of man take on light" *(Gaudium et Spes,* no. 22).

Central to the second dwelling place is the following of the

Crucified One. The Christian must be immersed in the Passion and Resurrection. We must look at Jesus and reflect on what we owe him and the death he suffered for us. For Teresa, "looking on Jesus" means "looking on him in faith." It is much more, for there is mutual regard, as Teresa put it in L, 13: "If a person is able he should occupy himself in looking at Christ who is looking at him, and he should speak, and petition, and humble himself, and delight in the Lord's presence . . . " According to contemporary exegetes, the New Testament phrase, "looking on Jesus," is to be taken eschatologically, that is, for faith in the glorified Christ. It means contemplating the glory of Christ the Savior, and work of the Holy Spirit, a contemplation in faith and love, as in the statement from the prophet Zechariah that the Evangelist John applies to the Calvary scene, "They shall look on him whom they have pierced," words that mean the loving contemplation of the followers of Christ.

In dwelling place three, speaking of the rich young man who turned away from the Lord, Teresa reminds her daughters that the Lord is calling them to be perfect, and "He must give the reward in conformity with the love we have for him." The final stage of the ascetic life is reached in the third dwelling place. There is no hint of gnostic self-purification; the emphasis is on the imitation of Christ, especially in his Passion. As she stated in her L, let people meditate on other subjects too, if they are so inclined, on hell or heaven, on death, on God's forgiveness. All very admirable, she adds, "provided one does not fail to meditate often upon the Passion and the life of Christ, which are, and have always been, the source of everything that is good."[3]

The prayer of recollection or the prayer of quiet takes place in the fourth dwelling place. Here the soul hears the soft whistle of the Good Shepherd. The whole human being is anointed in intellectual and affective faculties by meeting Jesus Christ. God makes himself present in Christ. The shepherd's gentle call pulls the sheep away from other attractions. There is an intuitive and joyful understanding of the mystery of Christ, preparing the will for union with him and making his presence felt. Working again with the imagery of water Teresa explains that in this prayer of quiet the soul is enlarged like a marvelous fountain whose capacity increases to accommodate the greater flow of water.

In the fifth dwelling place all the powers of the soul are captivated and absorbed by the presence of God. According to Teresa, "The Lord doesn't have to grant us great delights for this union; sufficient is what he has given us in his Son, who would teach us the way." Teresa's good sense appears again when she notes that being conformed to the will of God does not mean she would not feel sorrow at the death of her father or brother, or that she suffers trials and illness happily. With equal directness she gets to the heart of holiness: "Here in our religious life the Lord asks of us only two things: love of His Majesty and love of our neighbor. These are what we must work for. By observing them with perfection, we do his will and so will be united with him."

The silkworm metaphor enters in the fifth dwelling place—the silkworm that changes into a butterfly. The cocoon or the little "house" that the silkworm spins is Christ; in Teresa's words, "our life is hidden in Christ or in God (both are the same) . . . our life is Christ." For Teresa contemplation is not an escape from the body, not evasion, but the concentration of all the faculties on the person of the Risen Jesus.

In the description of the sixth dwelling place, after announcing the theme of the espousals, Teresa devotes the balance of the chapter to Jesus Christ. It is also in this section of C that Teresa comments that "to always withdraw from corporeal things and be enkindled in love is the trait of angelic spirits, not of those who live in mortal bodies," hence, she says, she cannot imagine what souls are thinking of when they claim they cannot think about the Passion, or still less about the Blessed Virgin and the saints. Teresa says of such people, " . . . they just don't understand and they will do harm to themselves and to others."

In characteristically warm fashion she comments, "Life is long, and there are in it many trials, and we need to look at Christ our model, how he suffered them, and also at his apostles and saints, so as to bear these trials with perfection. Jesus is too good a companion for us to turn away from him and his most blessed Mother, and he is very pleased that we grieve over his sufferings even though we sometimes leave aside our own consolation and delight."[4] The comment of Kieran Kavanaugh, O.C.D., is, "The purification of the person is realized not merely through the sufferings inherent to the human condition but especially through contact with the person of Christ in his humanity and divinity."[5]

In L, 22, 5, looking back on her prayer experience, Teresa wrote, "Who can there be, like myself, so miserably proud, that when he has labored all his life long over every imaginable kind of penance and prayer and suffered every kind of persecution, he does not count himself very wealthy and abundantly rewarded if the Lord allows him to stand with St John at the foot of the Cross? I cannot imagine how it can enter anyone's head not to be contented with this . . . " Not that Teresa ever lost sight of the glorified Christ—as in the brilliant passage that continued immediately after the words just quoted:

> If our nature or health doesn't allow us to think always about the Passion, since to do so would be arduous, who will prevent us from being with him in his risen state? We have him so near in the Blessed Sacrament, where he is already glorified and where we don't have to gaze upon him as being so tired and worn out, bleeding, wearied by his journeys, persecuted by those for whom he did so much good, and not believed in by the apostles. Certainly there is no one who can endure thinking all the time about the many trials he suffered. Behold him here without suffering, full of glory, before ascending into heaven, strengthening some, encouraging others, our companion in the most Blessed Sacrament; it doesn't seem it was in his power to leave us for even a moment . . . The Lord helps us, strengthens us, and never fails; he is a true friend . . . God desires that if we are going to please him and receive his great favors, we must do so through the most Sacred Humanity of Christ, in whom he takes his delight. Many, many times have I perceived this truth through experience. The Lord has told it to me. I have definitely seen that we must enter by this gate, if we desire his sovereign Majesty to show us great secrets.[6]

It is significant in Teresa that even with respect to the sufferings of Jesus, to which she was always most sensitive, there is always a clear sense of the Resurrection. We who live in the recovered aura of the restored Easter Vigil and the rediscovered saving significance of the Resurrection must marvel yet again at the depth of St Teresa's grasp of the unity of the paschal mystery, as in the L, 29, 4:

> Almost invariably the Lord showed himself to me in his resurrection body, and it was thus, too, that I saw him in the Host. Only occasionally, to strengthen me when I was in tribulation, did he show me his wounds, and then he would appear sometimes as he was on the Cross and sometimes as in the garden. On a few occasions I saw him wearing the crown of thorns and sometimes he would also be carrying the Cross—because of my necessities, as I say, and those of others—but always in his glorified flesh.

In the sixth dwelling place the soul relives the biblical dialogue of love between God and his people, in preparation for the definitive transformation into Jesus Christ. The desire to see God, to enter into contact with the absolute which is the patrimony of every rational creature, is converted in Teresa's doctrine into the necessity of seeing Jesus, meeting with him, speaking with him, for he is the living expression of God for us. For St Teresa the human situation was openness to God, the God who comes to us in Christ Jesus. In the final seventh dwelling place Teresa finds St Paul's words realized, "For me to live is Christ, and to die is gain," and "He that is joined or united to the Lord becomes one spirit with him." (Phil 1:21; 1 Cor 6:17) She understands both Pauline quotations as throwing light on the union of the spiritual marriage. "The soul can say these words (that is, the words of St Paul) now because this state is the place where the little butterfly we mentioned dies, and with the greatest joy because its life is now Christ. And that its life is Christ is understood better with the passing of time by the effects this life has."[7] The process silkworm-cocoon-butterfly serves as an image of the whole adventure of the interior castle. The story has two stages linked by a transition. The inner movement toward God begins in earnest as the fully-grown silkworm begins its cocoon; there in the dark cocoon the interior process of transformation occurs, just as in the second stage of the castle journey; and Teresa reminds her readers what intense effort the weaving of the cocoon requires. In the recent book by my confrere, John Welch, *Spiritual Pilgrims: Carl Jung and Teresa of Avila,* Teresa's butterfly image is presented as an image of healing, with remarkable likeness to Jung's understanding of symbols and their importance for psychic wholeness and the resolution of conflict between the ego and the self. According to Fr Welch, "the complete image of the silkworm-cocoon-butterfly is representative of a uniting symbol."[8] Teresa likely saw in this image an expression of experiences of transformation; she uses the image to describe the effects of union with God. "The butterfly symbolizes the paschal mystery as well as psychic growth."[9] Entering into the dying and rising of Christ we enter into union with God. The Lord's words are effective, bringing light and peace, as Teresa wrote, "So, too, with the Lord's words to the glorious Magdalene that she go in peace."[10]

The Christian images Teresa used prepared her to be open to the transforming experiences that occurred to her on her journey through the castle. Even in the loftiest stages Teresa warns against jettisoning the Christian images of faith. When she wrote that God wants us to ask creatures who it is who made them, she was defending symbolism.

CHRIST HER MASTER

Christ is the teacher on Teresa's way of perfection. She tells us in her L that much of what she wrote was not out of her own head, but she was told it by "this heavenly Master of mine." Like St Paul she is careful to distinguish her own views from the Lord's, although like St Paul also she would not have hesitated to say she felt she had the mind of Christ, who was acting from within her. Her great love for the Scriptures (although since no vernacular translations were permitted and she did not know Latin she had to take her knowledge of the Bible from the portions incorporated in the Divine Office and quoted in other books) sprang from her conviction that she found Christ revealed in word and deed in the Scriptures. She constantly checked her own experience in prayer against biblical parallels. In her thought Christ is master doubly —from without, through the Bible and the Church, from within through the direct and personal experience of his mystery. Jesus is both the master and the object of prayer; successive degrees of prayer are progressively more profound meetings with Jesus.

As she says in L, 25, 13: "from what I see and know through experience, a locution bears the credentials of being from God if it is in conformity with Sacred Scripture." When she consulted theologians she held them as spokesmen "for what the Church holds," as experts "in the truths of Sacred Scripture." Theologians and preachers were for her the ecclesiastical arm of the Church, and to this arm rather than to the secular arm she looked for deliverance from the threat of the Reformation that was raging beyond the borders of Spain. The little groups of women in her convents would be friends of the Lord, following the evangelical counsels, living the life of prayer, backing up the preachers and theologians in defense of the Church; the lives of the nuns would be for the Church, in the service of Christ.

Yet women were held particularly prone to false mysticism. With a shift of ground as quick as her woman's intuition and as sharp as her wit Teresa turns the mistrust of women into a argument on behalf of mental prayer. Relaying some typical objections from those who were sceptical about convents of women dedicated to lives of prayer Teresa summarized, " . . . it's harmful to virtue; it's not for women, for they will be susceptible to illusions; it's better they stick to their sewing; they don't need these delicacies; the Our Father and the Hail Mary are sufficient."[11] Turning the tables, Teresa agreed that the Our Father and the Hail Mary were indeed sufficient, so long as they were properly prayed, and that meant mental prayer. She never achieved the commentary on the Hail Mary she had projected, although a good commentary could be pieced together from her many reflections on our Lady. The W does include her famous commentary on the Our Father, which has taken its place among the classic interpretations.

Without downplaying vocal prayer Teresa insists strongly on mental prayer. Defending its necessity she explains enthusiastically, "Hold fast, daughters, for they cannot take from you the Our Father and the Hail Mary." The hit was scored! In the Valladolid manuscript of the W the censor's comment is still to be seen in the margin, "It seems she is reprimanding the Inquisitors for prohibiting books on prayer."[12] And indeed in 1559 the list of forbidden books put out by the Grand Inquisitor (Ferdinand de Valdés) included many books on prayer that he thought might harm simple souls. The prohibition became blessing, as Teresa explains in her L, 26: "When a great many books written in Spanish were taken from us and we were forbidden to read them, I was very sorry . . . " Her obedience brought a quick reward: "Then the Lord said to me, 'Be not distressed, for I will give thee a living book' . . . the Lord showed me so much love and taught me by so many methods, that I have had very little need of books—indeed, hardly any. His Majesty himself has been to me the Book in which I have seen what is true . . ."[13]

THE OUR FATHER

Teresa's approach to the Our Father begins with active recollection. Turning to the indwelling God is the foundation of prayer life and Christian life. All Christian life is simply entering into deeper union with the indwelling Trinity; the greater the union the more fruitful the apostolate. Teresa describes active recollection, "the soul collects its faculties together and enters within itself to be with its God." God is near; "he never takes his eyes off you . . . who can keep you from turning the eyes of your soul toward this Lord?" Her method is one of presence, as she puts it, "being fully present to God in our prayer, for he is fully present to us at all times . . . I'm not asking you to do anything more than look at him."[14] This prayer of active recollection, accompanying vocal prayer, disposes one for contemplative prayer, for the divine Master comes to teach and to give the prayer of quiet. "Sisters, out of love for the Lord, get used to praying the Our Father with this recollection, and you will see the benefit before long . . . " Yet she also warns the sisters that not all will enjoy contemplation; it is not necessary for salvation. But recollection does dispose one for contemplation. Of the prayer of quiet she writes, "The Lord puts the soul at peace by his presence, as he did for the just Simeon, so that all the faculties are calmed."[15] Such souls see that "they are within the palace, near the King, and they see that he is beginning to give them here his kingdom."

With Jesus teaching us to pray we discover new depths to the Our Father. "Certainly," writes Teresa, "it never entered my mind that this prayer contained so many deep secrets, for now you have seen the entire spiritual way contained in it, from the beginning stages until God engulfs the soul and gives it to drink abundantly from the fount of living water, which he said was to be found at the end of the way."[16]

"Hallowed by your name; your kingdom come within us." Teresa comments on these phrases to explain how vocal prayer can lead to pure contemplation, using the example of an elderly nun who used to spend several hours reciting a certain number of Our Fathers in memory of the times Our Lord shed his blood. She came to Teresa, quite upset she could pray only vocally; Teresa was able to assure her "that though she was tied to the Our Father she experienced pure contemplation and that the Lord was raising her up and joining her with himself in union . . ."[17] And then there is a side remark, a sally typical of Teresa's delightful style, "So I praised the Lord and envied her for her vocal prayer. If this account is true, as it is, those of you who are the enemies of contemplatives should not think that you are free from being a contemplative if you recite your vocal prayers as they should be recited, with a pure conscience."[18]

On "thy will be done on earth as it is in heaven" Teresa stresses we should not say the words unless we mean them. The Jesus who taught us this prayer also exemplified it. "Consider that Jesus acts here as our ambassador and that he has desired to intervene between us and his Father, and at no small cost of his own. It would not be right for us to fail to do what he has offered on our behalf; if we don't want to do it we shouldn't say these words . . . Oh, what a great loss there is when we do not carry out what we offer to the Lord in the Our Father."[19]

"Do you want to know how the Father answers those who say these words [thy will be done . . .] to him sincerely? Ask his glorious Son, who said them while praying in the garden. Since they were said with such determination and complete willingness, see if the Father's will wasn't done fully in him through the trials, sorrows, injuries, and persecutions he suffered until his life came to an end through death on a Cross."[20]

"Give us this day our daily bread" reminds Teresa of the Eucharist. The love and courage of Jesus bring us strength in our cowardice and weakness not just once but every day; that is why the Lord resolved to remain with us in the Blessed Sacrament. "His Majesty gave us . . . the manna and nourishment of his humanity that we might find him at will and not die of hunger, save through our own fault. In no matter how many ways the soul may desire to eat, it will find delight and consolation in the most Blessed Sacrament."[21] When Teresa heard people say they would have liked to live when Christ walked the earth she used to laugh to herself, for she wondered what more they wanted when in the Blessed Sacrament they had the Lord just as truly present as he was then.

The living faith which was our Lord's gift to Teresa led to deep faith in the Eucharist, even to the healing of bodily ills, as she personally experienced. After all, she writes, "Now, then, if when he went about in the world the mere touch of his robes cured the sick, why doubt, if we have faith, that miracles will be worked while he is within us, and that he will give what we ask of him, since he is within our house. His Majesty is not accustomed to paying poorly for his lodging if the hospitality is good."[22]

At the end of the chapters on the Our Father she alludes to a popular Spanish spectacle in order to show that prayer is a safe road:

Unless it is very much due to their own fault, souls who practice prayer walk so much more securely than those who take another road. They are like those in the stands watching the bull in comparison with one who is right in front of its horns. I have heard this comparison, and it seems to be true to the letter . . . Prayer is a safe road; you will be more quickly freed from temptation when close to the Lord than when far. Beseech him and ask him to deliver you from evil as you do so often each day in the Our Father.[23]

Encouraging her sisters to serve God joyfully, without constraint, she recommends love and fear of God, calling them signs that even the blind can see. Love and fear of God "are like two fortified castles from which one can wage war on the world and the devils."

Teresa experienced and described the virtue of faith almost entirely in reference to Christ, contemplated in prayer, seen in visions, heard in locutions. She is describing herself when she writes in C of the person who was praying before the crucifix, deeply afflicted she had nothing to offer to God, nothing to give up for him. "The Crucified himself in consoling her told her he had given her all the sufferings and trials he had undergone in his passion so that she could have them as her own to offer his Father." The reason God grants great favors is to fortify human weakness. "His Majesty couldn't grant us a greater favor than to give us a life that would be an imitation of the life his beloved Son lived."

TITLES FOR JESUS

I would like to end this study with five favorite titles Teresa used for Jesus: son, teacher, bridegroom, king and judge. All five are professions of faith. It was during the sixteenth century that Louis of León, O.S.A. (d. 1591), an early biographer of St Teresa, wrote his book, *The Names of Christ,* although it was not known to her.[24] It has become common in the twentieth century to approach christology through the New Testament titles for Jesus; here again the theology of Teresa proves its lasting value. The titles of Teresa all contain a strong saving sense "for us and for our salvation."

The title "Son" looks above all to the Incarnation. Along with the eternal relationship of the Son to the Father in the Holy Trinity there is the temporal, yet now everlasting, relationship of Jesus to the Father in loving obedience, and his relationship to us as Savior, fulfilling the loving designs of the Father on our behalf. An example is from the first line on the Our Father in W: "Our Father who art in heaven. O my lord, how you do show yourself to be the Father of such a Son; and how your Son does show himself to be the Son of such a Father."

"Teacher" is very common in Teresa. Jesus teaches us the way to God, indeed he is the Way. Not only does Jesus teach doctrine, he is the truth. "What wisdom will be attributed to the man who rejoiced at being accounted mad, since madness was attributed to him who is wisdom itself. Alas, alas . . . no longer are there any whom men account mad because they see them perform the heroic deeds proper to true lovers of Christ."[25] The wisdom of God comes to us through the man Jesus: "The Lord himself says that he is the way; the Lord says also that he is the light and that no one can go to the Father but through him, and anyone who sees me sees my Father."

On the role of Christ as "bridegroom" Teresa had much to say in her reflections on the Canticle of Canticles (or Song of Songs). She saw this great Old Testament love poem completely centered on Christ. Christian life is a nuptial event, and among the followers of Christ no one illustrates this better than the Mother of Jesus. "O blessed Lady, how perfectly we can apply to you what takes place between God and the bride according to what is said in the Song of Songs."[26] These words are Teresa's commentary on the line, "The king brought me into the wine cellar and set charity in order within me . . . " In the same book she writes of the divine intoxication of the Samaritan Woman who went shouting through the streets after meeting Christ at the well of living water.

In Teresa's use of the word "king" grandeur and dignity combine with proximity and closeness. The kingship of Christ has aspects of both suffering and joy, passion and exaltation. "His Majesty" is very frequent phrase for the Lord, a phrase filled with tenderness. We who live in a democratic (republican?) country and in the late-twentieth century may find such a title as "His Majesty" much too monarchical, but it was well-suited to the Spain of Philip II and in Teresa's use takes on a most amazing tenderness, similar to the Psalms and the Song of Songs. In the sixth dwelling place she writes, "His Majesty, as one who knows our weakness, enables the soul through (these) afflictions . . . to have the courage to be joined with so great a Lord and to take him as its spouse."

Finally, Jesus is "judge," again with a marvelous blend of distance and nearness. The only fear that thought of Jesus as judge should bring, writes Teresa, is the fear of not being faithful in love. "May it please His Majesty to give us his love before he takes us out of this life, for it will be a great thing at the hour of death to see that we are going to be judged by the one whom we have loved above all things . . . It will not be like going to a foreign country but like going to our own, because it is the country of one whom we love so much and who loves us."[27]

CONCLUSION

At the very end let me express my gratitude to my Discalced Carmelite brothers and to Catholic University for inviting me to give this paper. St Augustine once wrote, "Too late, Lord, have I loved thee." To a degree, I fell tempted to say to St Teresa, "Too late, Mother Teresa, have I found you," but now, thanks to the necessity of preparing this study, I have learned far more about the great lady of Spain that I ever knew before, and have been enriched by the other presentations of this glorious weekend. I now have a better understanding of my beloved elder sister in Carmel than ever before, my brilliant sibling in the family of Our Lady of Mount Carmel, humorous and tender writer, tireless traveler and reformer, loving disciple of Jesus Christ, Son of God, King, Teacher, Judge, her beloved Bridegroom.

NOTES

1. As I acknowledge the debt I owe to the authors whose works I now wish to list I am reminded of the comment of the Canadian classicist and humorist Stephen Leacock: "We writers all act and react on one another; and when I see a good thing in another man's book I react on it at once."

In the first place enormous gratitude is owed to Secundino Castro, *Cristologia Teresiana* (Madrid: Editorial de Espiritualidad, 1978). Readers familiar with Castro's study will notice how much in debt I am to him, and his work has been saluted by such Teresian scholars as Tomas Alvarez.

See Tomás Alvarez, "Humanité du Christ: L'ecole carmélitaine," *Dictionnaire de Spiritualité,* 7, cols. 1096-1110; also "Jesucristo en la experiencia de Santa Teresa," *Monte Carmelo,* 88 (1980), 335-65; and A. Moreno, "St Teresa: Contemplation and the Humanity of Christ," *Review for Religious,* 38 (1979), 912-23.

2. Pope Paul VI, "St Teresa of Avila: The Message of Prayer," *The Pope Speaks,* 15 (1970), 218-22.

3. L, 13, 13.

4. C, 6, 7, 13.

5. Kavanaugh, *Introduction to C,* p. 276.

6. L, 22, 6.

7. C, 7, 2, 5.

8. John Welch, *Spiritual Pilgrims: Carl Jung and Teresa of Avila* (New York: Paulist Press, 1982), p. 153.

9. Ibid., p. 141.

10. C, 7, 2, 7.

11. W, 21,2.

12. Ibid., 21, 8 and Kavanaugh's note 8, p. 468.

13. L, 26, 5.

14. W, 26, 3.

15. Ibid., 31, 2.

16. Ibid., 42, 5.

17. Ibid., 30, 7.

18. Ibid.

19. W, 32, 3 and 4.

20. Ibid., 32, 6.

21. Ibid., 34, 2.

22. Ibid., 34, 8.

23. Ibid., 39, 7.

24. Louis of León, *The Names of Christ,* trans. Edward Schuster (Saint Louis: B. Herder Co., 1955). "Cross and Crown Series of Spirituality," 6.

25. L, 27, 14.

26. *Meditations on the Song of Songs,* 6, 8.

27. W, 40, 8.

St Teresa's Presentation
of Her Religious Experience

◆ ◆ ◆

Joseph Chorpenning, Ph.D.

Fr Chorpenning is an Oblate of St Francis de Sales who holds the rank of Assistant Professor of Spanish and Theology at Allentown College. He has a doctoral degree in Medieval and Renaissance Spanish Literature from Johns Hopkins University and an S. T. L. degree in Historical Theology from Catholic University.

INTRODUCTION

One of the most obvious features of St Teresa of Avila's literary style is the diffuseness of her writing: she had a constant tendency to ramble, to digress from the point at hand. St Teresa herself was not only aware of the diffuse nature of her writing (see, for example, 12, 1, and 13, 22; and C, 3, 1, 5) but attempted to offer an explanation for it: "I want to explain myself further, for I seem to be getting involved in a great many subjects. I have always had this failing—that I cannot explain myself, as I have said, except at the cost of many words" (L, 13, 17).[1] Perhaps St Teresa's digressive style accounts for the fact that scholars who have studied the literary method of the L (completed in 1565 and first published in 1588) and of the C (composed in 1577 and first published in 1588) like Gaston Etchegoyen,[2] Helmut Hatzfeld,[3] and, more recently,

Victor Garcia de la Concha[4] have overlooked St Teresa's use in these two works of a variety of elements other than allegory to speak of her experience of God's presence and activity in her soul.[5] Some of these elements are derived from her personal experience; others are inherited from her literary and religious milieu; and still others are used to explain her experience. Moreover, this oversight on the part of these commentators calls into question their seemingly implicit thesis that allegory is the unifying principle of the L and C because allegory does not encompass the diverse elements which come together to make up these two works. The way in which St Teresa synthesizes the various elements of her L and C to present her personal religious experience, however, is not only of interest to literary scholars; it also crucial for defining the contribution she made to the history of theology, specifically to the development of theological method.

In this study I intend to demonstrate that St Teresa's L and particularly her C are narrative units composed of a variety of elements and that, considered as such, these works offer a method for resolving one of the major theological issues of St Teresa's day, namely, the relationship between subjective religious experience and objective truth. A secondary purpose is to make available a practical and useful way of reading the texts of St Teresa's L and C. My presentation will be divided into four parts. First, I will trace the development of the question of the relationship between subjective religious experience and objective truth, a question raised in the contrast that emerged in the twelfth century between monastic theology an scholasticism, from the twelfth century to sixteenth-century Spain, and I will relate St Teresa to that development. Second, I will list and explain briefly the different elements St Teresa uses to speak of her life and experience in the L and C. Third, I will demonstrate how these elements can be seen as forming a coherent narrative. Finally, I will explain how St Teresa's assimilation of the spectrum of elements found in her L and G into a coherent narrative offers a method for resolving the medieval dilemma of the relationship between subjective experience and objective truth.

THE PROBLEMATIC

In 1950 the late French hispanist Marcel Bataillon published the first Spanish edition and translation of his monumental *Erasmo y España: estudios sobre la historia espiritual del siglo XVI,* in which he described all sixteenth-century spiritual movements in Spain as having "actitudes *afines* a la de Erasmo."[6] At the same time he noted that if he had the book to rewrite, he would have gone back further into the fifteenth century to trace the origin of certain spiritual currents; he also marked the need for a close investigation of the history of the *devotio moderna* in Spain and elsewhere.[7] Two years later in a review-article of Bataillon's book, Eugenio Asensio faulted Bataillon for drawing too simplistic a picture of sixteenth-century Spanish spirituality precisely on the grounds that he failed to trace its roots back far enough.[8] Asensio suggested that Bataillon should have sought the origins of this spirituality in the Biblicism, Franciscan reform, and Italian reform movements of the fifteenth century.[9] However, it is necessary to view sixteenth-century Spanish spirituality from an even broader perspective than Asensio suggested, for if we are to understand this spirituality in general and St Teresa's life and writings in particular, we must go back to the twelfth and thirteenth centuries, because they are the starting-point for the major theological issue which sixteenth-century Spanish spirituality and St Teresa confronted: the relationship between subjective religious experience and objective truth.

The twelfth and thirteenth centuries are pivotal in the history of theology. From the sixth to the twelfth century theology was usually done within the context of monasticism, which was the mainstay of both religion and civilization during the first half of the Middle Ages.[10] And, as Dom Jean Leclercq has demonstrated, medieval monasticism was essentially a continuation of the Patristic period.[11] One of the most important instances of this continuity was the formula monasticism adhered to concerning the relationship between learning and piety: following St Augustine and St Gregory the Great, the monks held that learning was always to be subordinated to piety.[12] A concrete example of how this formula was put into practice is provided by the monastic method of interpreting Scripture. Basically this interpretation turned on the twofold sense of Scripture: Scripture expresses a truth (the literal sense) which conceals a deeper meaning (the spiritual sense).[13] During the Patristic period the relationship between the two senses of Scripture had been given classic expression by Origen in the East and Augustine in the West: the literal sense was subordinate to the spiritual sense.[14] The monks would follow this rule. The goal, then, of the monastic reading of Scripture was contemplation, personal union with the Lord in this life and later in beatitude.[15]

With the rise of Scholasticism in the twelfth and thirteenth centuries, the situation changes considerably. The theoretical grounding for Scholasticism was supplied by the rediscovery of Aristotle, and Scholasticism consequently came to be characterized by Aristotelian confidence in the intellect, speculation and human knowledge. The context for the development of Scholastic theology was not the monastery, where the love of learning was subordinated to the desire for God, but urban schools for clerics.[16] Just as Scripture was the beginning and foundation of the monastic *meditatio* and *contemplatio,* it was also the foundation and beginning of the scholastic *quaestio* and *disputatio.*[17] In contrast to the monks, though, the Scholastics, following Aristotle, for whom a substance could only be known by its sensible manifestations, believed that the literal sense of Scripture was the only one which could be known with certainty. Eventually the scholastic *quaestiones* drifted away further and further from the Scriptural text which produced them, and even became more important than the text commented upon.[18] Moreover, as Scholasticism developed, theology became autonomous from spirituality: the Scholastics focused on the objective content of Revelation, for example, the dogmas of the Trinity, Christ, grace, etc., rather than on personal experience of the data of Revelation, which had been the primary focus of monastic theology. In the twelfth and thirteenth centuries, however, Scholasticism, with its emphasis on the literal sense of Scripture, helped foster an important movement of spiritual renewal known as the "evangelical awakening," which was a healthy and much needed reaction to monasticism's neglect of apostolic poverty and preaching.[19]

Although there were attempts to unite theology and spirituality, for example, the Rhineland School, by the end of the fourteenth century there was a strong reaction against theology which pursued speculation for itself, because, in the words of Yves Congar, it was "not subordinated to the direct needs of the Church, to the defense of doctrine, instruction of the faithful, or evangelization in general."[20] One of the most important examples of this reaction is the *devotio moderna*. This movement turned to the monastic authors of the Middle Ages for inspiration, called for a return to the concrete imitation of Christ and the virtues of love, humility and detachment, and stressed the subjective, individual and psychological side of piety. Through the medium of the sixteenth-century Spanish spiritual masters, who were able to read the works of the principal authors of the *devotio moderna* such as Thomas à Kempis' *Imitation of Christ*, the *devotio moderna* had a decisive influence on the subsequent evolution of spirituality. Consequently, what began as a contrast between monasticism and scholasticism in the twelfth and thirteenth centuries deteriorated into a rift, a fissure, a divorce between theology and spirituality by the end of the fourteenth century.[21] As Dom François Vandenbroucke observes, "Spirituality was henceforth a psychological experience, which in itself could dispense with revelation and dogma, and, even more, with theology, Scholastic or otherwise."[22]

Despite efforts to reunite theology and spirituality in sixteenth-century Spain, for example, the foundation of the University of Alcalá de Henares and religious orders' reforms of their programs of study, no such rapprochement was achieved.[23] On the contrary, theology was further compartmentalized into various branches, for example, dogma, moral theology, Scripture, ascetical-mystical theology, pastoral theology. By the second half of the century, the divorce between theology and spirituality deteriorated into an antagonism between Scholastic theologians and spiritual writers.[24] This is the milieu in which St Teresa of

Avila lived and wrote. When she was commanded by her superiors to give a written account of her spiritual life, she came face to face with what had developed as the central theological issue since the twelfth and thirteenth centuries, the relationship between theology and spirituality, between objective truth and subjective personal religious experience. Teresa had to present her experience in a way which would clearly distinguish it from Illuminism and Lutheranism, so that it would not be considered suspect or condemned by the Inquisition, hence her constant preoccupation with orthodoxy and her frequent recourse to her spiritual directors and confessors. To present her experience, she had recourse to her spiritual reading—St Jerome's epistles, Gregory the Great's commentary on Job, Augustine's *Confessions* and the pseudo-Augustinian *Soliloquies,* the lives of the saints, Ludolph of Saxony's *Vita Christi,* Thomas à Kempis' *Imitation of Christ,* Fray Francis of Osuna's *Tercer abecedario espiritual,* Fray Bernardine of Laredo's *Subida del monte Sión,* and so on—as well as to her confessors and spiritual directors, Dominicans and Jesuits formed in speculative Scholasticism.[25] In order to discover how St Teresa presents her religious experience, it is necessary, first of all, to sort out the diverse constitutive elements of her L and C, and then to examine how she combines these elements in the composition of these works.

ELEMENTS OF THE L AND C

Previous commentators on St Teresa's L and C[26] have singled out and focused on primarily one element of these works, allegory, almost to the exclusion of others. Nevertheless, there are a number of elements, other than allegory common to the L and C, which St Teresa uses to speak of her experience of God's activity and presence in her soul, the subject matter of these works; at the same time they influence Teresa's presentation of this experience. These elements are neither presented in any systematic fashion nor clearly separated from each other. I will now list and briefly discuss the elements I have discerned in my reading of the texts of the L and C. While my list is not exhaustive, it does, I believe, include the most important elements of these works. For the sake of clarity and order, I group these elements into three major categories: the first group is directly derived from St Teresa's personal experience; the second consists of elements inherited from her literary and religious milieu; and the third is comprised of elements Teresa uses to explain her experience, when this is her obvious intention.

Personal Elements

Elements derived from St Teresa's personal experience include her emphasis on the humanity of Christ, her use of the analogy or comparison of friendship, and the presence of doxology and prayer in her works. These elements may be described as "personal," because they are part of the saint's first-hand religious experience, and they convey something of that experience to her readers.

In the debate in sixteenth-century Spain over whether or not in contemplation corporeal aids to devotion, including the humanity of Christ, must be abandoned,[27] St Teresa unequivocally states that devotion to Christ in his humanity was never an obstacle to the most perfect contemplation for her. In her L Teresa recommends devotion to the humanity of Christ from the earliest through the higher stages of the spiritual life (see 4, 8; 9, 4; and 22, 6-7). In the sixth dwelling place of the C, written fifteen years after her L, St Teresa affirms her earlier position with even stronger conviction (see 6, 7, 5-6). For Teresa, the humanity of Christ is the way to the highest mystical states: in both her L (15, 13; and 22, 7) and C (6, 7, 13), she says that the life of Christ is the pattern for our lives. These states consist precisely in imitating the humble and suffering Christ:

> For His Majesty can do nothing greater for us than grant us a life which is an imitation of that lived by his beloved Son. I feel certain, therefore, that these favors are given us to strengthen our weakness ... so that we may be able to imitate him in his greatest sufferings.

> We always find that those who walked closest to Christ Our
> Lord were those who had to bear the greatest trials (C, 7, 4, 4-5).

This quotation indicates that the humanity of Christ is part of a larger concept in St Teresa's writings. Her discussion of the humanity of Christ is filled with the language of friendship, as this passage from chapter 22 of her L, which treats the role of Christ's humanity in contemplation, illustrates: "No trial has come to me that I cannot gladly bear when I look at thee as thou stoodest before thy judges. With so good a friend, so good a captain at our side, who came forward first of all to suffer, one can bear everything. He helps us; he gives us strength; he never fails; he is a true friend" (22, 6). The broad context in which the humanity of Christ is situated, then, is that of the analogy or comparison of friendship, which is the most extensive way that Teresa consistently describes her relationship with God. The humanity of Christ is the means whereby this relationship develops from its initial to its most advanced and intimate phases.

In general terms, this relationship is characterized by divine benevolence, constancy, patience and forbearance, and by, alternately, human responsiveness and tepidity (see L, 8, 5). While the analogy of friendship pervades the L, the C offers a more chronological account of Teresa's relationship with God in these terms. The first three dwelling places recount the origins of this friendship; in the remaining dwelling places it grows, matures and deepens. This comparison is most developed in the sixth and seventh dwelling places, those of the spiritual betrothal and marriage, where Teresa focuses on experiences common to human relationships such as presence, separation, desire and distress.

In telling the story of this friendship, St Teresa is sometimes overwhelmed and tempted to burst into prayer and doxology: "at times when, as I write, the greatness of the debt I owe him rises up before me, it is only by a supreme effort that I can refrain from going on to sing praises to God" (L, 14, 12). More often than not, though, Teresa succumbs to this temptation, and the comparison of friendship yields to prayer and direct discourse with God. Her L and C are frequently punctuated with prayers and doxologies. Not surprisingly, in the C doxologies occur much more frequently in the later dwelling places than in the earlier ones, due no doubt to the former's greater intensity. Doxology is "giving glory to God."[28] St Teresa's are usually brief, and their form is that of the hortatory subjunctive, for example, "May he be for ever blessed and praised. Amen. Amen." (C, 6, 4, 18). By contrast, her prayers are longer and in the form of direct address (see, for example, L, 8, 6). Moreover, prayer itself is the *locus* of intimacy with the Lord: "mental prayer, in my view, is nothing but friendly intercourse, and frequently solitary converse, with him who we know loves us" (L, 8,5).

Elements from St Teresa's Milieu

No writer writes in a vacuum. The culture and institutions that surround him or her, the people he or she knows, the books he or she reads—all influence his or her writing. Accordingly, there are elements in St Teresa's L and C which are reflective of her cultural, social, religious and literary milieu: her readings; her recourse to confessors, learned men and holy persons; her concern for orthodoxy; and the themes of martyrdom, monasticism and poverty.

In order to present her experience, the primary source of her writings, Teresa turned for help to her spiritual reading (see, for example, L, 23, 12), to confessors and theologians, principally Dominicans and Jesuits, and to holy persons such as St Francis Borgia, Blessed John of Avila, St Peter of Alcantara and so on (see L, 15, 15). It is from these sources, as we will see, that other elements of her writings originate, for example, her use of the language of the faculties, her comparisons and images, and the themes of martyrdom and its substitutes and of the desire for heaven.

Inseparable from St Teresa's consultation of spiritual directors and theologians is her concern for orthodoxy. St Teresa wrote under obedience. Recent research has attempted to impress upon us how urgent it was for Teresa, in composing her works, to establish her orthodoxy under the watchful and menacing eye of the Inquisition: her writings were nothing less than an *apologia pro vita sua.*[29] When she wrote the C in 1577, her L was being examined by the Holy Office. In many places the saint says that she is unlearned and ignorant, and that she needs instruction and direction to comply with the mandate to give a written account of herself. To be assured of orthodoxy and of the authenticity of her experience, she freely submits herself to her directors: "as what I write is to be seen by persons who will know if I am wrong, I am going on without worrying about it. I know I have no need to worry from the point of view either of learning or of spirituality, as this is going into the possession of those who will be able to judge it and will cut out anything which may be amiss" (L, 14, 6). An even stronger statement of this attitude and her submission to the Holy Roman Catholic Church is found in the Epilogue to the C.

A variety of themes found in St Teresa's works are derived from her readings. One such set of themes are those of martyrdom and its substitutes, monasticism, prayer, poverty and almsgiving. These themes, inspired by the New Testament, surface in the Patristic period, and subsequently continue to remain constants in Christian spirituality.[30] St Teresa would have come into contact with them especially in her reading of the lives of the saints. For example, in her L she tells how in childhood she and her brother Rodrigo "used to read the lives of the saints together; and, when I read of the martyrdoms suffered by saintly women for God's sake . . . I had a keen desire to die as they had done . . . I used to discuss with this brother of mine how we could become martyrs. We agreed to go off to the country of the Moors . . . so that they might behead us there . . . (L, 1, 5). When this plan is thwarted, substitutes are found: they play at being hermits; she gives alms and tries to become more devoted to prayer (1, 6). Although the theme of actual martyrdom persists in St Teresa's writings (see, for example, L, 13, 4; and 35, 7; and C, 6, 1, 7), it is eventually transformed into the martyrdom of daily death to self and love (see, for example, L, 20, 11), exemplified by, among others, St Mary Magdalen (see L, 21, 7; and C,

6, 7, 4; and 7, 4, 15).[31] Similarly, childhood games of hermits and nuns are replaced by religious life, and in later life Teresa herself became a monastic foundress. Lastly, material poverty is an important part of Teresa's reform of Carmel; it is to be the basis for St Joseph's: "it had not come to my notice that our *Rule*, before its severity became mitigated, had ordered us to possess nothing . . . I had never doubted that poverty was the soundest basis for a foundation" (L, 35, 2). However, the theme of material poverty pales in comparison with that of spiritual poverty, a far more radical notion, for St Teresa insists on total detachment not simply from material possessions and wealth but from one's will, consolations, and favors (see, for example, C, 3, 2, 1-4; and 5, 2, 6).

Explanatory Elements

The final group of elements are those St Teresa uses to explain her religious experience: her method of explaining individual favors; mystical theology, which she equates with the Scholastic language of the faculties of the soul; imagery; and theological themes.

In the L Teresa distinguishes three levels of favors: "For it is one favour that the Lord should grant this favour; but quite another to understand what favour and what grace it is; and still another to be able to describe and explain it" (17, 5). A similar idea is found in chapter 1 of the fourth dwelling place of the C: "Although I think I have now a little more light upon these favours which the Lord grants to some souls, it is a different thing to know how to explain them" (4, 1, 1). The distinction Teresa draws is that of an event, an insight into the event, and the communication of the insight into the event. In both her L and C, she aspires to communicate her insights into her experiences, hence the question of her method of explaining favors. Her central concern is to convince the *letrados,* that is, the Scholastic theologians, "that her experiences and her spirit were not of the devil."[32]

St Teresa is consistent in her method of explaining favors. A hermeneutical aid in discovering and appreciating this method are the following four questions:[33] What happened? Why did it happen? What happened as a result of this? How do I now view what happened? If we ask these four questions of chapter 25 of the L, which concerns the experience of locutions, we get the following results. What happened? Teresa begins by describing the experience: "Though perfectly formed, the words are not heard with the bodily ear; yet they are understood much more clearly than if they were so heard, and, however, determined one's resistance, it is impossible to fail to hear them" (25, 1). Why did it happen? Teresa goes on to discuss the possible origins of this event: God (a favor), the devil (a trick or deception), or herself (self-deception). What happened as a result of this experience? The need arose to distinguish true from false locutions, a distinction Teresa makes in the course of her discussion of the possible origins of this event. How does Teresa now view this event? She regards it in terms of the comparison of friendship, that is, in the context of her personal relationship with God, prayer and doxology (see 25, 17). These questions can be used to approach virtually any account Teresa gives of a favor, and the pattern of responses will be very similar: a precise description of the event, the enumeration of its possible sources, the distinction between a true and false experience, and a consciousness of the role of the event in the total context of her relationship with God. This pattern attests to St Teresa's wish to be as complete and comprehensive as possible in her reflection on her religious experience.

Sometimes Teresa will try to describe a particular experience in the language of mystical theology, which she equates with that of the faculties of the soul (see, for example, L, 10, 1).[34] The sources for her use of this language were the ascetical authors she read, specifically Osuna and Laredo, and the theologians who directed her. Nevertheless, her theoretical ignorance of psychology was profound, as she readily admits, and she does not understand fully, and sometimes misuses this language (see L, 18, 2; and C, 4, 1, 8). Despite these difficulties, however, Teresa was able to describe all she observed. As Hoornaerthas remarked, "Though she sometimes gets involved in her terminology, she never confounds realities . . . We understand her thoughts not so much by the exact denomination of the faculties as by a description of their action."[35]

If Teresa's margin of error is somewhat wide in her use of the language of the faculties, she expresses herself much more comfortably and accurately when she uses images to explain her experience (see, for example, L, 18, 2). St Teresa draws her images from a variety of sources, both oral and written. Hatzfeld has aptly described Teresa as having "eidetic propensities" and her literary method as being that of "image concatenation."[36] E. Allison Peers and, more recently, Frs Kieran Kavanaugh and Otilio Rodriguez have made very complete lists of the numerous images Teresa uses in her works.[37]

Another way in which Teresa explains her experience is by theological themes like the desire for God and devotion to heaven, and the virtues of charity, humility and detachment. Leclercq has convincingly demonstrated that the desire for God and devotion to heaven permeated monastic culture.[38] This eschatological tendency is also very strong in St Teresa's L and C.[39] Desire for God inspires the first stages of the spiritual life (see L, 8, 5) and, crescendo-like, gradually builds and increases in intensity in the subsequent stages. This desire is born of the consciousness of the sharp contrast between the misery and mutability of this life and the beatitude and immutability of life in the hereafter (see L, 21, 7). This desire reaches its zenith in the sixth and seventh dwelling places of the C (see 6, 11, 1). A variation on the theme of devotion to heaven is that of tears, to which Teresa often refers (see, for example, L, 4, 3; 4, 6; 5, 11; 6, 4; and 11, 10), for the desire for God gives rise to tears.[40]

The theme of the virtues of charity, humility and detachment is linked to St Teresa's view of the humanity of Christ and to her concern for orthodoxy. She insists time and again that true union with God consists in one thing alone: reproducing the pattern of the life of Christ in one's own life by love of neighbor, humility and detachment (see C, 5, 3, 11). Humility and analogous virtues (see L, 12, 4; and C, 7, 4, 9), not simply prayer and contemplation, are the foundation of the edifice of the spiritual life: "you must not build upon foundations of prayer and contemplation alone, for, unless you strive after the virtues and practice them, you will never grow to be more than dwarfs" (C, 7, 4, 10; see 2, 1, 7). The practice of virtue is the test and gauge of the authenticity and sincerity of one's spiritual life.

ALLEGORY AND HAGIOGRAPHY IN THE L AND G

I have now identified and discussed the principal elements other than allegory which St Teresa not only uses to speak of her religious experience but which also influence the presentation of her experience in the L and C. No single element of the L and C has dominated the scholarly commentaries on these works as much as allegory has. This is most likely because scholars have discerned allegory to be the most systematic element of these works. According to Etchegoyen, St Teresa's best known allegories, those of the four ways of watering a garden in the L, chapters 11-22, and of the castle in the C, present the complete evolution of her spiritual life.[41] Hatzfeld, as I have already noted, identifies St Teresa's literary method as that of "image-concatenation": an initial allegory, specifically that of the four ways of watering a garden or that of the castle, soon begins to be filled with new images, diverting metaphors and an avalanche of clarifying similes.[42] For Hatzfeld, St Teresa's imagery is "pedagogical rather than of a poetical kind"; her aim is to make her experimentally gained insights as clear as possible.[43] St Teresa's literary method is also Garcia de la Concha's focus. He conceives of the C's structure as a network of isotopes, that is, allegories: St Teresa's method consists in developing the nuclear simile of the interior castle into an allegory, which in turn generates a network of similes which simultaneously remain part of the larger allegory as well as develop into other allegories. The structure and method of the watering allegory of the L are similar.[44]

Before proceeding further, I would make some observations on these commentaries.

(1) Etchegoyen, Hatzfeld, and Garcia de la Concha have judged allegory to be the most systematic element in the L and C. For these

scholars, it accounts for the most orderly section of the L, the thematic unity of which as a whole may not at first sight be apparent.[45] In the C allegory aspires to control the whole work. And yet, Teresa's allegories are not all that systematic. The introduction of secondary images and similes, which themselves may be developed into smaller allegories, dissipate the central allegory, as both Hatzfeld and Garcia de la Concha note.[46] St Teresa herself readily confesses that she is not all that comfortable with allegory, as her introductory remarks to the watering allegory of the L reveal:

> I shall have to employ some kind of comparison, though, being a woman and writing simply what I am commanded, I should like to avoid doing so; but this spiritual language is so hard to use for such as, like myself, have no learning, that I shall have to seek some such means of conveying my ideas. It may be that my comparison will seldom do this successfully and Your Reverence will be amused to see how stupid I am. But it comes to my mind now that I have read or heard of this comparison: as I have a bad memory, I do not know where it occurred or what it illustrated, but it satisfies me at the moment as an illustration of my own (11, 6).

Allegory provides an alternative to the language of mystical theology, the Scholastic language of the faculties, with which Teresa is very uneasy; but, even so, she chooses it less than enthusiastically.[47]

(2) Etchegoyen, Hatzfeld, and Garcia de la Concha stress the expository, didactic, and pedagogical function of allegory in the L and C. The passage just cited from the L corroborates this view of allegory. But it is also very one-sided. Literary critics like Robert Scholes and Robert Kellogg have pointed out that allegory is not only a mode of thought but also a mode of storytelling.[48] The constant erosion of the central allegories of watering in the L and of the castle in the C highlights allegory's inadequacy as a mode of thought in these works: St Teresa's improvisation and rambling occupy more space than her systematiza-

tion.[49] Similarly, if we consider allegory as a narrative technique in these works, principally in the C, we discover that it also falls short on that count, because it is incapable of integrating into a harmonious and meaningful unit the other elements of these works which I have singled out. The inadequacy of allegory as both a mode of thought and storytelling undercuts its ability to function as the unifying principle of these works, especially the C. Evidently an alternative needs to be searched out.

In a paper read at convocations, which also commemorated the fourth centenary of St Teresa's death, at the Carmelite Monasteries of Boston and of Philadelphia last spring, I attempted to reflect on St Teresa's L from the perspective provided by the contemporary narrative theology or theology of story. This theology takes as its starting-point human experience, which has an intrinsically narrative or story quality about it. The story, then, is the most common and universal means of communicating human experience, and human beings are essentially storylistening and storytelling beings, with storylistening being a precondition for storytelling.[50] This perspective serves to make us more aware than we have been previously of St Teresa as both a storylistener and a storyteller. I believe that St Teresa's storylistening and storyreading is the key to understanding her storytelling, specifically how the various elements of her L and C may be seen as having a narrative unity. Before St Teresa wrote her L and C, she had read other stories. She had read, for example, the *Life of Christ* by the Carthusian Ludolph of Saxony (d. 1378) which first appeared in Spanish translation at the beginning of the sixteenth century and was reprinted several times during the first half of that century; St Augustine's *Confessions,* the Spanish translation of which by the Portuguese Augustinian friar Sebastian Toscano was published at Salamanca in 1554; and one or more of the Spanish language editions of the various collections of the lives of the saints and of the Fathers as well as of the full-length lives of such saints as Catherine of Siena, Mary Magdalen, and Francis of Assisi, which were available and immensely popular in sixteenth-century Spain.[51] According to St Teresa's own testimony, the stories which had a profound impact on her throughout her life were this last group, the lives of the saints. In general, though, Teresian scholars have tended to overlook the influence of hagiography on Teresa's literary composition.

Leclercq lists hagiography among medieval monasticism's favorite literary genres. The monks not only read the hagiographical narratives which had been passed on to them by preceding generations but composed their own narratives, usually about a saint associated with their own monastery. These narratives were intended to be read aloud and listened to during the Divine Office.[52] St Teresa spent the greater part of her life within the monastic context, in which hagiography had traditionally enjoyed a privileged position. In Teresa's day this position is attested to not only by her own personal reading of the lives of the saints but by, for example, her instruction in the *Constitutions* that a compendium of the lives of the saints was to be included among the "good books" the prioress of each monastery was to provide for the spiritual nourishment of the community.[53]

Beyond the confines of the monastery, however, hagiography was also a very important part of sixteenth-century Catholic, and in particular Spanish, piety. During the late fifteenth and early sixteenth century, the lives of the saints and of the Fathers were among the great many religious books translated into Spanish which would serve as sources for the Catholic Reform. Moreover, a number of hagiographical collections, modeled on the medieval hagiographical collection of the Dominican bishop Jacobus de Voragine, the *Golden Legend,* as well as *vitae* of individual saints were written in Spanish and published.[54] The most popular of these collections was the *Flos sanctorum* of the Hieronymite friar Peter de la Vega which was first published at Zaragoza in 1521 and reprinted numerous times throughout the sixteenth century.[55] Several Teresian scholars believe St Teresa most probably read Vega's compendium, which included a life of Christ and a collection of lives of the saints inspired by the *Golden Legend*.[56] The importance and popularity of hagiography is further exemplified by the impact the lives of the saints had on St Ignatius of Loyola during his initial conversion.[57] It is

also shown by the place Ignatius gave to the lives of the saints in his
Spiritual Exercises, the spirituality of which was disseminated by the
Society of Jesus, one of the principal agents of the Catholic Reform:
Ignatius recommends that the lives of the saints be read during the second week and thereafter, and, in the "Rules with regard to eating," he
suggests that while eating, one occupy oneself with consideration of the
lives of the saints.[58] However, the diffusion of the lives of the saints
among the faithful was not limited to printed texts; it also included oral
and aural media because printed hagiographical collections were used
by preachers of the period as source books of *exempla* for their sermons.
This is yet another way St Teresa came into contact with hagiography,
as several scholars have recently suggested.[59]

The veneration and invocation of the saints was given even more positive encouragement by the Council of Trent, which instructed bishops
to foster the invocation and veneration of the saints and their images
"because through the saints of God miracles and salutary examples are
put before the eyes of the faithful, so that they may give thanks to God
for them, that they may fashion their lives and their actions in imitation
of the saints, and that they may be spurred on to adore and love God and
to cultivate piety."[60] In post-Tridentine Spain there is ample evidence that
this instruction was quickly put into practice. The veneration of the saints
as models of Christian life, workers of miracles, and heavenly intercessors
was a frequent and popular theme in the preaching of the period. New
collections of the lives of the saints began to be written such as Alonso
de Villegas' *Flos sanctorum,* which was published between 1578 and 1589
and subsequently reprinted in numerous editions. Incidentally, Villegas'
compendium was dedicated to the cardinal-archbishop of Toledo and
Inquisitor General Gaspar de Quiroga, who personally read the text of St
Tereas's L, and whose encouragement of the veneration of the saints was
considered by his contemporaries to be the most significant accomplishment of his archiepiscopate. Finally, a significant portion of the art of the
period was devoted to representations of the saints, as the painting of St
Teresa's contemporary El Greco affirms.[61]

Hagiography, therefore, was no small part of the cultural, institutional, religious and literary environment in which St Teresa read, listened and wrote. As we have already seen, Teresa began to read the lives of the saints as a child, but she would continue to find them helpful and encouraging throughout her life, even at the most advanced stages of the spiritual life (see L, 30, 17; and C, 6, 7, 6). Furthermore, throughout the L Teresa is conscious that her experiences are comparable to those of the saints, and that their lives are the clearest precedent for her own life and experience. For instance, in chapter 38 she tells us that, like St Paul and St Jerome, she was granted the favor of living, with surprising intensity, the communion of saints in heaven while still on earth (38, 1-6). I would like to suggest that the structure, themes and point of view of hagiography function as the unifying principle of St Teresa's L and C. I should immediately add a word of clarification: my emphasis on the impact of hagiography on St Teresa must not be considered as diminishing the effect of the story of the life of Christ on her; on the contrary, the life of Christ is itself mediated through the conventions of hagiography,[62] as we will see.

My suggestion that hagiography is the unifying principle of St Teresa's L is not entirely original. In a paper read at the annual convention of the Modern Language Association of America in 1979, Colbert Nepaulsingh suggested that the L be considered an autohagiography.[63] However, the arguments he marshals to support his hypothesis seem neither weighty nor persuasive. In the paper I gave in the spring of 1982 entitled "St Teresa of Avila: Theologian of Story," I fully critique Nepaul-singh's presentation. Suffice it to say here that its most serious flaw is its failure to consider hagiography as a literary form. Such a consideration would have made his arguments cogent. I will attempt to build a case for seeing hagiography as the unifying principle not only of the L but also of the C by focusing on the literary genre of hagiography.

The prototype of the literary genre of hagiography is St Athanasius' *Life of St Antony* (composed ca. 357), "which was to serve as a model for all subsequent Greek and Latin hagiography."[64] The plot of the *Life of*

Antony is biographical, that is, it is structured by the events of Antony's life (his nationality, parentage, education and youth, lifetime, death, post-mortem cultus and miracles). In turn it presents a structural model for its successors. Furthermore, in the plot of the *Life of Antony*, a pattern of thematic motifs emerge: the saint as a devout youth, demonology, miracles, virtues, the themes of martyrdom, monasticism, prayer, poverty, almsgiving, and so on. This pattern becomes normative for subsequent hagiography, where these themes evolve into commonplaces. Although specifics and emphases may vary, the form and general content of hagiography remains fairly constant because of its conformity to an established structure and pattern of commonplaces. While the biographical plot structures the hagiographical narrative, what enables the plot to unify the narrative is the point of view from which the life-story of Antony, or any saint for that matter, is told: a unity is perceived in the life of the saint—the friendship of the saint with God—and the whole story is told from this point of view.[65] The point of view serves to unify the thematic motifs of the plot: the saint being devout from youth, his struggles with demons and miracles, his virtues are all concrete expressions of his friendship with God as well as his conformation to and identification with Christ. In imitation of Christ, who went into the desert to meet the devil and undergo temptation, the saint faces his own demons; he also, as Christ did, goes about doing good, and emanates and exercises supernatural power over demons, the elements and irrational creation, sickness and death, which are all facets of the war against Satan. The biography which results may not be so much a factual account of the saint's life as a theological reflection upon and an enthusiastic presentation of the life of the saint, who sometimes becomes more an ideal than a person.[66] Finally, Athanasius' purpose in composing his biography of Antony was "to present a model of a life consecrated to the service of God. He wants to induce his readers to imitate the holiness of his hero, not his miracles and visions."[67] In general, therefore, the hagiographer's major aim is not only to interest people but to inspire and edify them.[68] The lives of the saints in the

Golden Legend are very representative of the hagiography St Teresa read and conform precisely to the structure, thematic pattern and point of view established by the *Life of Antony*. For example, this conformity can be demonstrated by a close examination of the life of St Martin of Tours in the *Golden Legend,* with which St Teresa's works indicate she was familiar.[69]

I would propose that St Teresa consciously or unconsciously found in hagiography not only an interpretative aid for understanding but a method for presenting her life and experience. In contrast to allegory, hagiography is capable of assimilating all the elements of Teresa's L and C which I have singled out. In fact, many of these elements are commonplace of hagiography. More specifically, hagiography's structure, plot, and point of view are present in the L, and its plot and point of view predominate in the C. Situating these works within the hagiographical tradition enables us to see how what might otherwise seem to be disparate elements in them come together to form a unified narrative. In my paper referred to above, I showed how the presence of the conventions of hagiography in the L justify describing this work as an autohagiography, and I suggested how the hagiographic element functions in the C. I will now briefly summarize the principal points of the former demonstration and then work out in detail my suggestion concerning the C.

My earlier discussion of the L can be summarized in five points.

(1) In her L Teresa uses hagiography not only to understand and present her own life and experience but also that of St Peter of Alcantara, which was simultaneously part of her experience (see 27, 16-21; 36, 20; and 38, 32). Her presentation is divided into his lifetime and post-mortem cultus and shows her to be a very able hagiographer.[70]

(2) In the prologue to the L St Teresa clearly establishes its focus and theme: her method of prayer and the favors God has bestowed on her. At the same time she stresses her sinfulness, only this does not detract from her focus on favors but accents it: in spite of her weakness, God greatly blesses her. The point of view from which the story is nar-

rated is the analogy of friendship, Teresa's friendship with God.

(3) Teresa's presentation begins with her giving her parentage (1, 1-3) and continues with her lifetime. Teresa uses the pattern of hagiography, the main purpose of which is to show how God is working in the life of the one whom he calls and cares for to present her youth. Providence provides her with devout parents, and God already awakens in her the desire for martyrdom, puts good books into her hands, and watches over her to guard her against the devil. When her desire for martyrdom is frustrated, she finds the traditional substitutes for this primordial experience: the eremitical life, almsgiving, and prayer (1, 5-6). At age twenty-one Teresa enters Carmel, and henceforth monasticism becomes the context in which her life and experience unfold. Blessed by God from her earliest years, Teresa is thus prepared for the extraordinary favors she will enjoy in later life.

(4) In the course of Teresa's life, the phenomena associated with hagiography occur, not the least of which are demonology and the miraculous. Favors are a regular part of her life. To try to explain the development of her relationship with God in prayer, Teresa adopts the allegory of the four ways of watering a garden (chapters 11-22). The remaining chapters of the L stress the miraculous and even greater favors Teresa enjoyed, for example, raptures, visions, locutions, her being on familiar terms with the saints in heaven while she is still on earth, the special efficacy of her prayer. Teresa is always careful to verify the authenticity of these favors by ascertaining that their source is God and not the devil or herself. In chapters 30-31 she repels fierce interior and exterior assaults by the devil. Chapters 32-37, which recount the foundation of the reformed convent of St Joseph, portray Teresa as a monastic foundress and bring out her devotion to the virtue of poverty. At this point Teresa begins to exercise what might be called a "spiritual maternity," another commonplace of hagiography;[71] through her reform God touched and continues to touch the lives of many people. God also works miracles through Teresa to make known his friendship with her, for example, her prayer restores sight to the blind and cures the sick

(39, 1-2). She also has dominion over demons (39, 4). While favors and miracles occupy the foreground of the L, Teresa is well aware that genuine spirituality is founded not on them but on the practice of virtue: "as the foundation of the entire edifice is humility, the nearer we come to God, the greater must be the progress which we make in this virtue: otherwise, we lose everything" (12, 4).

(5) In the L the structure, pattern of commonplaces and point of view of hagiography are present. Identifying the literary form of the L as autohagiography enables us to discover that the diverse elements which constitute this work form a unified whole. Moreover, in the L allegory structures about a quarter of the work, but the watering allegory is completely integrated into the hagiographical pattern as a way of explaining how Teresa's relationship with God in prayer develops.

The way hagiography functions in the C is a bit more complicated. By contrast with the L, allegory more or less structures the whole work. Moreover, the content of the C is couched in the form of teaching: its principal addressees are St Teresa's sisters, whom she, as monastic foundress, is instructing in the life of sanctity. But Teresa speaks more objectively and impersonally; she speaks in the third rather than in the first person, referring to the soul which progresses through the consecutive stages of the spiritual life and of a person she knows (patently herself) who has had this or that experience. Teresa thus presents her experience more systematically, schematically and abstractly, raising it to the level of principle. What, then, happens to the hagiographical conventions? While allegory may provide a structural principle for the C, it is the hagiographical pattern and point of view which unify its content and make it intelligible, for the same elements are present in the C as in the L.[72] In other words, despite the change of form in the C, its subject matter is fully comprehensible only to the extent that it is viewed from the perspective of hagiography. While allegory is the structural principle of the C, hagiography is its thought form and unifying principle. In the C the spiritual life is charted from the viewpoint of the soul's friendship with God, and according to the hagiographical pattern of commonplaces, specifically demonology, favors, virtues, and the mystique of martyrdom and its substitutes.

Etchegoyen observed that in the C there is a more balanced presentation of favors and virtues than in the L, which presents a minute analysis of mystical states and supernatural favors but says comparatively little about virtues.[73] While this is true, at the beginning of the C, St Teresa establishes its focus in much the same way that she does in the prologue of the L: "You must think over this comparison [that is, the soul as an interior castle] very carefully; perhaps God will be pleased to use it to show you something of the favors which He is pleased to grant to souls, and of the differences between them, so far as I have understood this to be possible, for there are so many of them that nobody can possibly understand them all, much less anyone as stupid as I" (1, 1,3). This statement serves to underscore the C's purpose, which is that of hagiography: to show how God is working in the life of the one whom he calls and cares for.

The first dwelling place sets forth the prerequisites for the life of sanctity: purgation from mortal sin, purification from affections for worldly affairs and pleasures and disposing oneself toward God by prayer, the door of the castle (1, 1, 7; and 2, 1, 11). Although in much hagiography the fulfillment of these requirements is a given since the saint is customarily portrayed as devout from youth and subsequently experiences a conversion from a less to a more profound spiritual life, at the same time hagiography's demonology, which focuses on the saint's confrontation with and defeat of the demons, the evil within himself, helps us to understand these prerequisites better. In fact, the soul's success in this initial struggle with evil can be considered the first favor it receives from God, for without his grace such a victory would be impossible (see 3, 1, 5).

The key to success in this struggle is introspection and self-knowledge (1, 1, 6). At the outset, then, St Teresa grounds the life of holiness in the virtues of self-knowledge and humility, the foundation of the castle (7, 4, 9); her emphasis on the practice of these virtues is constant throughout the C (1, 2, 9). Teresa also stresses the primacy of charity in the pursuit of holiness: "Let us realize, my daughters, that true perfection consists in the love of God and of our neighbour, and the more nearly perfect is our observance of these two commandments, the nearer to perfection we shall be" (1, 2, 17). In the course of making known the foundation of the relationship of the soul and God, Teresa also touches on another motif of hagiography, which underlies its demonology, miracles and favors, and which will be a constant feature of the C, Christocentrism: "we must set our eyes upon Christ our good, from whom we shall learn true humility, and also upon his saints" (1, 2, 11).

In the first dwelling place, therefore, St Teresa lays the groundwork for leading the life of sanctity, and in so doing introduces most of the principal commonplaces of the hagiographical pattern, which will be present in each of the subsequent dwelling places. In the second mansion this pattern begins to function even more strongly as the soul receives the favor of the Lord calling it to enter into an interpersonal relationship with him. This call can come in a variety of ways: the conversations of good people, sermons, the reading of spiritual books, sickness and trials, prayer (2, 1, 2-3). Teresa hastens to add, though, that one should not become dependent on spiritual favors, "for that is a very poor way of starting to build such a large and beautiful edifice" (2, 1, 7). Rather, our principal occupation should be the imitation of and the conformation of ourselves to the life of Christ, especially his sufferings: "embrace the Cross which your Spouse bore upon his shoulders and realize that this Cross is yours to carry too . . . All other things are of quite secondary importance: if the Lord should grant them to you, give him heartfelt thanks" (2, 1, 7). The reason God grants favors is not for our aggrandizement but to reveal his power (1, 1, 3).

The soul's responsiveness to the Lord's call, however, is not left uncontested by the devil, who now mounts a strong attack against the soul. In the face of this adversity, the soul must persevere in its resolution and, above all, keep its gaze fixed on God (2, 1,9). But not only the devil tests the soul's resolution to persevere in its friendship with

God; so does God himself, who, in the third dwelling place, withdraws spiritual sweetness *(contentos)* from the soul. God's allowing the soul to emerge victorious from its struggles with the devil in the second dwelling place is a great favor (3, 1, 5). Sometimes such souls are anxious to advance quickly in holiness. While God grants the soul favors, he also sends it periods of aridity for various reasons: to teach the soul to be humble and not to be restless (3, 1, 9); to provide it the opportunity of conforming itself to Christ by suffering (3, 1, 9); to make it conscious of its misery, limitations, and shortcomings and of his mercy and goodness (3, 2, 1); and to test its detachment and mastery over the passions (3, 2,6). This period of probation demands total self-renunciation: "And believe me, what matters is not whether or not we wear a religious habit; it is whether we try to practice the virtues, and make a complete surrender of our wills to God and order our lives as His Majesty ordains: let us desire that not our wills, but his will, be done" (3, 2, 6). Total self-renunciation is a *conditio sine qua non* for moving on to the subsequent dwelling places (3, 2, 9).

Beginning with the fourth dwelling place, the relationship between God and the soul attains a higher and deeper level. Teresa herself puts it this way: "For we now begin to touch the supernatural . . . " (4, 1, 1). While the main purpose of hagiography is to show how God is working in the life of the one whom he calls, and this aim is fulfilled in the first three dwelling places, it comes even more to the fore in the fourth through the seventh dwelling places, in which the soul experiences ever greater and increasing favors.

In the fourth dwelling place the soul experiences the favor of consolations *(gustos)*, which in the L St Teresa termed the "Prayer of Quiet." In the face of this favor, Teresa admonishes the soul to put more store by its practice of the virtue of humility than by it (see 4, 2, 10). She also advises special watchfulness against the devil in this dwelling place: "As the natural is united with the supernatural in it, it is here that the devil can do the most harm; for in the dwelling places of which I have not yet spoken the Lord gives him fewer opportunities. May he be for ever praised. Amen" (4, 3, 15).

In the fifth dwelling place God bestows upon the soul the favor of the Prayer of Union (see 5, 1,9), which is a prelude to the spiritual betrothal of the sixth dwelling place (5, 4, 4). In the second chapter of the fifth dwelling place, St Teresa uses the comparison of the process of how the silkworm becomes a butterfly to illustrate her description of this favor and its effects. The accent is, again, on self-renunciation and the practice of penance, prayer and good works (5, 2, 6-7). Teresa then enumerates the effects of this union on the soul: "it finds itself longing to suffer great trials and unable to do otherwise. It has the most vehement desires for penance, for solitude, and for all to know God" (5, 2, 7). The effects of this dwelling place and the remaining ones are very similar in kind, but differ in intensity (5, 2, 7). At this point the soul even attaches little importance to what the saints endured, for it understands by first-hand experience how God transforms the soul, so that it no longer seems to be itself (5, 2, 8). For Teresa, the essence of union with God consists in the practice of the virtues of humility and perfect love of neighbor, which conforms the soul to Christ (5, 3, 12). Throughout this dwelling place, Teresa advises watchfulness for the deception of the devil, who will try to hinder the forthcoming betrothal. "For there is no enclosure so strictly guarded that he cannot enter it, and no desert so solitary that he cannot visit it" (5, 4, 8). The best way to avoid his deceptions are: "First, we must continually ask God in our prayers to keep us in his hand . . . we must never have any confidence in ourselves . . . But most of all we must walk with special care and attention, and watch what progress we make in the virtues . . ." (5, 4, 9)

In the sixth and seventh dwelling places, St Teresa uses the comparison of betrothal and marriage, respectively, to describe what happens in them.[74] In the sixth dwelling place "The soul is now completely determined to take no other spouse; but the Spouse disregards its yearnings for the conclusion of the betrothal, desiring that they should become still deeper and that this greatest of all blessings should be won by the soul at some cost to itself (6, 1, 1). Consequently, the soul experiences exterior trials, for example, persecution by friends, praise and grievous infirmities, which make actual martyrdom preferable (6, 1, 4-7). These provide the soul further opportunities to conform itself to Christ: "I should always choose the way of suffering, if only to imitate Our Lord Jesus Christ, and even were there no other special benefit to be obtained from it—and there are always a great many" (6, 1, 7). There are also interior trials, for example, a scrupulous and inexperienced confessor (6, 1, 8-11) and severe distress (6, 1, 13), the best remedy for which is "to occupy oneself with external affairs and works of charity and to hope in God's mercy, which never fails those who hope in him" (6, 1, 13).

While the soul experiences these trials, it is also the recipient of great favors in this dwelling place: its Spouse, who is in the seventh dwelling place, calls (chapter 2), locutions (chapter 3), raptures (chapters 4-5), intellectual visions (chapter 8), imaginary visions (chapter 9), and a number of other favors (chapter 10). Teresa is very careful to establish the source of these favors in her presentation of them, lest they proceed from the devil, whose activity is curtailed in this dwelling place (see 6, 1, 14), or from herself. The effect of these favors is an increase in the soul's desire for God and also its distress at its own sinfulness and miserableness, which becomes a martyrdom for the soul (6, 7, 4). Some help, though, is afforded at this point by meditation on the humanity of Christ and the lives of the saints: "For life is long and there are many trials in it and we have need to look at Christ our pattern, and also at his apostles and saints, and to reflect how they bore these trials, so that we, too, may bear them perfectly" (6, 7, 13). A further effect of this phase is that the soul is "filled with a determination to suffer for God's sake and to desire to have many trials to endure, and to be very much more resolute in withdrawing from the pleasures and intercourse of this world, and other things like them" (6, 2, 6).

Finally, in the seventh dwelling place the friendship between God and the soul is consummated in the spiritual marriage. The difference between the type of union with God which St Teresa describes in this dwelling place and the prayer of union and spiritual betrothal is that once the spiritual marriage takes place, the soul no longer suffers separation from God, as it does in the prayer of union and spiritual betrothal (chapter 2). Among the effects of this marriage upon the soul are self-forgetfulness and a great desire to suffer (see 7, 3, 1): "In short, the desires of these souls are no longer for consolations or favours, for they have with them the Lord himself and it is His Majesty who now lives in them. His life, of course, was nothing but a continual torment and so he is making our life the same, at least as far as our desires go" (7, 3, 6). Moreover, this state does not result in pride: "The more they [that is, the souls in this dwelling place] are favoured by God, the more timorous and fearful do they become concerning themselves . . . " (7, 3, 14)

The temptation which assails the soul in this dwelling place is to rest (7, 4, 17), but rest is not the aim of the spiritual marriage: "if the soul is much with him [the Lord] . . . it will very seldom think of itself; its whole thought will be concentrated upon finding ways to please him and upon showing him how much it loves him . . . this is the purpose of the spiritual marriage, of which are born good works and good works alone" (7, 4, 6). One of the good works which Teresa mentions is praying for others, especially those in mortal sin, which, she says, is "the best kind of almsgiving" (7, 1, 4). But nothing pleases the Lord so much as a life lived in conformity with his own (7, 4, 9). We thus return to the leitmotif of the C: "His Majesty can do nothing greater for us than grant us a life which is an imitation of that lived by his Beloved Son . . . these favours are given us to strengthen our weakness . . . so that we may be able to imitate him in his greatest sufferings" (7, 4, 4).

The union with God which St Teresa describes in the seventh dwelling place can be best appreciated in the context of hagiography's Christocentrism and emphasis on martyrdom. The saint's dominion over demons, miracles, favors, and, most importantly, virtues are all expressions of his conformation to Christ and of the abiding presence of Christ in him/her. The effects and fruits of the spiritual marriage, for example, self-forgetfulness, the desire to suffer, the practice of the virtue of humility and charity, which are all aspects of the bloodless martyrdom of daily death to self, attest to this conformation and pres-

ence. The martyrs desired martyrdom because it afforded the most perfect conformation to Christ.[75] In turn, Christ himself was deemed to
be present in the martyrs as the object of experience.[76] For Teresa, the
abiding union with God of the seventh dwelling place is a life lived in
conformity with the life of Christ, which, she says, was a "continual
torment" (7, 3, 6). God awakened the desire for martyrdom in Teresa
in childhood; in the seventh dwelling place it attains maturity and perfection. Teresa's constant focus on this mystique testifies to its centrality in her own spiritual doctrine and experience in particular and in
Christian spirituality in general.

RECONCILIATION OF THE OBJECTIVE AND SUBJECTIVE

Despite St Teresa's difficulties with the Scholastic language of the
faculties and expository allegory, she is able to present her experience
clearly and accurately in the L and C, because hagiography prevails over
these elements by unifying and giving intelligibility to her presentation.
The conventions of hagiography enable us to see how the personal, cultural and explanatory elements of the L and C form a unified narrative.
Moreover, hagiography also offers a method for resolving the medieval
dilemma of the tension between subjective religious experience and
objective truth, with which St Teresa necessarily had to come to terms
in composing these works.

The principal contribution which St Athanasius' *Life of St Antony*
made to the history and development of narrative as well as of theological method was that, by making the life of the monk Antony arche-
typal, it provided a method of relating the experience of a particular
individual to the ways of divine Providence and to an objective pattern of spiritual growth. Subsequent hagiographers set out to show how
the life of a saint, in its own particularity, belonged to the literary and
theological tradition initiated by the *Life of St Antony*.[77] They did this
by demonstrating that the life of the saint in question conformed to its
biographical structure, pattern of commonplaces and point of view. At

the same time they proposed to present this life as a model and archetype of holiness in its own right. In this way personal, subjective, experience is given objectivity and universalized. Hagiography thus served as a way to understand and present the life and experience of another person. However, it could also fulfill this function for one's own life and experience, without veering from Church teaching and tradition, and without having to renounce anything of one's own experience. Hence the case of St Teresa.

St Teresa consciously or unconsciously found in hagiography not only an interpretive aid for understanding but also a method for presenting her life and experience in an objective way. Consequently, hagiography provides Teresa a way of resolving the medieval dilemma of the tension between subjective religious experience and objective truth, without resorting to the abstract concepts and theorems of Scholasticism. The objective is embodied in the hagiographical tradition, and the life of Teresa in its particularity is shown to belong to this tradition. At the same time her life is presented as a model of Christian holiness in its own right by being recounted according to the conventions of hagiography.[78] Hagiography thus serves Teresa as both an interpretive aid and a method for presenting her own experience, without veering from Church teaching and tradition but also without having to renounce anything of her own experience, because hagiography was an established part of Church teaching and tradition which offered a formal model for assimilating personal experience into that teaching and tradition.

Revisionist interpretations of literary works often are overstated and do not come to terms with the richness and complexity of the works they aspire to interpret. In the final analysis my reading of L and C is but an attempt to understand and, even more importantly, to appreciate something of St Teresa of Avila, an extraordinary woman, who, because she was so much a part of her times and culture, was able to contribute such a rich and complex spirituality to her Church.

NOTES

1. All references to St Teresa's L and C are to E. Allison Peers' English translation of these works in the paperback editions (Garden City, NY: Image Books, 1960 & 1961).

2. Gaston Etchegoyen, *L'amour divin: essai sur les sources de Sainte Thérèse* (Bordeaux: Feret et Fils, 1923), pp. 316-53.

3. Helmut Hatzfeld, *Santa Teresa de Avila* (New York: Twayne, 1969), pp. 23-61.

4. Victor García de la Concha, *El arte literarw de Santa Teresa* (Barcelona: Ariel, 1978), pp. 228-74.

5. My own earlier essay "The Literary and Theological Method of the *Castillo Interior*," *Journal of Hispanic Philology*, 3 (1979), 121-33, can also be faulted for this oversight.

6. Marcel Bataillon, *Erasmoy España: estudios sobre la historia espiritual del sigh XVI*, trans. Antonio Alatorre, 2nd ed. (Mexico: Fondo de Cultura Económica, 1966), p. xiv.

7. Ibid., p. xiii.

8. Eugenio Asensio, "El erasmismo y las corrientes espirituales afines," *Revista de filología española*, 36, (1952), 31-99. Bataillon's book should also be read in light of José C. Nieto's *Juan de Valdés and the Origins of the Spanish and Italian Reformation* (Geneva: Droz, 1970), which makes substantial revisions in Bataillon's presentation of Valdés and the Illuminists *(alumbrados)*. Nieto's book has recently been translated into Spanish and published together with five of his subsequent articles on Valdés and related topics which appeared between 1970 and 1977 (Mexico: Fondo de Cultura Económica, 1979).

9. A more recent, and thorough, attempt to relate sixteenth-century Spanish spirituality to the fifteenth century is Melquóades Andrés, *La teología española en el sigh XVI*, 2 vols. (Madrid: Editorial Catolica, 1976-77). Coll. "Biblioteca de Autores Cristianos," Serie Maior, 13 and 14.

10. See Bouyer, Leclercq, Vandenbroucke and Cognet, *A History of Christian Spirituality*, 3 vols., trans Benedictines of Holme Eden Abbey (New York: Desclee, 1963-69, repr. New York: Seabury, 1977), II, pp. 3-220.

11. Jean Leclercq, *The Love of Learning and the Desire for God: A Study of Monastic Culture*, trans. Catherine Misrahi, 2nd ed. (New York: Fordham Univ. Press, 1961).

12. See ibid., pp. 13-44 and St Augustine, *On Christian Doctrine*, trans. J. F. Shaw (Grand Rapids: Eerdmans, 1979), pp. 519-79. Coll. "Nicene and Post-Nicene Fathers," 2; and Letter 118 (To Dioscorus), St Augustine, *Letters II (83-130)*, trans. Sr. Wilfrid Parsons (New York: Fathers of the Church, 1953), pp. 262-94. Coll. "The Fathers of the Church," 18.

13. On the question of the relationship between the literal and spiritual senses of Scripture during the Middle Ages, see Henri de Lubac, *Exégèse médiévale: les quatre sens de l'Ecriture*, 4 vols. (Paris: Aubier, 1959-64).

14. See Origen's *Commentary on the Song of Songs*, trans. R. P. Lawson (Westminster, MD: Newman Press, 1957), pp. 25, 58 and 81-82. Coll. "Ancient Christian Writers," 26; and Augustine's *On Christian Doctrine* which became the textbook on exegesis in the Middle Ages.

15. Leclercq, *The Love of Learning*, pp. 3-15.

16. See ibid., pp. 3-4 and 237-41.

17. Robert E. McNally, *The Bible in the Early Middle Ages* (Westminster, MD: Newman Press, 1959), p. 9. Coll. "Woodstock Papers," 4.

18. See M.-D. Chenu, *Nature, Man and Society in the Twelfth Century: Essays on New Theological Perspectives in the Latin West*, trans. Jerome Taylor and Lester Little (Chicago: Univ. of Chicago Press, 1968), pp. 270-309.

19. See ibid., pp. 202-69.

20. Yves Congar, *A History of Theology*, trans. Hunter Guthrie (Garden City: Doubleday, 1968), p. 137.

21. François Vandenbroucke, "Le divorce entre théologie et mystique," *Nouvelle Revue Théologique*, 82 (1950), 372-89; and Bouyer et al., *History of Spirituality*, II, pp. 373-406, 428-39, and 532-43.

22. *History of Spirituality*, II, p. 506.

23. See Andrés, *La teología española* I, pp. 32-43 and 82-197. Andrés himself advances the highly debatable proposition that Spanish Scholasticism achieved a reunion of theology and spirituality—see ibid., pp. 386-424.

24. Otger Steggink, *Experiencia y realismo en Santa Teresa y San Juan de la Cruz* (Madrid: Editorial de Espiritualidad, 1974), pp. 165-67.

25. For complete inventories of St Teresa's reading, see A. Morel-Fatio, "Les lectures de Sainte Thérèse," *Bulletin Hispanique*, 10 (1908), 17-67; Rodolphe Hoornaert, *Sainte Thérèse écrivain: son milieu, ses facultés, son oeuvre* (Paris: Desclée, 1922), pp. 303-91; and Etchegoyen, *Essai sur les sources*, pp. 13-22 and 33-46.
On St Teresa's relationship to the Dominicans and Jesuits see William Barden, chap. 10 "St Teresa and the Dominicans," and James Broderick, chap. 11 "St Teresa and the Jesuits," *St Teresa of Avila: Studies in Her Life, Doctrine and Times*, eds. Frs Thomas and Gabriel (Westminster, MD: Newman Press, 1963), pp. 206-21 and 222-35 respectively. See Jeannine Poitrey, *Introduction à la lecture de Thérèse d'Avila* (Paris: Beauchesne, 1979), pp. 36-49. Coll. "Bibliothèque de Spiritualité," 13; Damaso Chicharro's introduction to his edition of Santa Teresa de Jesus, *Libro de la Vida* (Madrid: Catedra, 1979), pp. 39-53, and García de la Concha, *El arte literario*, pp. 47-90.

26. That is, Etchegoyen, Hatzfeld and García de la Concha: see notes 2, 3 and 4 *supra*.

27. For a survey of this debate see Andrés, *La teología española* II, pp. 152-58.

28. Recently theologians have become more concerned with seeing doxology as a part of theology. For instance, Geoffrey Wainwright, in his work *Doxology: The Praise of God in Worship, Doctrine and Life* (New York: OUP, 1980) expresses this concern. A synopsis of this book by the author himself can be found in "In Praise of God," *Worship*, 53 (1979), 496-511.

29. See, e.g., Francisco Márquez-Villanueva, "Santa Teresa y el linaje," in his *Espiritualidad y literatura en el sigh XVI* (Madrid-Barcelona: Alfaguara, 1968), pp. 141-205; and Teófanes Egido, "The Historical Setting of St Teresa's Life," *Carmelite Studies*, 1 (1980), 122-82. The latter is an English translation of three-fourths of an essay originally published in Spanish in *Introducción a la tectum de Santa Teresa*, ed. Alberto Barrientos (Madrid: Editorial de Espiritualidad, 1978), pp. 43-103.

30. See Bouyer et al., *History of Spirituality*, II, pp. 190-210.

31. St Teresa's transformation of the theme of martyrdom may have also been influenced by the courtly love tradition, in which, at least in Spain, it was a commonplace that the lover was a martyr: see A. A. Parker, "An Age of Gold: Expansion and Scholarship in Spain," in *The Age of the Renaissance*, ed. Denys Hay (New York: McGraw-Hill, 1967), pp. 222-48, esp. pp. 240-41; and Keith Whinnom's introduction to his translation of Diego de San Pedro, *Prison of Love (1492, together with the Continuation by Nicolás Núñez (1496),* (Edinburgh: Edinburgh Univ. Press, 1979), p. xv.

32. Egido, *Historical Setting*, p. 131.

33. These questions are derivative of John Dowling, "Ethics and Personal History," *Philosophical Studies* [Dublin], 22, (1973), 90-120. See David B. Burrell, *Exercises in Religious Understanding* (Notre Dame: UND Press, 1974), pp. 11-41.

34. This element of St Teresa's writings has been studied by Etchegoyen, *Essai sur les sources*, pp. 125-28; and R. Hoornaert, *St Teresa in Her Writings*, trans. Joseph Leonard (New York: Benziger Bros., 1931), pp. 314-17. The latter is an English translation of the greater part of Hoornaert's *Sainte Tkérèse écrivain*. EDITOR'S NOTE: the English translation, however, failed to include chap. 2 of the French original's Part Three, viz., "Les sources," a regrettable omission.

35. *St Teresa in Her Writings*, p. 316.

36. Hatzfeld, *Santa Teresa,* pp. 16 and 40, respectively.

37. See Peers ed., 3, pp. 393-97, and I.C.S. ed., 1, pp. 397-98 and 2, pp. 515-20. Also see the catalogue of the castle imagery of the C and its applications in St Teresa's own words in I.C.S. ed., 2, pp. 544-52.

38. Leclercq, *The Love of Learning*, passim.

39. At the same time it must be kept in mind with Hatzfeld, *Santa Teresa*, p. 153 that "The divine love analyzed by Santa Teresa in its yearnings, sufferings and torments, as well as her concept of the Beloved as prisoner of the lover might have been impossible without another tradition, mat of human love, idealized, by the way, and offered for the first time with an exact love psychology in the short novel *Cárcel de amor . . .* "

The courtly love tradition, with its description and analysis of human love, then, probably also affects St Teresa's analysis and description of her relationship with God. More concretely, desire played an important part not only in the sentimental romance *Cárcel de Amor,* where it is personified in the initial allegory by the wild-man knight—see Diego de San Pedro, *Obras completas,* 3 vols., ed. Keith Whinnom (Madrid: Castalia, 1971-79), II, pp. 81-88-but also in the Chivalric romances like the *Amadis de Gaula* which St Teresa read—see O. H. Green, *Spain and the Western Tradition: The Castillan Mind in Literature from El Cid to Calderón,* 4 vols. (Madison: Univ. of Wisconsin Press, 1963-68), I, pp. 106-07.

40. See Leclercq, *The Love of Learning*, pp. 72-73 and Kilian McDonnell, "Prayer in Ancient Western Tradition," *Worship*, 55 (1981), 34-61, esp. 59-60.

41. Etchegoyen, *Essai sur les sources*, pp. 316-53.

42. Hatzfeld, *Santa Teresa*, pp. 23-61.

43. Ibid., p. 23.

44. Garcia de la Concha, *El arte literario*, pp. 228-74. It should be noted that

Etchegoyen and Hatzfeld use the terms "simile," "allegory," "metaphor," and "symbol" without ever specifying what they understand by them, whereas Garcia de la Concha explicitly situates his use of these terms within the context of contemporary literary criticism, e.g., Northrop Frye, *Anatomy of Criticism: Four Essays* (Princeton: Princeton Univ. Press, 1957) and Angus Fletcher, *Allegory The Theory of a Symbolic Mode,* 4th ed. (Ithaca: Cornell Univ. Press, 1964), to name two critics he cites.

45. See Jeannine Poitrey, "Qu'est-ce que le livre de la vie?," *Les Langues Néo-latines,* 72 (1978), 3-15, esp. 10 and Chicharro, *Libro de la Vida,* pp. 74-75. For three recent studies of the L's structure see Garcia de la Concha, *El arte literario,* pp. 184-222; Enrique Llamas, "Libro de la Vida," in *Introductión a la ledum de Santa Teresa,* pp. 219-23; and Chicharro, *Libro de la Vida,* pp. 74-81.

46. See Hatzfeld, *Santa Teresa,* pp. 39 and 59-61; and García de la Concha, *El arte literario,* pp. 245-74 and passim.

47. By contrast, St Teresa appears to be more at home with some of the secondary images she introduces, as the freedom and spontaneity with which she does so suggests. Occasionally, they seem to be attempts to convey something of her experience, much the same as prayer and doxology are.

48. Robert Scholes and Robert Kellogg, *The Nature of Narrative* (New York: OUP, 1966; repr. of the 1968 ed., 1971), p. 109.

49. Cf. Hatzfeld, *Santa Teresa,* p. 59.

50. See Stephen Crites, "The Narrative Quality of Experience," journal *of the American Academy of Religion,* 39 (1971), 291-311.

51. See note 25 *supra.*

52. See Leclercq, *The Love of Learning,* pp. 199-206. On the use of hagiography in the Divine Office, also see Pierre Salmon, *The Breviary Through the Centuries,* trans. Sr David Mary (Collegeville: The Liturgical Press, 1962), pp. 62-94 and passim.

53. Peers ed., 3, p. 220.

54. See Andres, *La teología española* II, pp. 178-82; Morel-Fatio, *Les lectures,* pp. 42-44; Hoornaert, *Sainte Thérèse écrivain,* pp. 305-11; and Etchegoyen, *Essai sur les sources,* pp. 36-37.

55. See Andrés, *La teología española,* II, p. 181; and García de la Concha, *El arte literario,* p. 53, no. 10. *Flos Sanctorum* was the general tide given to these collections. In sixteenth-century Spain these compendia, with their emphasis on the miraculous, were the religious counterparts of the romances of chivalry and competed with them as "best sellers" of the day—see Chicharro, *Libro de la Vida,* pp. 36-37 and 41.

56. See Etchegoyen, *Essai sur les sources,* p. 36; Efrén Montalva and Otger Steggink, *Tiempoy vida de Santa Teresa,* 2nd ed. (Madrid: La Editorial Catolica, 1968), p. 32, n. 27. Coll. "Biblioteca de Autores Cristianos," 283; and García de la Concha, *El arte literario,* p. 53.

57. San Ignacio de Loyola, *Obras completas,* eds. Ignacio Iparraguirre ad Candido de Dalmases, 2nd ed. (Madrid: La Editorial Catolica, 1963?), pp. 91-94. Coll. "Biblioteca de Autores Cristianos," 86.

58. Ibid., pp. 220 and 240 respectively.

59. See Garcia de la Concha, *El arte literario,* pp. 88-90; and Chicarro, *Libro de la*

Vida, pp. 52-53.

60. *The Church Teaches: Documents of the Church in English Translation,* trans. Clarkson, Edwards, Kelly and Welch (Saint Louis: Herder, 1955), p. 216.

61. See Jonaman Brown, William E. Jordan, Richard L. Kagan and Alfonso E. Pérez Sánchez, *El Greco of Toledo* (Boston: Little, Brown and Co., 1982), pp. 49-50, 56-57 and 113-16; and Sarah Schroth, "Burial of the Count of Orgaz," in *Figures of Thought: El Greco as Interpreter of History, Tradition and Ideas,* ed. Jonathan Brown (Washington, DC: National Gallery of Art, 1982), pp. 1-17, esp. p. 6. Coll. "Studies in the History of Art," 11.

62. See the "Foreword" to Granger Ryan's and Helmut Ripperger's translation of *The Golden Legend of Jacobus de Voragine* (New York: Longmans, Green and Co., 1941; repr. New York: Arno Press, 1969), p. xiii.

63. Colbert Nepaulsingh, "Santa Teresa's Libro de la Vida: Auto-hagiography," paper presented at the 94th annual convention of the Modern Language Association of America, San Francisco, December 28, 1979; and Joseph Chorpenning, "St Teresa of Avila: Theologian of Story," unpublished paper presented to Fourth Centenary Lecture Series at Boston Carmel, March 14, 1982.

64. Johannes Quasten, *Patrology,* 3 vols. (Westminster, MD: Newman Press, 1962-63), III, p. 43. The best English translation of the *Life of St Antony* is that of Robert T. Meyer (Westminster, MD: Newman Press, 1950; repr. New York: Paulist Press, 1978). Coll. "Ancient Christian Writers," 10.

65. See Ryan and Ripperger, *The Golden Legend,* p. x.

66. See Hippolyte Delehaye, *The Legends of the Saints,* trans. Donald Attwater (New York: Fordham Univ. Press, 1962), p. 54; and Ryan and Ripperger, *The Golden Legend,* pp. xi-xiii.

67. Quasten, *Patrology,* III, p. 39.

68. See Delehaye, *Legends,* p. 54; and Ryan and Ripperger, *The Golden Legend,* p. xiii.

69. See Hoornaert, *Sainte Thérèse écrivain,* p. 308; and my unpublished 1981 Catholic Univ. of America S.T.L. thesis, "The Theological Method of St Teresa of Avila's *Interior Castle,*" pp. 46-51. The present study is based on this diesis. I should, then, like to take this opportunity to record my deep appreciation to Fr David N. Power, who patiently supervised its progress, for his inspiration, guidance, constructive criticism and continuing encouragement.

70. Her presentation is still considered to be one of the principal sources of information about St Peter—see Donald Attwater, *A Dictionary of Saints* (New York: Penguin Books, 1965; repr. 1979), p. 275.

71. See *Life of St Antony,* pp. 32-33; and Bouyer et al., *History of Spirituality,* I, pp. 314-17.

72. Scholars are divided on the question of whether there is a continuity or connection between the L and C. See, e.g., Etchegoyen, *Essai sur les sources,* p. 350 and Louis Cognet, *Historie de la spiritualité chrétienne: la spiritualité moderne,* I (*L'Essor: 1500-1650*) (Paris: Aubier-Montaigne, 1966), p. 89. My presentation obviously lends support to the position that there is a continuity between these two works.

73. Etchegoyen, *Essai sur les sources,* p. 350.

74. This comparison is introduced in the final chapter of the fifth dwelling place. See C, 5, 4, 3-5.

75. Bouyer et al., *History of Spirituality*, I, pp. 197-99; and Paul Molinari, "Martyrdom: Love's Highest Mark and the Most Perfect Conformation to Christ," *The Way*, suppl. no. 39 (1980), 14-24, esp. 17-22.

76. Bouyer et al., *History of Spirituality*, I, p. 204; and Molinari, *Martyrdom*, p. 19.

77. See Quasten, *Patrobgy*, III, p. 43; and Leclercq, *The Love of Learning*, p. 202.

78. St Teresa's presentation of her life and experience was taken as a pattern in subsequent hagiography. See Bernard Plongeron, "Concerning Mother Agnes of Jesus: Themes and Variations in Hagiography (1665-1963)," in *Models of Holiness/Concilium* no. 129, eds. Christian Duquoc and Casiano Floristan (New York: Seabury, 1979), pp. 25-35, esp. p. 33.

◆

Teresa of the
Living Spirit

◆

St Teresa of Avila and Centering Prayer

◆ ◆ ◆

Ernest Larkin, S.T.D.

Fr Ernest Larkin's name is familiar to persons who follow developments in contemporary American spirituality. He is much in demand as a lecturer and retreat master.

INTRODUCTION

The purpose of this study is to locate St Teresa of Avila in the contemporary terrain of centering prayer. Centering prayer is a new term but an old reality, originating with Thomas Merton's insight into centering as the movement from the false to the true self and developed as a prayer form by the Cistercians Basil Pennington, Thomas Keating and others, and by the Benedictine John Main. This form of prayer seeks to maintain a contemplative contact with God beyond any particular images and concepts through the use of the holy word or mantra. The prayer is contemplative in thrust but active in method, inasmuch as it is within human possibility and choice and recommends itself to mature Christians, who have thought and prayed *about* God enough and now are looking for the "more," that is, a deeper, more personal contact with God.

Following the suggestion of Thomas E. Clarke, S.J. in a philosophical reflection called "Finding Grace at the Center,"[1] I believe that centering prayer is a broader category than the one form described above and that it should apply to at least three forms: (1) mantric way of dark faith as above; (2) the prayer of fantasy or guided imagery; and (3) the prayer of life experience or consciousness examen.[2] The latter two forms involve the use of imagery, reflection and affections. Guided imagery is designed to evoke God from the unconscious; and consciousness examen, as the name suggests, identifies God working in one's conscious experience. For the purposes of this study only the dark faith form and guided imagery will be addressed, since Teresa's practice and reflection veer between these two forms. Consciousness examen as a prayer form does not seem to have entered her purview.

Broadening centering prayer in this fashion is neither arbitrary or pointless. Teresa's experience and doctrinal exposition include elements from both methods; far better then to put the two under a common umbrella. The very nature of contemplation and the privileged ways of achieving it are at stake in this inquiry. Contemplation, as the obscure, infused, loving knowledge of God, is beyond images and concepts. But it does not follow that this gift of wisdom is always experienced as apophatic, that is, dark, negative and contentless. Contemplation can also be experienced as kataphatic, that is, as light, positive and concrete. In this case God might be experienced *in* as well as beyond the image.

The classical question of the role of the Sacred Humanity in prayer enters here. Teresa reacted against a widespread opinion of her contemporaries that held that all created reality, even the Sacred Humanity, had to be bypassed in the highest mystical union. Teresa wavered on the point and eventually disagreed. What was her position in this matter in the active forms of contemplative prayer, which she called "recollection" and others subsequently named "simplified affective prayer?" Did she find God in the Man Jesus Christ, and therefore in image, or was she striving to get beyond image and concept? In what sense are aspiring mystics to "empty" themselves of images and concepts? Are they to leave aside normal thinking and even the expression of spiritual affections, as the mantric form of centering prayer directs? Or is simplified affective prayer a viable bridge from meditation to contemplation? The question is how does one best tune into the Reality of Christ, in dark faith or in image? We would search out the Holy Mother's teaching in this matter as a practitioner and theorist of centering prayer.

Her "method" of centering prayer was inspired by Francis of Osuna in his book, *The Third Spiritual Alphabet*.[3] The theme of this book is recollection, which means presence and intouchness with the indwelling God; the way to recollection is the *via negativa,* journeying inward beyond all creature competitors. Teresa on reading this book "resolved to follow that path" (L, 4, 7).[4] At prayer her basic thrust was "to keep Jesus Christ, our God and Lord, present within" herself, using her imagination, not in the style of discursive meditation, but by simple representations of Christ "interiorly," in some mystery of his life, especially the Passion (L, 4, 7). She bolstered up the austere approach of relating to the transcendent Reality of the living Christ by making simple gospel reflections. Both contemporary methods of centering prayer seem to be involved. The prayer that resulted was Teresa's active mental prayer, her "practice of prayer" from 1538, when she first came in contact with Osuna, to the end of her life.

How are we to evaluate this prayer of Teresa? Is it centering prayer, and if so, which form? Does contemporary theory on centering prayer throw any light on Teresa's experience? Or does Teresa illuminate this area of spirituality today, helping us to better understand and appreciate the way of dark faith and the way of fantasy?

Our aim is to examine the way Teresa prayed in her pre-mystical days, especially in the eighteen-year period between 1538 and 1556 when she struggled to bring more of her life to the Lord. The method she developed became her normal way of prayer both in the liturgy, vocal prayer and in her daily mental prayer for the rest of her life. It is an important area of inquiry both for understanding Teresa and for spiritual theology today.

To this end we shall first examine Osuna's capital teaching on recollection in order to see where Teresa is coming from. Then in the second part we shall examine briefly the theory and practice of the two forms of centering prayer to provide points of comparison. Finally we shall examine Teresa's procedure and her doctrinal statements about this "practice of prayer."

FRANCIS OF OSUNA

The term recollection *(recogimento)* was an important one in sixteenth-century Spain. It described, not so much a method of prayer, which it has come to mean from St Teresa, as a whole way of interiority, a withdrawal from ordinary occupations and even normal thinking processes in order to be caught up in God. It was the way of illuminism and of the *Alumbrados,* both terms with questionable connotations now but originally orthodox and positive. Adherents sought interiorization and downplayed externalism; eventually they split into an heretical faction and an orthodox one. The former were the "dejados," who cultivated abandon *(dejamiento)* and so emphasized the divine action that no place was left for human cooperation. All behavior, however immoral, was accepted as God's working, and the result was an excessive, sometimes scandalous quietism.

The other group, the "recogidos" or recollects remained orthodox. They were the vanguard of the revival movements in the religious orders. They too emphasized the divine initiative and action, but they saw the need for human collaboration, for concentration on the Sacred Humanity, and for affective prayer.

Osuna belonged to the recollects. For him recollection meant getting in touch with the indwelling God, the faculties "collected" and attentive to the fountain of living waters within. Recollection was a way of life, designed for the perfect or would-be perfect (163). The goal was "mystical theology," that is, infused contemplation, the hidden, loving knowledge imparted exclusively by the indwelling Christ (161). Ascetical efforts of "pious love and exercising moral virtues to prepare and purge the soul" (162) prepared for this gift. The whole process was best called recollection out of a whole thesaurus of synonyms, says

Osuna, because it gathered together what was dispersed and achieved a union with oneself, with others and with God (169-173).

Recollection was the popular word then for what is called centering today. Both are a life's work accomplished by multiple exercises, attitudes and supernatural gifts. For Osuna no one method is *the* prayer of recollection, *the* centering prayer. Teresa speaks of recollection in a similarly inclusive way, but she also designates two specific prayer forms that she calls "recollection," one of them active (W, 28-29), the other passive or semi-passive (C, 4, 3). Both consist in silencing the faculties and shutting oneself within oneself. Active recollection is self-directed, passive recollection divinely induced, as by the shepherd's whistle.

Osuna, on the other hand, designates three kinds of prayer of recollection: vocal, prayer of the heart, and "mental or spiritual prayer," the latter two being meditation and contemplation respectively. Teresa's prayer of recollection, as we shall see, hovers between these latter two and leans heavily toward contemplation. It is a specification of Osuna's "special recollection," by which he means formal prayer, in which "you are to retire into your heart and leave all created things for the length of two hours: one hour before and one hour after noon, at the most quiet time possible" (388).

Ousna is a typical proponent of the "via negativa," that is, the approach of downplaying the created and seeking God directly beyond all images, concepts and representations. But he is not a purist, any more than Teresa, and in his presentation of recollection as the way to perfection he does not limit the search to negation. Along with his decided preference for seeking God in silence and solitude, beyond human props, he is a strong advocate of reflection on the Sacred Humanity, especially in the mystery of the Passion, holding with St Bonaventura that "no one can call himself devoted to the sacred passion unless he spends most of the day contemplating it in one manner or another" (177).

The *via negativa* for Osuna is primarily affective detachment. Effective detachment, which means actual by-passing, such as living in silence and solitude, is the right climate; it is a necessary means to the freedom that is affective detachment, whereby one is willing to use or forego the object according to God's will. Early in the text he counsels the developing contemplative to be blind, deaf and dumb: blind to God by "holding fast to what is in our hands without understanding it" (100) and blind to "everything that is not God" (103); deaf to "imagination and distractions" (104); and dumb to words and reflections (105-106). This strategy quiets the three faculties of the soul and prepares the way for the real and experiential knowledge of God that is "the state of recollection" (106). The following typical directive is repeated over and over again:

> For life to rise up from the heart like a richly abundant spring, we have only to guard the heart with all vigilance, unburdening and clearing it of all created things so that the one who created it may emerge with the life of grace (132).

Usually he is calling for a decision of the heart for God and not the wholesale rejection of the created and human. Osuna's way is the gentle search for God in quiet and solitude. He ends his first foray into his method of emptying and despoiling with a beautiful chapter on meekness, the "quality of repose" that characterizes the bypassing of the normal human mode in favor of the *via negativa* (107-112).

Osuna is as inexorable as St John of the Cross. But like John his demand is to reject competitive thoughts and loves and to rise above one's own mental processes as inadequate to attain God as he is. He is not fostering a frontal attack on all mental activity as a simplistic, literalist reading of the text would suggest. He is not saying that any image, however subtle and unassuming, is the enemy of recollection. Images run wild, yes; imagery and reflection as the main burden of the consciousness, yes; but image as image, no. It is doubtful if the psyche can even function without an image, even in the contemplative states. So the language and categories of Osuna need to be read in the context of his century; his spiritual writing suffers from the cultural and philosophical limitations of the period. Almost aware of this fact Osuna writes in the prologue:

> Because some matters of mystical theology cannot be understood in ordinary language nor comprehended without immediate experience of them, we shall clarify that the most blessed Humanity of Christ Our Lord and God in itself neither impedes nor hampers recollection, regardless of how refined or lofty it is (39).

Absolutist statements, such as "empty your heart and pour out all created things" (131), tediously abound in the treatise and continue to raise doubts, if not about the Sacred Humanity, at least about thinking at prayer.

"No pensar nada" (thinking nothing) is a case in point. Osuna espouses the shibboleth and interprets it to signify the movement into God's level of being and understanding, beyond reason, beyond the human mode. It does not mean coma or even ecstasy, but zeroing in on God beyond created analogues. As a matter of fact, in its highest actuation "no pensar nada" means "pensarlo todto" (thinking everything) (565). "No pensar nada," in other words, is a mystical phrase that expresses a direction; in itself it says too much and too little. But it must have captured Teresa's mind. Who cannot imagine the youthful Teresa de Ahumada delighting in these words of Osuna:

> It is not without reason that Scripture so often commands us to enter within ourselves and turn to our hearts. Each person is to rest within himself and not go outside; he is to close the door over himself, sealing himself inside, so that God may commune secretly with the soul. The soul must not open the door of the senses nor slip the bolt of vigilance that locks the door. Otherwise he will depart who comforted you in that closing of the door . . . (566).

Francis of Osuna was not the only significant spiritual master forming Teresa. Besides her Carmelite heritage she was in touch with the main spiritual movements of the time, all of them emphasizing interiority and mental prayer. Osuna had the honor of launching Teresa on the project of second conversion. She found the world of *The Third Spiritual Alphabet* congenial and immensely appealing. Osuna gave direction to her thinking. He did not deliver ready-made answers, certainly not in the questions of this study; on the contrary, he left open the practical questions on how to proceed. Teresa did not have to contradict anything she read in the book; she had only to specify it. Her debt to Osuna is obvious to anyone who reads the two authors. And without invidious comparisons it is also clear that the disciple in this case is greater than the master.

CENTERING PRAYER

Morton Kelsey distinguishes between religious experiences which are "usually called contemplative experiences" and the "meditative use of images."[5] The contemplative experiences are imageless; they have been promoted in Western Christianity since Plotinus in the third century and they have a long pedigree of mystical writers behind them, preeminent in modern times being Teresa of Avila and John of the Cross. Kelsey, strong proponent of the imaged way, wants to right the balance and reinstate the validity and advantages of imaged meditation.

The choice of the two epithets, contemplative and meditative, is felicitous. Contemplation connotes encounter, and meditation suggests integration. In both cases centering is the goal, contemplation locating one's true self beyond one's self in God, and meditation bringing order and calm self-possession in the midst of multiplicity in a human life. The two forms of centering prayer come out of two different spiritualities: the imageless out of the classical, contemplative spirituality of the past, the imaged from the holistic spirituality of the present. The first zeroes into God in a sheer, unhampered way, beyond the nitty-gritty; the other searches for the center in the bodiliness, the emotionality, the piecemeal, historical and social character of human life.

Imageless centering prayer is contemplative in orientation, but in itself it is not contemplation. Contemplation is always from the inside out, pure gift from God communicating himself; centering prayer is the active effort to enter within and to stand at the threshold of the inner chamber where God dwells, waiting to be touched by God. Contemplation is that divine touch; all other contemplative disciplines are preparation and disposition. When contemplation occurs, when there is "total silence in darkness," the practitioner is to "remain quiet, receptive," even stopping the mantra according to one school of thought.[6] There is no need to split hairs and define exactly when centering prayer leaves off and contemplation begins. Centering prayer is active prayer, contemplation is passive, and the incipient contemplative will often be at a loss to distinguish the two moments.

Imageless centering prayer is practiced in the following way. After the initial physical predispositions of good posture, deep breathing, and an alert, relaxed state of mind the person gets in touch with his/ her deepest reality, where he/she is image and dwelling place of God. This initial act of faith gets beyond words and formulas to the Reality beneath them. There is a sense of Presence and a loving attention to God, both of which are maintained and deepened over the period of the prayer, usually about eighteen minutes, by the rhythmic repetition of the holy word or mantra synchronized with the breathing. The mantra has no magic power. It is a name of God, like "Abba" or "Jesus," or a short phrase like "Maranatha" or "Jesus, mercy." The mantra specifies this prayer form and is repeated throughout. It becomes less obtrusive with time, being listened to and then heard within rather than spoken.

The mantra is a focusing agent, not a source of insights that call forth affective responses. Insights and affections, holy thoughts and desires, resolutions and aspirations are all distractions in this prayer form. Pennington compares the mantra to piped-in music in a bus or store; it is to occupy the imagination and mind, so that the heart can give full attention to God. The mantra is to help change the flow of consciousness from the outside in, from the plethora of thoughts and feelings of the psyche to the silence and quietude before the Mystery within, the ineffable God who is *Toda y Nada,* everything and nothing. Content-wise the holy word is a confession of poverty, an acknowledgement that there is no adequate thought or feeling for God, that the emptiness of objectless "pure consciousness," which is the source and ground of normal consciousness, is closer to the truth and closer to God than the tangled translations of our own understanding. Human thoughts hopefully dissolve into the "learned ignorance" of unknowing, and human desires are traded off for the one capital Desire that is God. The genius of the *via negativa* is being applied with the one important addition of the mantra. It remains to be seen in our time, as Philip Novak argues, whether guided imagery can ever take the place of this proven and universal contemplative discipline.[7]

The exercise is concluded with the slow recitation of the Our Father. The purpose here is to facilitate return to normal consciousness from the Alpha level likely to be induced by the centering prayer. The Our Father here is an example of imaged prayer. The words bring holy thoughts and desires to awareness, but even more importantly they trigger in the unconscious personal images and feelings. The latter allow us to get a deeper hold on ourselves for the surrender of faith to God. This is the genius of imaged prayer.

Kelsey, like many modern authors, especially those influenced by Jungian theory, sees spiritual growth in terms of integration and wholeness. Imaged prayer is encounter with God, through the Risen Christ, who is the Icon of God, contacted by us in the image. Kelsey is fond of pointing out that for ten centuries preceding Teresa and John of the Cross the imaged way was the normal way of Christian contemplation. Since Teresa and John the *via negativa* has dominated the tradition and prejudices spiritual persons against image and feeling at prayer. If, however, one thinks of transcendence as wholeness, as the integration of the parts in a unity that is greater than the sum of the parts, a new perspective opens up on spirituality and the image can be rehabilitated. This integration is not cheap grace. One must quiet down to hear what the inner person is saying through its own language of the image. Kelsey writes:

> ... The idea that inner images, which can appear spontaneously to any of us, might lead beyond one's personal psyche was never considered. Therefore, mysticism was no longer seen as something which ordinary people might hope to experience.[8]

Imaged centering prayer uses concrete human experiences—a gospel story, a fantasy, a dream, pictures, music, bodily movement like the dance—to help one enter the hidden and deeper levels of one's life. These outside factors are the instrument, but the inside image from one's life is the vehicle of self-revelation. Inside images are the agents of integration, becoming "symbols," a word whose etymology is the Greek *syn* and *bolein,* meaning to place together. Symbols unite the outer and inner levels, the conscious and the unconscious, ego and Self, the human and the divine.

These images, which stir up profound affective activity within us, represent us as we are—our moods, feelings, brokenness, yearnings, freedoms and unfreedoms, sinfulness and union with God. The image allows us, not only to think about, but to experience these parts of ourselves, and the experience gives self-knowledge. The process is not heady or speculative but a matter of "feel," of the hallowed word in Ignatian spirituality "sentir," which is not just sensible or emotional feeling, but intellectual evaluation as well. These feelings are nurtured by the image, so that a person cultivates self-knowledge and self-possession by befriending the inner symbols of one's being such as the dream. Integration takes place and higher meanings about one's life surface in the consciousness. With the eyes of faith one gets beyond the nuts and bolts of the psychological dynamics and peers into the emergent human being, oneself, who is image of God and symbol of God. This experiential revelation of ourselves in our dissimilarities and similarities is the revelation of God, since we are a word bespoken by God. In getting more in touch with ourselves we touch God.

The encounter with self can thus be the encounter with God. Guided imagery, it is true, can be merely psychic and need not include supernatural transcendence. Transcendence in this sense is gift and grace, a matter of God's self-disclosure in the human experience. Without this graced aspect guided imagery could be an endless procession of images and feelings that never get beyond themselves, a merry-go-round that never moves closer to the Center. In this case there would be no referent outside the created image itself, no relationship to God, no Mystery, no cosmic Christ. This is the hazard in imaged prayer, just as projection is the hazard in imageless prayer. The self experienced in the image must be the God-self, the Christic self, just as the God experienced in silence and darkness must be the real God and not the projection of one's imagination or understanding or unconscious needs.

John of the Cross seems to relegate imaged prayer to a non-contemplative status, thereby identifying this prayer with discursive meditation. He writes:

> . . . We must also empty [the imaginative power and phantasy] of every imaginative form and apprehension that can be naturally grasped by it, and demonstrate the impossibility of union with God before the activity relating to these apprehensions ceases . . . The advice proper for these individuals is that they must learn to abide in that quietude with a loving attentiveness to God and pay no heed to the imagination and its work.[9]

Commentators either accept this evaluation or by rethinking the Sanjuanist synthesis in different philosophical categories explain it differently.[10] The contemporary theology of Karl Rahner or Edward Schillebeeckx would have no difficulty agreeing with a revision of this teaching. Without entering into the hermeneutical debate, a more accepting attitude toward the image in prayer and one not in contradiction to St John and certainly more hospitable to St Teresa is well stated by Robert L. Schmitt, S.J., in his study of the image of Christ as feudal lord in the *Spiritual Exercises:*

> The image is obviously not Christ and yet is meant to describe him. The image interprets and points to Christ, Christ as he has been encountered and experienced by Ignatius. It is meant to facilitate the encounter, to act as a type of introduction, to help the exercitant understand what Christ has been and is saying to him and doing for him.[11]

This point of view will be useful in evaluating Teresa's method of prayer. She seeks the transcendent Christ and God, even as she comes by experience to recognize the never-ending role of the Sacred Humanity in prayer. To speak the Humanity of Jesus is to speak image. Teresa, heir of the eschatological spirituality of the *via negativa,* is also a realist, who presents a holistic teaching on prayer.

TERESA'S METHOD OF CENTERING PRAYER

Until Teresa read Osuna, she "did not know how to proceed in prayer or how to be recollected" (L, 4, 7). As a child she had a natural bent for real prayer, which is personal relationship and contact with God. Her initial training in the convent of the Incarnation disrupted this spontaneous style, according to Efrén Montalva, because it foisted artificial and arbitrary meditation forms upon her and left her uncoordinated in the use of her mind and heart in prayer.[12] Osuna restored order by returning her to her original direct approach to Christ. From this point forward Teresa was launched on the project of resolving her ambivalence and her lack of psychological and spiritual integration in order to bring her whole self to Christ in the surrender of faith.

Our purpose in this third part is to address one factor in this project, her way of praying. We shall examine first her own experience on the background of the imageless and imaged forms of centering prayer.

Then we shall look briefly at the doctrinal formulations of her method both under the rubric of recollection and simple, affective prayer.

In 1538 Teresa, twenty-three years old and a Carmelite nun for three years, found herself mysteriously ill for the second time in her young adulthood. The illness has still not been adequately diagnosed. It was a severe physical breakdown aggravated if not caused by the conflicts and pressures in this exuberant nun of high idealism and fledgling wings. With her father and another religious from the Incarnation she had come to Becedas to consult a "curandera." The cure prescribed could not begin till the following spring and it was autumn at the time. The trio returned to Uncle Peter's home where Teresa was introduced to one of her most favored books, Osuna's *Third Spiritual Alphabet*. For the next nine months Teresa devoured this book, finding the appropriate solitude there in the country to cultivate the life-giving recollection Osuna taught. One of the key occupations she restructured was the way she prayed.

How did Teresa pray after this? Her prayer was founded on the presence of Christ within her. The prayer was not an imagining of his presence; it was a realization of his presence experienced in faith.[13] Maintaining the contact was the struggle. Her contact point was pure love (L, 9, 5), the "naked intent" of *The Cloud of Unknowing,* without any support system of reflection. The way was "most laborious and painful," Teresa wrote and gave the following reasons:

> For if the will is not occupied and love has nothing present with which to be engaged, the soul is left as though without support or exercise, and the solitude and dryness is very troublesome and the battle with one's thoughts extraordinary (L, 4, 7).

A beachhead was secure: she was in touch with the living Christ, presence to Presence. But she was praying "over her head." She did not love God enough or was she integrated psychologically or spiritually to practice this simple loving attention to God. The method belonged to the advanced, who proceed by way of love (L, 9, 5) without a lot of reflection. Teresa knew that she should have been meditating discursively, but she was unable to use her imagination or her discursive intellect. Dicken suggests that the reason for the impossibility was the unrecognized presence of the dark night of the senses;[14] Efrén Montalva[15] and Tomas Alvarez[16] speak of lack of coordination in her thinking and the uncontrollable wanderings of her imagination, the faculty she was later to call "the madman in the house." My opinion is that both causes were at work. Her solution was to have a book at hand, to read it as needed, and to use holy pictures (L, 9, 4; 22, 4), nature scenes like "fields, or water, or flowers" (L, 9, 6), and above all, to use simple gospel reflections, especially to "represent" Christ "interiorly" (L, 4, 7).

All these "strategies" belong to the same one category of image. They do not include a mantra; Teresa does not seem to have favored the repetition of formulas. Her supports captured her mind and spoke to her heart. Most of them were exercises of active imagination. Even the book served to collect her wandering mind and pull herself together by a special power (L, 4, 9), a function Holy Communion also performed and rendered the book superfluous. The pictures (W, 34, 6-7), nature, and the representations of Jesus were more obvious guided imagery.

Teresa described her early gospel reflections in this way: "since I could not reflect discursively with the intellect, I strove to picture Christ within me in those scenes where I saw him more alone" (L, 9, 4). This picturing is not speculative but personal; there was no picture (she could not use her imagination: L, 9, 6) but a sense of his person which was quickly integrated with the real Presence within her soul. The anonymous monk of the Eastern Church who wrote a little spiritual classic called *Jesus* may well have caught Teresa's "representation":

> This union with the person of Christ is only possible if we set up before us, if we carry within ourselves, an intensely real image of Jesus. An image does not mean imagination nor a mental picture (although at the beginning that can be useful), but a definite interior vision, with hazy definition, which cannot be described outwardly.[17]

The images were not a parallel track. The sweat on Jesus' brow, for example, which she would have wiped away but held back because of shame and embarrassment, was perceived marking his face now. In the famous *Ecce Homo* incident the sight of the vivid statue "broke her heart" and she fell down "before Him" with "the greatest outpouring of tears" (L, 9, 1). The recall of the gospel statement, the stirred affectivity and the resultant affect-laden perception *of Jesus passus* alive now in his glorified state within her were the imaged centering prayer that added to the original sense of presence and concretized, maintained, and nurtured her union with Christ.

This was not discursive meditation (L, 9, 5). It is looking at Jesus through the windows of a gospel vignette and perceiving, that is, imaging the gospel that was being relived at that moment in Teresa. Full presence was the objective, and the imaging collected her soul in "remembrance" and recollection (L, 9, 5), two words that eventually name the prayer described. The Reality, the Christ, was not seen; he was in darkness, as happens between two friends in a dark room (L, 9, 6). The imaging process puts the Presence in better focus and makes for a more integrated experience.

Sometimes the total experience is strong as in the peak experience of the *Ecce Homo* (L, 9, 1) or relating St Augustine's conversion to herself (L, 9, 7). In both cases there is a deep grasp of her whole self as well as the Lord and a profound self-offering in love. At other times the images are relatively weak pointers to Jesus, of a piece in the early years with her fragmented psyche and her moral ambivalence, and in later years the limited input possible to her in the face of the pervasive graces of infused contemplation. Similarly, the peak experiences were probably watersheds that gathered the daily streamlets and showed the cumulative effect of many lesser efforts, or else they were significant mystical graces such as the *gustos* (the grace of "quiet" or infused love) in the *Ecco Homo* incident.

Teresa's prayer seems to manifest the same ebb and flow, summits and plains that marked her ecstatic experience later on. In her practice of prayer from the beginning there are high points of contact in which she is present to Jesus in pure faith; when this sense faltered and needed shoring up, she moved into a simple gospel reflection. The first moment is the counterpart of imageless prayer; the second corresponds to imaged prayer. This order was reversed in her mystical years (L, 23, 1), when she learned to begin with the gospel scene and let herself be transported into absorption in God. Whatever the order of these two elements of her experience, her prayer seems to include both approaches, neither one in its pure state, but custom-made to suit her own personality and the grace of the time. Her prayer was a combination of encounter and integration, immediate presence and the "meditative use of images."

When Teresa lost sight of the role of the image in her prayer, as she did toward the end of her eighteen-year struggle, thus from 1554 to 1556, she was in danger of floundering (L, 23-24). She seemed to be falling too facilely into mystical absorptions without bringing her "self" into the prayer. At least this was the fear of the two directors she consulted, when she continued to observe a lack of improvement in her life. Eventually they concluded she was deceived by the devil (L, 23, 14). This erroneous judgment was a blessing in disguise. While the verdict almost crushed her, it did lead her to consult some young Jesuits, who returned her to the pattern of imaged contemplative prayer. This was liberation for Teresa.

Through their help she was able to see through the excessively abstract and possibly unrealistic prayer and reinstate the role of the image as well as mortification outside prayer as guards against illusion (L, 22, 1-3; 23, 16-17; 24, 2). In her religious climate once there was an experience of felt presence to God, particularly in an intense, apparently mystical way, there was a tendency to abandon all human effort and think it unnecessary if not an intrusion. Teresa "strove to turn aside from everything corporeal," including the Sacred Humanity (L, 22, 3). Her delight in mystical absorptions was so great, that "there was no one who could have made me return to the humanity of Christ" (L, 22, 3). This was a temporary and much regretted departure from her Beloved (L, 22, 4). This error was not only prejudicial to the Risen Lord; it fostered an illusory prayer unconnected with her life, as Diego de Cetina told her. Such prayer lacked foundation, the foundation or real life mediated by the image of the Sacred Humanity (L, 23, 16). According to Cetina technique was less important than her affective state. He proceeded to urge her to free herself for a full surrender to God by cultivating a more authentic prayer, that is, a more wholehearted desire for God ("a return again to prayer") and the denial of contrary desires ("mortification"). She was not to repeat this mistake again. For the rest of her life she never took her eyes off Jesus.

Teresa translates her experience into doctrinal terms in the description of active recollection (W, 28-29), passive recollection (C, 4, 3), in discussing the role of the Sacred Humanity (L, 22), and in distinguishing meditation and simplified affective prayer (C, 6, 7).

Active recollection moves the center of consciousness from the outside to the Presence within, closing one's eyes literally and as the symbol of rejection of outside competitive forces (W, 28, 6). In passive recollection the movement within just happens and an intense recollection ensues. Until the Lord moves in this sovereign way, Teresa counsels the readers to practice, not discursive prayer, but simple attention to what the Lord is doing. She vehemently opposes "stopping the mind" (C, 4, 3, 4), or holding one's breath (C, 4, 3, 6), or trying not to stir or to allow the intellect or desires to stir. The ill-conceived effort to "stop thinking" *(no pensar nada)* will likely produce the opposite effect (C, 4, 3, 6). Simple attention to the experience or to supportive imagery is the best human cooperation. In Teresa there are no dichotomies between imageless and imaged contemplative prayer. Attention to the divine Presence is capital; "shutting oneself within oneself" is the defense against exteriority; whatever contributes to one or the other of these two basic attitudes is valid centering prayer.

Teresa's teaching in the later dwelling places does not change. In the higher stages of spiritual growth we are to seek the presence of God if it is not already a given reality in our prayer. We are not to sit around like "dunces wasting time waiting for what was given us once before" (C, 6,

7, 9). Two ways of seeking are available, one "discursive thinking," the other "representing truths to the intellect by means of the memory" (C, 6, 7, 10). The former is meditation, and that is no longer an option at this stage (C, 6, 7, 11). But recalling the mysteries of Christ's life and letting them speak to the contemplative "whom God has brought to supernatural things and to perfect contemplation" is another (C, 6, 7, 11). Teresa states her position in a clear synthesis of much that we have said. Referring to the simple loving recall of the mysteries of Christ's life, she writes:

> . . . I say that a person will not be right if he says he does not dwell on these mysteries or often have them in mind, especially when the Catholic Church celebrates them. Nor is it possible for the soul to forget that it has received so much from God, so many precious signs of love, for these are living sparks that will enkindle it more in its love for our Lord . . . The mere sight of the Lord fallen to the ground in the garden with that frightful sweat is enough to last the intellect not only an hour but many days, while it looks with a simple gaze at who he is and how ungrateful we have been for so much suffering (C, 6, 7, 11).

CONCLUSIONS

By way of summary I would like to draw the following conclusions from what we have considered:

(1) Teresa's method of mental prayer was neither purely imageless or merely imaged. Her emphasis on real encounter has affinity with the Pennington form of centering prayer, but her use of the image places her more properly in the Kelsey stream. If we must choose one or the other category, it would be imaged centering prayer with the rider that the sense of the real Presence is the heart of her prayer. The older name, simplified affective prayer, or even active recollection, which is basically Teresa's own choice are probably more accurate designations but less likely to be immediately intelligible and attractive to our contemporaries.

(2) This form of imaged contemplative prayer is neither meditation nor contemplation in a Sanjuanist sense; it is not the equivalent of "loving attention," which is imageless contemplative prayer in St John of the Cross (A, 2, 12, 8; 2, 13, 4). Does this face pit the two saints against each other in their teaching about the transition to contemplation? This is an age-old debate, which deserves study in the context of centering prayer. My own bias is that they differ in emphasis but not in substance. Their divergences are due to the nature of their writings and to their own personalities. Teresa is the pragmatist who deals in the concrete order; John is the theoretician who deals in absolutes and not in "how-to" teachings.

(3) Teresa's method is not pure guided imagery since she starts from a deep awareness of the presence of Christ in faith and constantly returns to this base. The guided imagery does not seek to find the Lord but to bring more of the self into the prayer. Simple reflections and affective outpourings serve to bring together the imaginative-intellectual affective self before the Lord.

(4) Teresa's teaching on the beginnings of contemplation is an immense contribution for our generation, which prefers the holistic, incarnational, human way to God over any exaggerated spiritualism. At the same time she is a corrective against horizontalism. Placing her in the context of today's literature on centering prayer serves to make her teaching more actual. Her method is a model of simplicity: get in touch with the Lord present within and nurture that presence by simple reflections and affections. The way from meditation to contemplation is rendered more smooth, a gradual shift, perhaps without the rupture of the crisis form of the dark night described by St John of the Cross (N, 1, 8, 3). Once again Teresa vindicates her title as "Doctor of the Church" and "teacher of prayer," especially for practical spiritual direction. May God be glorified in this beautiful "Daughter of the Church."

NOTES

1. Thomas E. Clarke, "Finding Grace at the Centre," *The Way*, 17 (1977), 12-22 and also in *Finding Grace at the Center,* eds. Basil Pennington and Thomas Keating (Still

River, MA: St Bede Publications, 1978), pp. 49-62. In the latter collection the last two pages of the article are edited, so that only one method of centering prayer is suggested, that of dark faith. One of the chief contributions of this article is thereby lost.

2. A full presentation of these three forms of centering prayer is recorded by Ernest E. Larkin in eleven audio cassette tapes under the title "Centering and Centering Prayer," (Kansas City, MO: NCR Audio Cassettes, 1982).

3. Francis of Osuna, *The Third Spiritual Alphabet* trans. Mary E. Giles (New York: Paulist Press, 1981). Coll. The Classics of Western Spirituality." References to this book will be by page within parentheses in the body of this article.

4. References to the works of St Teresa are from the I.C.S. ed.

5. Morton Kelsey, *The Other Side of Silence* (NewYork: Paulist Press, 1976), p. 129.

6. Thomas Fidelis, OCSO, of Conyers, Georgia, has printed these directives on a prayer card. John Main, OSB insists that the mantra is always retained in centering prayer.

7. Philip Novak, "Spiritual Discipline and Psychological Dream Work: Some Distinctions," *Studio Mystka,* 2 (1979), 47-58.

8. Kelsey, *The Other Side,* p. 130.

9. St John, A, 2, 12, 2, and 8.

10. For a literal following of John's terms and obvious teaching, see Marilyn M. Mallory, *Christian Mysticism: Transcending Techniques* (Amsterdam: Van Gorcum Asen, 1977). For a re-evaluation in Hegelian categories, see Georges Morel, *Le sens de l'existence selon S. Jean de la Croix* (Paris: Aubier, 1960-61).

11. Robert L. Schmitt, "The Christ-Experience and Relationship fostered in the *Spiritual Exercises* of St Ignatius of Loyola," *Studies in the Spirituality of Jesuits,* 6, (1974, 5), 242-43.

12. Efrén Montalva, *Santa Teresa por Dentro* (Madrid: Editorial de Espiritualidad, 1973), pp. 126-32

13. Tomás Alvarez has written beautifully on this aspect, as so many others, of Teresa's prayer. See his "Una classica esperienza di preghiera," *Rivista di Vita Spirituale,* 29 (1975), 586-612, esp. at 606.

14. E. W. Truman Dicken, *The Crucible of Love* (New York: Sheed and Ward, 1963), pp. 173, 176 and 287-88. Teresa's solution to her inability to meditate discursively, according to Dicken, was the development of her method of "affective prayer," an ancient conversational form of prayer known to history but temporarily obscured in the sixteenth century milieu of highly organized discursive meditation. The prayer is affective activity with very little imagination and intellectual content, contemplative in orientation, and unlike highly intellectual discursive meditation compatible with the ligature and impossibility to meditate associated by St John of the Cross with the passive dark night of the senses. I heartily agree with diese observations, as will be seen in this third part of my study.

15. Montalva, *Santa Teresa,* p. 129.

16. Alvarez, *Una classica,* p. 597.

17. A Monk of the Eastern Church, *Jesus: A Dialogue with the Saviour,* trans. A Monk of the Western Church (New York: Paulist Press Deus Books, 1965).

St Teresa's Inspiration
for Our Times

◆ ◆ ◆

Monika Hellwig, Ph.D.

*Monika Hellwig's accomplishments as a lecturer and writer
are many. She has received three honorary doctorates in
the last ten years. She is also a Professor in the Theology
Department of Georgetown University in the District of
Columbia.*

INTRODUCTION

The colorful, lively and delightful figure of Teresa of Jesus which
emerges from the preceding papers in this symposium, obviously holds
great varied inspiration for our times. The problem in concluding and
reflecting on what has gone before is not that of finding but of selecting
material.

Much of Teresa's relevance and inspiration for our times has already
been explicitly or implicitly developed in the foregoing articles. Susan
Muto has given us the benefit of Teresa's keen understanding of what
constitutes true human growth and development in a deeply Christian
perspective. Her vivacious practicality and her perennial insights into
both the existential and the socially conditioned dimensions of living as
a woman, have been vividly presented in Sonya Quitslund's paper. Her
response to ecclesial and societal challenges of her time has been care-

fully placed in context in Jodi Bilinkoff's study, and her response to the paradoxes of a truly spiritual reform within a truly sinful Church has been brought alive by Keith Egan.

This would already have sufficed to show the immediate relevance of Teresa of Jesus to our times. But the symposium has offered more, because it also considered in depth particular aspects of Teresa's spirituality and theological understanding. The dogged return of Teresa to the humanity of Jesus, as set out in Eamon Carroll's lines, speaks directly and pertinently to the theological and pastoral issues of christology in our times. Ciriaco Morón-Arroyo, Elias Rivers and Joseph Chorpenning, each in his own way, have explored Teresa's radical approach to personal and mundane experience as a theological source, which speaks in the most direct way to many of our concerns today. Finally, Ernest Larkin has traced Teresa's helpful discernment of the pathways most apt to lead people in our times as well as hers into deep and authentic prayer.

Gathering up all these riches, one might well ask what is left to say. This Fourth Centenary symposium intends to celebrate not only a memory but also a legacy. Perhaps, therefore, a concluding reflection should be concerned with the question: what are we doing with this legacy? What does it all mean for us? If it is difficult to translate Teresa's writing from Spanish into English, it is nevertheless very easy to translate her legacy from the sixteenth century into the present and from the cloister into the market place. In particular, there seem to be three areas in which Teresa has important insights for us in our own times. They are: faith and theology; humility, especially in relation to the Church; and the connection between conversion, poverty and community.

FAITH AND THEOLOGY

In our times we have rediscovered with a new depth of experience that all in Christian life is built upon faith, that faith is not a matter of "believing that" nearly as much as it is a matter of "believing in," and that faith is indeed a gift of God. Within the Catholic community in this century we have been experiencing a new Reformation which echoes some of the issues of the sixteenth-century Reformation. The Second Vatican Council has been a strenuous effort to contain this new Reformation within the communion of the Catholic Church, but it necessarily brings its tensions and conflicts and struggles. There is a certain liberation in it from triumphalist certainties into a new search.

After the battering we have suffered from secularization, as it questioned and continues to question the language of our prayer and the symbols and imagery of our faith, and after the shock we sustained with the "Death of God" movement, bringing the possibility of radical atheism into the midst of our Christian consciousness, we find ourselves having to ask in new ways what faith is and on what it rests. We find ourselves relieved of those unshakable certainties attained step-by-step by our own efforts in an apologetic that offers a tightly argued and conclusive rational case. This loss is a crisis, a challenge and, finally, a call to a new quest for the living God.

Surprisingly, perhaps, Teresa offers herself as a guide on that quest through her teaching on the prayer of beginners.[1] It is true that Teresa's life was set within a culture that lived and breathed in a sacralized atmosphere, yet there are hints and suggestions in her writings of an interior experience that says much to us in our situation. For all the enculturated acknowledgement of the divine in the everyday life of her society, she was able to report that even in an observant convent life the rituals of worship and the devout practices could remain quite external to the intimate personal experience of the real.[2] The experience of the "absence of God" was not really alien to Teresa's own life or that of those about her.

Teresa's blunt approach to the problem of the "absence of God" seems very pertinent to our own experience as believers in a pluralistic and largely secular society. A personal God is perceived only in persevering, faithful personal presence to God. Moreover, personal presence to God is a matter of time, of solitude and of honesty. It requires great courage because of the imminent risk of transformation of one's vision and identity and goals, and the risk, therefore, of losing control of one's own life.[3]

Our sense of reality is shaped by the influences to which we open our imagination, hour by hour, day by day, week after week, year after year. Teresa's long campaign against the reality interpretation of the parlor conversations seems curiously apt as a model in our age of media madness. Teresa documents autobiographically the lengthy, tedious, onerous journey involved in leaving behind a perception of reality that is, in fact, unreal. Her autobiographical preoccupation with the frivolity and vanity of her teen-age years may seem to be grossly exaggerated, but the issue as she sees it has to do with the ability to be in touch with the real and therefore to be open to God's self-revelation and self-communication.

In our own times, we suffer so much from dissipation and distortion of personal focus, that it is time to take this concern of Teresa's to heart. The distortions are deliberately contrived for commercial profit by pervasive and psychologically clever forms of advertising and indirect persuasion. The struggle to experience reality in inner personal freedom is urgent and inescapable in our lives. Prayer is at first bound to be, as Teresa describes it, a long, hard and even bitter struggle to escape from this distorted perception of reality into communion with truth, communion with God.

This inevitably raises the question of what is truth. In our time, many people find all religious language and ceremony hollow. They find theology and the traditional teachings of spirituality so alien to their experience that they fear deception and illusion. This is a fear with which, sooner or later in their lives, contemplatives have always had to deal. Throughout the L Teresa makes it clear that she was no stranger to this fear, and that conventional answers were often not helpful to her.

Teresa's own answer to the challenge is not dogmatic but experiential. It is the kind of answer we can appreciate so well today. To be alone, to be quiet, to pay attention to what is happening at the center and depth of one's own being, to remain there patiently waiting, to open oneself to reality, allowing it to speak in nature, and in one's own bodily, psychic and interpersonal experience—this is, indeed, to come to terms with the Ultimate communicating itself to us. This is no longer a hearsay contact with truth, a second-hand and alien concept of reality; it is existential, personal contact with the real.

This is the rock bottom foundation from which one can move into the history and tradition that have been distilled for us by others. This is, indeed, to come to terms with the Ultimate communicating itself to us. This seems to be Teresa's point when she writes that God gave her "a living book" as the support and guide of her spiritual life. This, also, seems to be the starting point, the apologetic foundation or ground of credibility that persons in our own culture need. If in the context of such an unconditional personal quest, the God of our tradition is still heard to speak in the idiom and conventions that are culturally determined, there is nevertheless a firm assurance that what is encountered is reality and truth. Our grasp of truth moves from the inner personal experience to embrace the outward, common expression, and not in the other direction. It is in this context that Teresa's insistence on the need for perseverance in prayer becomes so practical—her insistence that the important thing is to keep giving God one's attention, for all the rest will follow as God's initiative.

It seems to be this kind of assurance of truth that allows Teresa that extraordinary personal detachment with which she can unhesitatingly insist on the content and truth of what she writes. She is quietly assured that it is true and that it will be seen to be true by the light of the reader's own experience; as, for example, when she writes:

This chapter is very beneficial;[4]
It contains good doctrine;[5]
    This should be read attentively, for the explanation is presented in a very subtle way and there are many noteworthy things.[6]

All this, of course, has implications not only for prayer and for the individual Christian's pursuit of a life of faith; it has far-reaching implications for theology. It implies universal direct access to God's self-revelation, as illustrated by the image of the "living book" given to Teresa by God.[7] This is surely one of the reasons for which Teresa was constantly suspect in her own time. In a time of reformation and rethinking, those charged with preserving the orthodoxy of the faith usually become very nervous when there appears to be a threat that they may lose control of the situation.

Because we also are in a time of reform and rethinking, Teresa's ways of coping with this are particularly helpful, for she has a subtle, carefully nuanced way of submitting herself to the judgment of the Church while never abandoning her conviction that God speaks in our experience and can be trusted to speak to us so that we understand and are not deceived. She admits no doubt that God speaks continuously to those who will listen, showing them both divine and created reality in its truth, and utterly transforming their consciousness and their lives in that truth.

Teresa's confidence that revelation is to be found continuously in all human experience, appears to be anchored in her personal discovery of the humanity of Jesus as the way of all wisdom and communion with God. It is a discovery we in our times share with her, for contemporary theology with its radical questioning of the philosophical underpinnings of our customary patterns of theology, has found itself with just one unquestionable point of entry into Christian theological discourse—the human Jesus. For this reason, among others, the spirituality of Teresa has much to offer to struggling Christians today, many of whom find that they must quite radically rethink their understanding of God and the relationship of the human to the divine.

HUMILITY BEFORE GOD,
THE WORLD AND THE CHURCH

Humility is a virtue and a demand that presents many problems to the contemporary Christian and perhaps especially to Christian women today who are confronted with the demand to resist sexist discrimination and to respond to "assertiveness training." It becomes very difficult in an age and culture heavily committed to "positive thinking" and "healthy self-love and self-acceptance," to respond to the evangelical counsel of humility without feeling that it falls somehow short of mental health.

Teresa's understanding of the role of faith in constituting human reality undergirds her straightforward sense of the definition of humility. Her understanding is as fresh and pertinent today as it was when it was first expressed. Humility means in the first place an enthusiastic "owning" of God's gifts to oneself—all of them without exception—because it shows little gratitude or respect or realism to hold the divine gifts in contempt or deny their bestowal.[8] This understanding explains how Teresa could make those evaluations of her own writings which were quoted before and whose boldness simply takes one's breath away. They are presented not as boasts but as acknowledgements of the generosity of God.

This attitude puts the contemporary promotion of self-esteem into a truly Christian perspective, because both virtue and talent are credited as divine favors, and properly so. Indeed, even achievements are so credited in keen awareness of total dependence on God both in the order of creation and in the realm of grace. But Teresa offers more than this. Humility involves a certain easy, realistic sense of limitations, and nowhere is this clearer than in what she says about being a woman.[9]

While it may at first dismay the contemporary reader to come across negative and self-deprecatory allusions to being a woman, the context puts these remarks in a very different light. There are no passages that suggest that Teresa thought it to be in itself a misfortune to be created female. There are many passages, especially those referring to her own youth, that suggest deep dissatisfaction with the current, culturally conditioned role definition that thrust women into utterly unsatisfying frivolity and triviality if they were well-born.

Teresa again-and-again acknowledges without hesitation that she is at a great disadvantage because she has not had the opportunity to study, especially to study Scripture and theology. Frequently, the apparently self-deprecating passages turn out to be simply a ruthlessly real-istic acknowledgement of her inability to make certain judgments and discernments because she has been systematically deprived of both the information and the training. As she tries to evaluate much that has happened in her own spiritual journey,[10] there is a startling recognition of a certain childishness and instability into which the enforced perma-nent dependence of this situation maneuvered her.

It seems to be the very acceptance of her own weakness and lack of foundation in theology, that enables her to admonish and criti-cize scholars and clergy unhesitatingly for their compromised preach-ing, their abstract theology and their lack of foundation in prayer and personal experience. She asserts the truth of her own experience but respects the different wisdom of the scholar. She is sure of her ground (once she has struggled through those agonizing years in which various confessors tried to persuade her she was under the direct influence of the devil), but she also wants to define that ground in the terms of the tradition, the terms of orthodoxy.[11]

Thus, it is not only when confronted with scholarly expertise that she has come to terms with her own limitations, but also when con-fronted with Church authority as authentically representing the truth of the Tradition. Yet it is interesting to note in the mature Teresa a quiet assurance that eventually the truth of her experience will be found to be in congruence with the truth passed down officially in the Tradition. The oft-quoted dying remark that she died after all a daughter of the Church, carries a certain note of triumph over considerable difficulties and misunderstandings.

Teresa has some extraordinary insights into the whole matter of humility. Perhaps the most pertinent to our own times is her remark that when a work is founded in humility it does not lead to frustra-tion.[12] Of course, Teresa is writing in this particular instance about the "work" of prayer, of long-term perseverance in prayer when there is little satisfaction in it. Yet, the remark is obviously pertinent to all types of apostolic work and offers an astonishing perspective on the contemporary, much discussed, problem of "burn-out" in active apostolates, particularly those dealing with conflict.

Writing, as always, directly out of her own experience and her own rather ruthless assessment of her own experience, Teresa sees for herself and is able to show us that discouragement and frustration imply a certain attitude and expectation. They imply reliance on oneself as the initiator and responsible agent and they imply the expectation of success in proportion to the effort invested. They imply that one has a right to expect success, a proprietary right. The lesson that Teresa has had to learn herself and which she intends to pass on, is a hard one. It is a matter of radical reliance on grace and radical acknowledgement of the primacy of divine initiative and the Lordship of God.

There is one other aspect of Teresa's grasp and practice of humility that offers a startling note of contemporaneity with ourselves. It is her way of studying the experiences of prayer and especially of extraordinary phenomena which occurred in her own prayer. There seems to be no fear of putting all under the sharpest psychological scrutiny to consider whether anything might be self-delusion or the outcome of illness or emotional instability. She is very ready to consider all of this a possibility and to work out in collaboration with others and with the traditional teachings, suitable and adequate criteria by which to assess the authenticity of mystical phenomena.[13]

Only a very solid humility could ground an individual in this kind of calm self-scrutiny, wide open to the possibility of finding oneself deluded. Teresa, of course, lived before the age of experimental psychology, analytical psychology and the social and human sciences in general. Yet this attitude of hers offers strong guidance to us today who are much besieged and often feel quite threatened by these disciplines.

CONVERSION, POVERTY AND COMMUNITY

The notion of sin causes contemporary Christians considerable difficulties. Much of what we learn from the social sciences and from psy-

chology questions even the intelligibility of the idea of sin. The extent
to which we are all conditioned by our experiences is constantly being
documented both in individual cases studies and in statistical analyses
of the incidence of crime, addiction, suicide, divorce and other human
tragedies. All of this challenges the notion of freedom and therefore the
idea of culpability. Moreover, there is strong and pervasive pressure to
identify all acknowledgement of guilt and sinfulness as psychologically
unhealthy—an aberration of human consciousness to be overcome by
proper professional counsel.

On the other hand, it becomes clear to thoughtful Christians that
the whole message of Christianity is nonsense unless we do indeed need
to be redeemed from sin. Moreover, it soon becomes clear to any sensitive person, Christian or not, that all is not right with our world or ourselves and that the traditional understanding of sin does in fact address
the situation in the world as it actually is. The question then arises as
to how the traditional teaching about a world warped by sin and about
the inevitability of each person's involvement in that sin, can be understood coherently in the context of contemporary experience and self-
knowledge.

In a fashion truly visionary and inspired, Teresa's own self-knowledge and her perception of the human situation anticipate our problem. Long before modern biblical scholarship demonstrated as much,
Teresa saw quite clearly that sin is not primarily to be defined in terms
of culpability but in terms of personal orientation. This is remarkable
because in her times as in ours, the Catholic perception of sin seems to
have been shaped largely by the experience of the sacrament of Penance
practiced in the form of individual, often devotional, confession of specific sins.

In the earliest ages of Christian history, the notion of sin was shaped
rather by the experience of adult baptisms with the dramatic change
of life-style, understanding, values, goals and community associations
which such baptisms entailed. Such an experience yielded a sense of sin
built on the contrast of life before and after Baptism into the Christian

community. The contrast was a total turning about of one's life, and sin was recognized as the state of being disoriented, turned in the wrong direction. Repentance, conversion, redemption, therefore, are seen as a matter of turning to face the other way. Any question of attribution of culpability becomes entirely secondary to the real issue of discerning and acknowledging the pattern of one's disorientation.

What is truly extraordinary is the extent to which the realization of this permeates Teresa's writings, more especially the L, in which so much is concerned with her perception of her own deeper conversion and her recognition of sinfulness in her own life.[14] Much of what she says about the "great sins" of her past life which her confessors would not allow her to spell out in her writings, seems ridiculously exaggerated if considered in terms of specific acts, their material gravity and the degree of knowledge and deliberate consent, and therefore of culpability, involved in them. However, the same laments and protestations are wholly comprehensible if what is being deplored is the disorientation of her earlier life in the light of her later clarity of focus and perception.

Not only in her understanding of sin but also in her approach to the call for repentance, Teresa is thoroughly modern and therefore helpful to us. Telling the story of her own struggling spiritual life and of her own long, reluctant road to a deeper conversion, she relates for us with disarming candor her long-term unwillingness and failure to "do penance" according to the accepted canons of her historical period and her monastic tradition. Readers of our own time may recognized in her refusal a not altogether unhealthy response, for she would not go through an outer performance that did not spring from an inner sense of authentic reality. This same trait that kept her from devout penitential practices earlier in her life seems to be what kept her doggedly faithful to the truth revealed to her throughout her life, and in the course of that life led her through a repentance and conversion that was very radical indeed.

What emerges from this, as Teresa reflects to others what she has learned from her own mystical and ascetical experience, seems to be a deep conviction that true repentance, penance, conversion, moves from the inside outwards rather than the other way around. Her advice seems to be, in effect, "give God your attention, give it seriously, perseveringly, generously, and God will draw your whole being until all is indeed reoriented".[15] This anticipates much of what we know about human behavior from modern depth psychology. We are never wholly aware of all that is happening at the deeper levels of our consciousness. We are apt to be caught in the dynamic of "hidden agenda." We cannot change our motivations, our desires, our fears, our fantasies directly. Divine truth must often break through in the passivity of contemplation, where it can take us by surprise. True penance, as the Shepherd of Hermas taught long ago, is "deep knowledge."[16] When it breaks through, behavior, life style, relationships eventually all fall into the right focus. Divine love, as Teresa portrays it, is somewhat like a Pied Piper.

It is wholly consonant with this understanding of conversion to God that Teresa should place such emphasis on the roles played by poverty, community and spiritual direction. It is also quite logical that her criterion of evangelical poverty is a matter of what it is that one worries about.[17] Although Teresa is very ready to excuse lay people from her demands in relation to poverty, one cannot help but observe that the criterion of what it is that one worries about is really universally applicable. Here again, the conversion comes from the inside and works outwards.

In a time and a monastic tradition in which contemplation and "favors" in prayer were greatly esteemed, though also seen as dangerous, Teresa never loses sight of the truth that salvation is by charity and that love of God is inseparable from love of neighbor. In her teaching and guidance of others there is a very strong emphasis on community as an essential dimension of conversion to God. Once again, Teresa's emphasis has an uncannily contemporary resonance. In our own time the predominant cultural thrust is toward individualism and a quest for self-fulfillment whether in material or spiritual ways. But simultaneously in many places "basic Christian communities" attest to the rediscovery of the centrality of community in conversion to God.

A more subtle aspect of this appears in Teresa's relationships and attitudes to confessors and spiritual direction. Her concern to submit her writings and her own life to the judgment of the Church in the persons of its officially appointed representatives, seems to be not only a matter of personal humility before the Church as God's agent. It seems to be also the community concern to be credible to others so as to be able to serve and teach and build the community. This seems to account for some of her clever strategies and maneuvers.

One might say, in conclusion, that Teresa is truly a model in many ways for our times because of the extraordinary human maturity that she attained. Her life gives testimony that maturity lies in the balancing of one's own experience and understanding with guidance from the community and tradition, and in balancing one's own needs and quest with self-gift to others.

NOTES

1. See, for example, L, 11-13 and W, 17ff.

2. L, 7 and W, 8-10.

3. L, 8.

4. L, 22, chapter heading.

5. L, 21, chapter heading

6. L, 18, chapter heading.

7. L, 26, 5.

8. See especially L, 10, 4.

9. The theme recurs throughout the L and is often echoed in W, for example, L, 10, 8 and W, 9-11.

10. L, passim. A particularly poignant example of the enforced dependence appears in L, 23 and 24.

11. This is evident in all her writings, but is particularly emphatic in the L, 10-22, where she discusses four degrees of prayer.

12. L, 12, 5.

13. For example, L, 25, passim.

14. See also W, 8-15, concerned with detachment and mortification.

15. L, 8, 4, 5 and 9.

16. "Fourth Mandate," Section 2 of *Shepherd of Hermas,* trans. Joseph M.-F. Marique (Washington: C.U.A. Press, 1947), p. 265. Coll. "Fathers of the Church."

17. W, 2.

The Institute of
Carmelite Studies

PURPOSE AND GOALS

The Institute works toward a richer understanding of the Carmelite heritage through studies in spiritual theology, scriptural exegesis, and other related fields. It encourages scholarship among its members and others who seek to deepen an .appreciation of the Order's spirit and traditions. Some of the members have produced new translations of the spiritual classics of St Teresa of Avila, St John of the Cross and St Thérèse of Lisieux, and other writings for the assistance of those who wish to understand better these Carmelite authors. Members of the Institute are available for conferences, seminars, courses, and other study group meetings held for the development and promotion of an awareness of the Carmelite Order's spirituality, charism and history. In recent years we have undertaken the collecting of various documents, papers and publications related to the Order. This collection, the Institute's library facilities and conference room are located at the Discalced Carmelite Monastery in Washington, D.C.

The Institute gathers regularly to discuss and encourage the research and other scholarly projects of the members. Since its founding in 1966, it has sustained an interest in the study of both Western and Eastern spiritual traditions, especially the meditative practices of the mystics.

At present membership in the Institute is open to Friars of the American Provinces of the Discalced Carmelites. During plenary meetings new members are proposed and their names referred to the Washington Province's Provincial Council for approval. We do not conduct a degree program, but we make every effort to share our facilities with anyone engaged in research on Carmelite topics requiring access to our library and archives. Our Washington library provides a convenient setting for our own scholars and others who obtain permission to consult our holdings. We have been receiving increasingly frequent requests for information about our study resources and for research guidance.

To continue and further its work the Institute of Carmelite Studies welcomes support from foundations, organizations and interested individuals. Contributions are tax deductible.

MEMBERS OF THE INSTITUTE

John Clarke
Adrian Cooney, M.A.   *Boston College*
Kevin Culligan, Ph.D.   *Boston University*
Michael Dodd, Ph.D. Cand.   *Catholic University of America*
Kieran Kavanaugh, S.T.L.   *Teresianum, Rome*
Christopher Latimer, M.A.   *Mt. Carmel College, Washington, D. C.*
Steven Payne, Ph.D.   *Cornell University*
Otilio Rodriguez, S.T.L.   *Teresianum, Rome*
Emmanuel Sullivan, Ph.D.   *Catholic University of America*
John Sullivan, S.T.D.   *Institut Catholique, Paris*
Lawrence Sullivan, S.T.D.   *Teresianum, Rome*

PUBLICATIONS OF THE INSTITUTE

The Institute is committed to providing accurate and contemporary translations of the works of major Carmelite writers and to keeping them in print in economical editions.

Volumes Already Published

The Collected Works of St John of the Cross, translated by Kieran Kavanaugh, OCD and Otilio Rodriguez, OCD (2nd ed., paper and hardbound, 1979).

The Collected Works of St Teresa of Auila, translated and edited by Kieran Kavanaugh, OCD and Otilio Rodriguez, OCD. Volume 1: The Book of Her Life, Spiritual Testimonies, and Soliloquies (1976). Volume 2: The Way of Perfection, Meditations on the Song of Songs, and The Interior Castle (1980).

Story of a Soul, The Autobiography of St Thérèse of Lisieux, translated from the original manuscripts by John Clarke, OCD (2nd ed., 1976).

St Thérèse of Lisieux, Her Last Conversations, translated by John Clarke, OCD (1977).

Letters of St Thérèse of Lisieux, General Correspondence. Volume 1 : Years 1877-1890, translated by John Clarke, OCD (1982).

Carmelite Studies, edited by John Sullivan, OCD. Volume 1: Spiritual Direction in the Teresian Carmel (1980) —OUT OF PRINT. Volume 2: Contemporary Psychology and Carmel (1982). Volume 3: Centenary of St Teresa (1984).

Volumes in Progress

The Collected Works of Edith Stein. Volume 1 : Life in a Jewish Family, and Open to God's Plan, translated by Josephine Koeppel, OCD [1984]; Volume 2: Woman, translated by Freda Mary Oben.

The Complete Works of Elizabeth of the Trinity. Volume 1: General Introduction and Major Spiritual Writings, translated by Aletheia Kane, OCD [1984].

The Collected Works of St Teresa of Avila, translated and edited by Kieran Kavanaugh, OCD and Otilio Rodriguez, OCD. Volume 3: The Book of the Foundations, The Constitutions, Poetry and Other Minor Writings [1984].

Letters of St Thérèse of Lisieux, General Correspondence. Volume 2: Years 1890-1897, translated by John Clarke, OCD.

Collaboration with other publishers has extended the use of our texts in *The Classics of Western Spirituality* (Paulist Press), in *St Teresa of Avila: A Spiritual Adventure* (El Monte Carmelo, Burgos-Spain), and in other volumes. Some of our translations have been rendered into Braille and recorded as "taped books" for the blind.

For inquiries about publications and for a catalogue, contact:
    Br Bryan Paquette, Director
    ICS Publications
    2131 Lincoln Road, N.E.
    Washington, D.C. 20002
    Tel. (202) 832-6622

Internet Resources

Generalate of the Discalced Carmelite Friars Web site available at
http://www.ocd.pcn.net

Discalced Carmelites Washington Province Web site available at
http://www.ocdwashprov.com/index.htm

Institute of Carmelite Studies Web site available at
http://www.ocdwashprov.com/id33.htm

ICS Publications Web site available at
http://www.icspublications.org

Christus Publishing, LLC Web site available at
http://www.christuspublishing.com

CPSIA information can be obtained at www.ICGtesting.com
Printed in the USA
BVOW082125090812

297529BV00007B/29/P